Reconstructing
American Literature

Reconstructing American Literature

Courses, Syllabi, Issues

Edited by Paul Lauter

THE FEMINIST
PRESS
Old Westbury
New York

Library of Congress Cataloging in Publication Data
Main entry under title:
Reconstructing American literature.
   1. American literature—Study and teaching (Higher)
2. American literature—Outlines, syllabi, etc.
3. American literature—Minority authors—Study and
teaching (Higher)   4. American literature—Minority
authors—Outlines, syllabi, etc.   5. American literature—Bibliography.
   I. Lauter, Paul.
PS41.R4   1983   810'.9   83-20730
ISBN 0-935312-14-5

Cover design by Lucinda C. Geist
Text design by Lea Smith
Typeset by Duarte Phototypesetting Co.
Manufactured by R.R. Donnelley & Sons Co., Crawfordsville

Contents

INTRODUCTION
Paul Lauter

This volume is a tool in a larger effort to change the teaching of American literature and, therefore, the definition of what we call American culture. It contains sixty-seven American literature syllabi that differ significantly from those of most courses in content and often in organization. Those differences reflect the efforts of instructors to incorporate in their teaching the fruits of two decades of scholarship in minority and women's history, art, literature, and culture. About a third of these courses are introductory, mostly chronological surveys, although the volume also contains a number of introductory courses that are organized along thematic or generic lines. In addition, the book includes three groups of more advanced courses, some focused on periods, some on genre, and others organized around themes.

In most respects these syllabi and the brief introductions provided by the instructors speak for themselves. They offer models, bibliographies, interesting ways of linking works, varying approaches to texts, differing frameworks—in short, practical assistance to the instructor interested in changing his or her teaching of American literature. Like the *Female Studies* series on which it was modeled, *Reconstructing American Literature* can also be helpful in addressing institutional reluctance to alter curricula. In the very early days of Women's Studies the *Female Studies* volumes helped to certify that, indeed, such courses were being taught at many institutions across the country. This book illustrates that the process of changing the teaching of American literature is well underway in every part of the United States, at colleges and universities of every description, and in a variety of forms. It provides alternative models for departmental or curriculum committees as they discuss ways in which courses can be redesigned to respond to the new literary scholarship, as well as to new student constituencies and their differing interests.

Beyond their practical usefulness, however, these syllabi implicitly raise some issues I wish to examine briefly in this introduction: Why has the imperative to change the teaching of American literature arisen? What are the underlying aesthetic, organizational, intellectual, pedagogical questions that must be addressed if, in fact, what we have called "American Literature" is to be altered significantly?

i

Next to where I type, I have tacked up the syllabi for two American literature courses recently taught at well-known, indeed prestigious, institutions in the United States—one in California, the other in Ohio. Both are survey courses, one called "The American Literary Imagination," the other "Life and Thought in American Literature." One covers, in one semester, thirty-two writers, including Philip Freneau, William Cullen Bryant, Washington Irving, John Greenleaf Whittier, John Crowe Ransom, and Ezra Pound; all are white and male, except for one assignment on Emily Dickinson and one poem by Marianne Moore. The other, a two-term course, includes twenty-three white male writers and Emily Dickinson. I do not want to argue that in 1983 such courses have no right to exist, for that kind of statement would engage the significant issue of academic freedom. But such courses are simply not truthful, nor professionally current. The pictures they present to students of the American literary imagination or of American life and thought are woefully incomplete and inaccurate. In the profession of literary study they represent what, in Psychology, was represented by generalizations about moral development based on interviews with a sample of white, male, college sophomores and juniors; or in History, was represented by conclusions about the "expansion" of opportunity under Jacksonian democracy when, in fact, white women's opportunities and those of black people were largely contracting. Were such courses titled "American Literature from the Perspective of 'Diner'" (a film set in 1958), they might have accurately represented themselves. But now, a quarter of a century later, a large new body of scholarship has transformed the intellectual base of our profession. To be responsive to this scholarship and to present an accurate picture of the development of the literary cultures of the United States, teaching has begun to change. This volume is a record of such change and a means for encouraging its systematic development.

The changes in our profession that I am describing are rooted in the movements for racial justice and sex equity. Those who worked in the movements came to see that to sustain hope for a future, people needed to grasp a meaningful past. Programs were created, often in the form of courses in "freedom schools" and "free universities," to explore areas like black history and culture. Soon after courses were developed that examined the lives and achievements of women; and still others focused on ethnic and racial minorities. In time, often accompanied by well-publicized conflict, such courses began to be incorporated into the curricula of existing colleges and universities, and in some secondary schools as well. The initial set of questions thus brought by the social movements into academe really involved efforts to understand the present: How did things get to be this way? What has been the historical experience that led to where we are? How have people like us responded to racism and sexism in the past? In turn, such questions led to an intense look at existing curricula. Students and faculty members began to ask what became the key questions for curricular change: "Where are the blacks?" "Where are the women?"

Once such questions had been asked, it was only a short step—at least for some—to begin designing courses that attempted to answer them. And so at the first stage of curricular reform in the late 1960s and early 1970s we began to see courses on Black Writers and Women Writers, and others that explored "images" of women in literature. Such courses were important in establishing that, indeed, such writers existed, were interesting to students, and even valuable to study. They were, in curricular terms, the equivalent of the first steps of the rich new developments in minority and feminist scholarship. But they remained essentially peripheral in the academy. The students who enrolled for them were often extraordinarily enthusiastic and motivated to unusual feats of reading and research; but they were relatively few in number. Meanwhile, in the "mainstream" introductory and major courses, the majority of students—a dwindling band they were in literature—encountered little change.

To be sure, some courses and the major anthologies added a few women and blacks (mostly male) and expectantly stirred. Kate Chopin's *The Awakening* and a bit of Frederick Douglass's *Narrative* of his life became standard fare; safe enough, even for the recalcitrant, since the excerpts from the latter preached literacy and the former "resolved" a woman's role conflicts through suicide. In fact, however, such works and the many others soon crowding to the barriers of our attention remained marginal to the structures of academic knowledge. Our accounts of cultural history, our understanding of aesthetic value had not changed. Even into the 1980s, for example, no portrait of the development of the American novel reflected at all adequately the fact that many if not most of the major fiction writers during the half century after 1870 were women: Elizabeth Stuart Phelps, Sarah Orne Jewett, Mary Wilkins Freeman, Edith Wharton, Willa Cather, Ellen Glasgow, Mary Austin, among others. Literary commentators continued to assert that the dominant mode of American fiction was the romance, and that the literature of the United States was peculiarly devoid of social novels—as if those women never wrote. Similarly, critics and instructors maintained that complexity, irony, and ambiguity were the only significant virtues for a poem; and thus they stood mute before the repetitive, deceptively simple text of an American Indian chant. Of course, the new scholarship has begun to say goodbye to all that, but courses have been remarkably slow to change.

Perhaps not remarkably. For there are major barriers to change that instructors continue to encounter much more directly than scholars or critics. The most practical of these is simply the availability of texts. As a scholar, I could locate in one or another library a copy, for example, of Phelps's *The Silent Partner*; thus I could read and think about the implications of that book for the history of working-class and women's literature. While there was money for photocopying, I could even reproduce the novel for a small class on the Literature of Industrialization and Work. But that money ran out during the 70s, a class of thirteen was too large for handouts and I had to give up the book until The Feminist Press recently reissued it. If I chose to use an anthology—and financial pressures on students have pushed strongly in that direction—the situation was considerably worse. For even the most "enlightened" anthologies provided me with one—and only one—predictable story by Charles Chesnutt, Freeman, or Cather—and absolutely nothing by Charlotte Perkins Gilman, Zora Neale Hurston, Leslie Silko, or Alice Walker.

This volume obviously does not resolve the practical difficulty of texts.[1] Indeed, in certain respects the book underlines that problem. Since these are almost all real courses taught in real institutions, their instructors had to use texts that were available. In some cases, one can practically feel the instructor pushing up against the edges of what could be ordered, or even reproduced, for students. As a result, this volume is more limited than it might be—not by the imagination of its contributors, but by the same constraint we all face of availability of texts. Only a few syllabi meaningfully integrate the work of Hispanic-American, Asian-American, or American Indian writers; in these respects, the state of the art in American literature is not very well developed. We chose to include three courses developed at the Institute on Reconstructing American Literature held at Yale University by this project in 1982 precisely because those materials were more "wish lists" than actual courses and reflected what might be taught if texts were actually available. To extend the usefulness of this book, the reader should also consult volumes devoted specifically to courses on the literature of one minority or of women, issues of journals like *MELUS*, and collections of minority and women's writings.

Instructors may also face an even more difficult practical barrier in the reluctance of departmental colleagues and deans to accept differences in curricular priorities—let alone to change their own ideas of them. That reluctance is not at all hard to understand—even, moderately, to sympathize with. At one level it derives from the same kind of psychological process that motivates women to seek out women's texts and Chicanos to seek out Chicano works. Many of us white, male professors were taught that writers like Hemingway, Bellow, or—God save the mark—Mailer expressed our own values, if not our own experiences. If such gods of our literary pantheon were to be displaced to make room for a Zora ("Zora who?"), were our values, *all* values, also to be displaced? Were *we* to be displaced? In a profession of displaced persons, were we to join the roaming ranks? To be sure, that progression of thought will stand neither the test of logic nor that of academic power realities. But it is a factor for all that, just as is the reluctance to take on works from different cultures about which we feel ignorant. Such ignorance, of course, can be overcome through study and experience, to which more and more of our colleagues have committed themselves in faculty development seminars, in institutes, and in their own changing research. But differences in theory persist: at more fundamental

levels, the reluctance to change involves questions of aesthetics and pedagogy. And it is to these that I wish now to turn.

ii

How do we decide what to include in a course or in an anthology? Once
we recognize that the answer to that question is not foreordained by God, the
curriculum committee, or even the Norton anthology, a spectacular and
dangerous world of choice opens before us. In a practical way, as I have
indicated, the real possibilities of choice are less brilliant than they might at
first appear, but in the end we will not be satisfied with selections dictated by
a base pragmatism. We want them to conform to some set of standards,
aesthetic principles, pedagogical theories. Let us, then, imagine ourselves
walking freely—as in fact we are—in a world of many hundreds of authors
and thousands of pages of texts. We recognize some old friends, we nod
familiarly here and there, we are startled by a few unforeseen apparitions,
and we are always asking, "Of these many—appealing, strange, unsettling,
ordinary—what few do we take back with us into a fifteen-week class?"
        This is a serious enterprise. And perhaps the beginning of wisdom here
is to recognize the peculiar way in which our profession has trivialized our
own work. We have largely made ourselves guides to the forms of language
in texts—no mean task, but not, especially in classrooms, the heart of the
enterprise. For as teachers of literature, we are mediators between fictions in
language and people we call students. If our profession draws us to the
formal aspects of literary art, the core for most of our students remains the
experiences they encounter in the books and poems we bring them to.
        Take, for example, the following comment by Tomás Borge, a poet and
also one of the leaders of the successful guerilla struggle to liberate Nicaragua from dictatorship:

> But as to my personal formation, my vocation, my dedication to just
> causes, to politics, was due greatly to reading a German author who
> wrote about the west of the United States. His name was Karl May. He
> might not be very well known, but he wrote some novels; and the people
> in those novels had some definite qualities: loyalty, courage, honesty.
> And I made the effort, not always successful, to imitate them. Writers
> thus contribute to the formation of men. Another such writer, whose
> individual history does not interest me, was John Steinbeck.[2]

Borge's comment illustrates one way in which books—the experiences and
people in them—influence consciousness and thus actions in the world.[3]
This may indeed be their main value. Thus, we must begin by considering
seriously the nature of the experiences we select for the classroom.
        This is an argument neither for "relevance" nor for "morality." We
must be aware that no culture values all experiences equally and that our

curricula have validated certain experiences at the expense of others. Some of the most popular texts in United States literature present hunting—a whale or a bear—as paradigms for "human" exploration and coming of age, whereas menstruation, pregnancy, and birthing somehow do not serve as such prototypes. We need to consider whether texts of quality which explore such crucial female experiences—like Edith Summers Kelley's *Weeds*, Meridel LeSueur's "Annunciation," Paule Marshall's *Brown Girl, Brownstones*—do not have important places in our curriculum. To take another example, do we define heroism or even courage as qualities exclusive to the battlefield and perhaps the bull ring? Or do we extend the definition to include the New England spinster struggling for a place to live and grow old with dignity, or the fugitive's quest for freedom in the North? Again, a significant portion of canonical literature presents men pushing toward frontiers, exploring, conquering, exploiting the resources of sea and land. But for many immigrant and female writers, removal to the frontier represents a tearing up of roots; their concern is less self-discovery or conquest of new territory than the reestablishment of family, community, and a socially productive way of life. To the extent that we concentrate exclusively on works from the anti-social, escapist tradition in United States letters, we keep our students from learning of that more socially-focused tradition concerned with how to make life work in the here and now.

My point here is not to argue for the importance of any one set of experiences or values. Rather, it is to bring to the surface the fact that an element in curricular choice is subject-matter, or perhaps more accurately the paradigms of human experience embodied in a work. And to propose— as these syllabi implicitly do—a wider set of experiences for our curricula. That would be desirable, I think, even if collegiate student bodies consisted as they once did predominantly of young white men. But broadening curricula becomes even more imperative when we perceive not only the heterogeneity of our students, but of the world into which they are growing. Literary study can become central once more to the academic enterprise precisely because it provides students imagined opportunities to learn of experience and cultures not their own and to encounter differing values.[4]

At this point we engage significant objections; I would summarize them as follows: "Accepting that your argument is not directed to a curriculum determined by the 'relevance' of its subject-matter, are you not, nevertheless, using as standards of choice criteria external to the world of literary art? Are we not obligated to teach 'the best' of what has been written, rather than works that are representative, either of experience or of history? Would you have us include *inferior* work because it is by or about women, or minority people? Or because it 'illustrates' some set of historical circumstances or contemporary issues? Do we not, if we use any but aesthetic standards for choice, make literature and its study into a handmaiden of history or sociology, or the servant of someone's politics?"

These issues are fundamental and therefore not to be disposed of by short answers, however valid. It is important to realize that most curricula— like those I described above—and all anthologies include works on bases other than absolute aesthetic quality. It would be hard to maintain on purely aesthetic grounds that Mather, Bryant, Irving, Holmes, Norris, Cummings, Mailer—all of whom are regularly anthologized and often taught—are more important than Douglass, Freeman, Wharton, Hurston, or Alice Walker— who appear far less frequently, if at all, in anthologies or courses. It is, in fact, perfectly reasonable to include a work because it is historically representative or influential. Further, it is naive to assume that *nothing* but aesthetic quality goes into making even such fine works as Crane's *Red Badge of Courage* or Faulkner's *Absalom, Absalom* part of our literary canon while excluding Gilman's "The Yellow Wallpaper" or Hurston's *Their Eyes Were Watching God*. Surely, the political system called "patriarchy" is at some level involved in choosing works that focus on male experience and perspectives.

Nevertheless, the problem of aesthetic standards needs to be encountered on its own ground. Unfortunately, however, such standards were not delivered on tablets of bronze into the hands of T.S. Eliot. They derive from social practice and they change over time. Fifty years ago, Wyndham Lewis and Joseph Hergesheimer were all the rage; *ubi sunt?* And then there was that *serious* fifties novelist from Maryland—Lord, what was his name? Few are the artists whose names persist through time, and—dare one say it?—no North American is as yet indisputably among them. One must ask, then, not how to apply a given and persisting set of standards, but where standards come from, whose values they embed, whose interests they serve.

iii

Common academic experience exaggerates the degree to which aesthetic standards appear to be "universal." Place a group of literature professors in a room, give us ten unidentified texts, and more than likely we will agree on the value of half of them, perhaps more. Not surprising. After all, we have very similar training and congeneric lives, whose profound impact on our consciousness is pervasive if difficult to discern. We have all been taught the formalist virtues: economy, irony, well-articulated structure, and the like. We know the modernist catechism: literature is a form of discourse that "has no designs on the world," that represents things rather than trying to change them, and that speaks a language whose claim is originality, not clarity or simplicity. We also know that for many of the works we have learned to value, standards like complexity and detachment are, indeed, appropriate. This does not make them universal in literary study.

In this context it may help to recall that our views of literary excellence derive largely from criticism of recent vintage, for only in the 1920s and 1930s was the professional focus on texts and structure developed. Such formalist criticism emphasized as the poetic virtues complexity, irony, emotional restraint, and verbal sophistication. Allan Tate, for example, argued that "tension—the full organized body of all the extension and intension that we can find in it"—determines greatness in poetry.[5] Such a standard responded to the modernist poetry then being written—Eliot, Pound, Hart Crane—and it provided a method for combating the moralistic and "subjective" writing of genteel critics. It brought back into vogue the metaphysical poets and tended to disparage poets like Percy Bysshe Shelley, Walt Whitman, and Edna St. Vincent Millay—one of Tate's favorite targets. But while formalist *explication de texte* was effective both as a classroom tactic and for exploring a great many powerful texts, it provided no useful basis for approaching that great body of literature that placed a premium on simplicity, transparency, and emotional directness—from American Indian chants and spirituals to Langston Hughes and Gwendolyn Brooks, from *Uncle Tom's Cabin* to *Daughter of Earth*.

Where did Tate's standards, so sophisticated and powerful yet so exclusive and limiting, come from? The answer is complex,[6] but one part of it concerns the social position of the "man of letters in the modern world." In a mass society, as Tate characterized twentieth-century America, the social and cultural power of the critic was in decline. In the sphere of language and literature, however, he (the pronoun is apt) could retain a degree of authority as part of a priesthood of the word. But that could be true only in interpreting works amenable to complex analysis by the enlightened. This is not the whole story, of course, nor is it meant to disparage formalism as a strategy for appropriate texts. But I do wish to underline the fact that when the demands of a critical style become fundamentally determinative over curricular choice, they become barriers to apprehending other kinds of literary merit.

In general when we talk about "literary" or "aesthetic" merit we are speaking of the interest the form and language of a text hold for us—even if its values are alien. What if one were to argue that merit resides as importantly in the capacity of a work to move us, to evoke authentic feelings, even to prod us into action? It seems to me that literary training—perhaps on the medical model—practices us in dissociating what a work is about and how it affects us from the ways in which it is put together. Thus we teach the shape and sinew and texture of a hand, not whether it offers us peace or a sword. It is, after all, far easier to talk of form than of feelings—especially in a classroom. And yet, the question persists: In what ways does aesthetic merit reside in the production of affect and in what ways in the details of structure?

Probably no American writer raises that question more vividly for us than Harriet Beecher Stowe. In his "Afterword" to the Signet edition of *Uncle Tom's Cabin*, John William Ward describes the novel as the "despair of literary critics and a puzzle for social historians." He continues:

> Its immense, incredible popularity puts a problem to both literary and historical understanding. For the literary critic, the problem is simply how a book so seemingly artless, so lacking in apparent literary talent, was not only an immediate success but has endured. More importantly, if one of the tests of the power of fiction is the way in which a novel provides images that order the confusing reality of life, then *Uncle*

Tom's Cabin ranks high. Uncle Tom, litte Eva, Simon Legree, Topsy who just growed—these are characters who now form part of the collective experience of the American people.
(p. 480)

But the puzzle may lie more in the questions the critic asks and the terms the critic uses than in the novel itself. Stowe is reasonably clear in the matter:

> The writer has given only a faint shadow, a dim picture, of the anguish and despair that are, at this very moment, riving thousands of hearts, shattering thousands of families, and driving a helpless and sensitive race to frenzy and despair....Nothing of tragedy can be written, can be spoken, can be conceived, that equals the frightful reality of scenes daily and hourly acting on our shores, beneath the shadow of American law, and the shadow of the cross of Christ.
>
> And now, men and women of America, is this a thing to be trifled with, apologized for, and passed over in silence? Farmers of Massachusetts, of New Hampshire, of Vermont, of Connecticut, who read this book by the blaze of your winter-evening fire,—strong-hearted, generous sailors and shipowners of Maine—is this a thing for you to countenance and encourage? ... And say, mothers of America, is this a thing to be defended, sympathized with, passed over in silence?
>
> ... But, what can any individual do? Of that, every individual can judge. There is one thing every individual can do,—they can see to it that *they feel right*.... See, then, to your sympathies in this matter!
> (pp. 471, 472)

The book is meant to produce the "right feelings" of sympathy and outrage which lie at the root of "right action." Clearly, there is nothing in the least "artless" about Stowe's capacity to generate such feelings. Indeed, she is as artful in achieving her goals as Henry James—who patronized the book as a "wonderful 'leaping' fish" flying about outside "the medium in which books breathe"—was in achieving his.

Yet for years, few critics apart from Leslie Fiedler treated *Uncle Tom's Cabin*, or Stowe's many other works, with anything like the seriousness they deserve. It may well be that she was the victim precisely of her success in generating, not so much sales, as Fiedler proposes, as emotion. The dominant view, certainly since the modernist revolution against nineteenth-century gentility and emotionalism, has been suspicion of literary sentiment; indeed, among the most damning terms in the critic's arsenal has been "sentimental." We much prefer the detachment and aesthetic distance of irony, the tight, masculine lip. If an affection for a pleasing sentimentality was the curse of Victorian literati—and it was—surely our own has been to clamp feeling at a distance, to teach that big boys don't cry, and to busy ourselves in cerebral linguistic enterprises. We are familiar enough with the dangers of sentiment, the slippery slope that leads downward past the death of Little Eva to Stella Dallas, All My Children, and the Harlequin romances. What is problematic about irony has been less obvious, though one can track the path down the slope opposite to that of emotionalism past "Icarus in

Flight," and "Is There an American Cinema" to the cocktail-party chatter
of the junior English major: "She did her dissertation on Elinor Wylie, you
say. I see. Elinor Wylie."

Beneath the questions of curriculum and what we choose to emphasize
in class are political issues. The allegation of "sentimentality" does not,
finally, explain the "puzzle" of Harriet Beecher Stowe. Of course Stowe can
be dreadfully sentimental but the curve of her reputation has little to do with
this, or indeed with any other purely aesthetic consideration. It does,
however, coincide remarkably with the fall and rise of interest in the rights of
black people and of women of all races. The restoration of *Uncle Tom's Cabin*
to a degree of literary grace in the last decades testifies more to the impact of
the civil rights movement than, as yet, to a shift in our literary aesthetic.

Similarly, the more recent interest in Stowe's later fiction, like *The
Minister's Wooing*, developed initially from concerns given new weight by
the women's movement. Such concerns led to the reexamination of critical
terms like "regionalist." Gradually, it became clear that such terms, far from
being neutral descriptives, embody assumptions about literary and, finally,
human value. Thus, designating certain works, like those of Stowe, Mary
Wilkins Freeman, Charles Chesnutt, or Hamlin Garland as "regionalist"
effectively helped limit perception of their value as well as their use in
curricula.

Stowe again helps focus these issues for us. For she could not only be
sentimental but she also wrote sketches whose primary interest was their
ability to capture the local color of New England and Florida dialect and
character. Yet she can also be a powerful and subtle writer about social and
psychological conflict. Implicitly, a number of the syllabi collected here
argue for the importance of including Stowe—and the many other writers
for whom I have posed her as a paradigm—in our changing curricula.

What I am suggesting is that standards of literary merit are not absolute
but contingent. They depend, among other considerations, upon the relative
value we place on form and feeling in literary expression as well as on
culturally different conceptions of form and function. Thus, in seeking to
teach "the best"—as we should—of the various literatures that constitute
our national culture, we need constantly to reexamine our cultural yardstick.
Otherwise, we shall confine ourselves to works that happen simply to
conform to standards with which we have been familiar or which will suit
our professional roles as traditionally defined in academe.

iv

Changing the curriculum is more than a matter of abstract theory. Too
many faculty have come to me after workshops and asked, "How can you
teach that? What is there to say in class?" These questions, painful and real,
suggest the connection of curricular revision not only to aesthetic but to
pedagogical strategy.

The classroom is only one of the many contexts in which we and our students engage literature. We assume that the classroom is in some sense neutral, that the forms of literary encounter it implies do not do violence to the essence of a given work. But is that in fact the case? An American Indian tale, for example, can be read in ethnographical publications, it can be recited aloud by a student or instructor, it can even be heard and its recitation seen on a video tape. But all of these forms of literary encounter lift the tale from the tribal context in which it takes its living shape. The actual audience for the tale would have received its ritualized clues as to the kind of tale about to be told and would thus have its expectations defined. Further, such an audience would generally be familiar with the central characters and thus need not be introduced to them. Often, beyond all that, the tale fulfills definable, perhaps sacred, functions within the life of the tribe. All these elements are missing or badly distorted in the classroom, where the tale becomes an artifact of study. The instructor's task thus begins to shift from interpretation of the text itself to recreation of the cultural, social, and performance contexts that shape it. But even the most successful *recreation* cannot reproduce the real function of such a tale *within* the tribe and thus its real impact on the people by and for whom it was created. This might appear to present a discouraging prospect for an instructor. But in fact, it provides us with an opportunity to explore the important problem of how responses to a work differ according to the circumstances in which it is encountered and depending, also, upon the reader's or listener's own position in the world.

Although the problem is, perhaps, somewhat more extreme with American Indian literature than with other cultural traditions, the difference is in degree only, not in kind. The circumstances in which culture is produced and encountered, the functions of culture, the specific historical and formal traditions which shape and validate culture—these all differ somewhat from social group to social group and among classes. In this respect, the problem of changing curriculum has primarily to do with learning to understand, appreciate, and teach about many varied cultural traditions.

A few other instances may be helpful here. From the beginning, African-American artists have drawn on two differing traditions: the variety of European-American traditions available to and often thrust upon them, and the indigenous and equally varied cultures of black Americans and, to some extent, black African and Caribbean people. The latter, largely an oral and to some degree a "folk" tradition, includes forms as different as the slave narrative, "spirituals" and work songs, the blues, dialect tales, the verbal play common in the black community. But form is not the only thing that has separated black community. But form is not the only thing that has separated black American culture, for clearly the circumstances in which such forms were created and performed and the functions they served *within* the black community and in relation to the white community were equally distinct.[7] A spiritual might be a mode of solace—or a signal hidden from the white listener. The teller of tales might provide amusement and distraction, but also a means of sustaining sources of power within the black community.

The debate about the extent to which black artists do or should draw on this popular tradition has long raged among African-American literary critics. For our purposes it is necessary only to point out that many black artists did so. It thus becomes necessary to establish that context in order to work fully with Charles Chesnutt's stories, Ralph Ellison's *Invisible Man*, poems by Langston Hughes or Gwendolyn Brooks, precisely as it is necessary to familiarize students with the western history and traditions upon which T.S. Eliot or William Faulkner draw. More necessary, since fewer of our students are likely to be at all familiar with even the popular, daily ground of African-American culture, much less its artistic forms. The point here is not, however, to provide "background," but to understand fully the narrative strategies of Uncle Julius as a character and Chesnutt as an author in *The Conjure Woman* tales, or to see the play of poetic lines based formally on the blues or other African-American genres. Similarly, Henry Louis Gates, Jr. has argues that the narrative structure of Hurston's *Their Eyes Were Watching God* is designed to call attention to itself in order to privilege speech, the oral tradition, as a means for sustaining value in the black community.

A decade ago, it would have been virtually impossible to undertake the pedagogical tasks upon which I have touched here. Many of the key texts were not in print, or available only in research libraries. More to the point, perhaps, very little analysis of the distinctive qualities of minority and white female literary traditions had been published, Now, however, we have entered a phase in teaching, as in research, in which we can look at the received tradition of American letters alongside those newly recovered and have at our disposal serious analyses of both. That process, as I have suggested, allows us to review not only the subject matter of texts, the standards of literary value we use to make curricular choice, and some of the pedagogical changes implies by altered choices; but it also forces us to examine the way in which revised courses should, or inevitably do, respond to the imperatives of historical study. It is to that final subject I wish now to turn.

v

To some degree, every text inscribes the social ground against which it was created. Indeed, one can argue that literary works arise in the intersection of historical reality with cultural tradition. It follows that if we are interested in a more comprehensive view of the past, we will select historically and culturally diverse texts. As I pointed out above, we do that now when we include the New England schoolroom poets or James Fenimore Cooper in a survey course. Along such lines, there is no logical bar to broadening selection to include Lydia Maria Child and Susanna Rowson. For the historical and cultural grounds they encode are surely as valid and interesting as those of the male writers with whom we are more familiar. My point here, however, is not to reify the previous discussion of content, nor to preach a sermon about the responsibility of literature courses to clarify the history and past culture of this nation for students who are too ignorant of them.

I want, rather, to consider the transformation of perception that, I believe, occurs when a traditional literary category is shattered by adding a range of different works to prior accounts of it. Begin with F.O. Matthiessen's definition of the "American Renaissance": Emerson, Thoreau, Poe, Melville, Hawthorne. Add to it, now, Margaret Fuller, including her "Woman in the Nineteenth Century" and her late reports from revolutionary Italy; and now, Frederick Douglass's 1845 *Narrative*; and, again, Linda Brent's *Incidents in the Life of a Slave Girl* and some of the domestic fiction which, together with the tradition of the slave narrative, she evokes. A curriculum that includes this variety will, of course, provide us with a more comprehensive view of cultural cross-currents in the period leading up to the Civil War. My argument, however, is directed to how our views of the traditonal texts of the American Renaissance will alter in terms both of classroom presentation and private reading.

I am suggesting that familiar works change when we read them alongside others, less familiar, but which grew from the same historical soil. One can, for example, consider *The Scarlet Letter* with *Incidents in the Life of a Slave Girl*; Douglass's *Narrative* with Emerson's "Self-Reliance" and "Politics." Or, to touch on other periods and categories, one might examine the "realism" of Crane's "The Bride Comes to Yellow Sky" and *Maggie* with that of Freeman's "Louisa" and "Old Woman Magoun"; or the captivities of Mary Rowlandson with those of the Keres' "Yellow Woman" story and Olaudah Equiano. Nor have we yet wandered far from the received curriculum—we might want to proceed a step further, setting beside Thoreau's evocations of American Indian Experience the Indians' visions of their own lives and those of the whites. In putting together differently a broader set of texts, the creators of many of these syllabi are engaged not only in historical clarification, but are providing renewed access to familiar texts alongside fresh perceptions of a range of newly-valued literary works. And, of course, they are reshaping the very terms—"American Renaissance" and "realism," for example—that we have used to organize literary study.

This historical approach to literary study implicitly brings into question the hierarchy of forms as well. These syllabi regularly use more diaries, letters, and other "discontinuous" forms than traditional curricula might, and they probably make greater use of autobiographical writing, at least by minority writers and white women. In part, such curricular broadening is a consequence of the new feminist scholarship. Not only have feminist scholars uncovered surprising riches in women's journals and letters, like those of Maimie Pinzer to Fanny Quincy Howe (*The Maimie Papers*), but they have shown why many women sought self-expression in discontinuous, non-fictive forms, and how the tendency to disparage these was both consequence and cause of the devaluation of women's writing. In part, too, this kind of curricular shift reflects a heightened concern for "private" as well as "public" worlds. Autobiographical writing by successful public men, like

Franklin and Henry Adams, has always been part of the American literature curriculum. It has been a relatively short step through the remnants of racism from their work to that of Douglass and perhaps even W.E.B. DuBois. Writers like Linda Brent and Maimie Pinzer represent a more substantial departure because they are not people of public importance and their concerns are the more "mundane" problems of sexuality, family, poverty, housing—"love and money," to adapt Jane Austen's formulation of the subject matter of the novel. The renewed interest in such works in literary study parallels the shift in history from an overwhelming emphasis on political, diplomatic, and military study to a new regard for social history, and especially history "from the bottom."

This more historical approach has one further significant virtue. Literary works are often presented as the production of individual genius, isolated from the social world in which all human beings live. That mystifies writing, for authors, like other people, are part of, not separated from, the world they inhabit. And they compose in response not only to their literary predecessors but also to their social circumstances—as well, of course, as to their personal qualities. To say it another way, works of literary art express—in different balance—both the distinctive subjectivity of individual writers *and* the social dynamics of the world in which they lived. Again, Stowe is helpful here. It was not she, Stowe said, who wrote *Uncle Tom's Cabin*, but God writing through her. As a metaphor, the statement has a certain validity, for the book does indeed inscribe the transcendent social and emotional forces shaping antebellum America. And it compels us as readers to engage those forces emotionally and not simply as objects of study. For in a certain sense, we do not read simply as private individuals, any more than writers write that way. We are people in a world, not merely students of an art form. As books speak out of social as well as private realities, so they speak to and help form us as social beings. They affect what we value, how we see and perhaps even how we act.

To examine and reflect upon a set of reasonably well-scrutinized texts can be intellectually rewarding, but it seems to me to hold us looking backward at fragments of the past. Implicit in the curricular changes advanced in this book is, I believe, an aspiration to shape an equitable future in this most diverse of nations. I read that as a healthy and cheering development in our profession. For it means we are endowing what we do with the energy of our values, that we have revived the seriousness with which we once regarded the work of "The American Scholar." The job of reconstructing American literature is thus part of a broader movement for equal and fulfilling education. And its importance lies precisely in placing the study of our national cultures at the heart of educational renewal.

Notes

1. Another part of the project on Reconstructing American Literature, of which this volume is one product, involves the development of a wholly new anthology of American literature.

2. Interview, Managua, Nicaragua, August 1983.

3. In *Gender, Fantasy and Realism*, Alfred Habegger points out how the novel provided the Victorian reader with the opportunity "to try on a certain role—to think out with the help of a book-length narrative the potential life-consequences of being a given kind of woman" (p. ix). New York: Columbia University Press, 1982.

4. A colleague, Diana Hume George, wrote concerning this issue: "Those exploring/ conquering/ aggressive texts, made the centers of literature and humanities curricula, turn our classrooms into the 'educational' equivalents of the prime-time TV world, where program after program captures and keeps its audience by feeding it myths about danger and excitement—as if such experiences were at the heart of being human. In an era that is seeing the demise of the word and the rise of the video image, we might offer something different, and not only generically; I mean that the issue of balance is not just internal to the classroom—there are new reasons in the hyper-TV generation to offer gentler, more humanistic, more complex versions of human experience; otherwise we give students only a more cerebral version of tube ethics."

5. Allan Tate, "Tension in Poetry," *The Man of Letters in the Modern World* (New York: Meridian Books. 1955), p. 71.

6. I have explored that question at some length in "Race and Class in the Shaping of the American Literary Canon: A Case Study from the Twenties," *Feminist Studies* 9, No. 3 (Fall, 1983).

7. See Lawrence Levine, *Black Culture and Black Consciousness: Afro-American Folk Thought from Slavery to Freedom* (Oxford: Oxford University Press, 1977).

INTRODUCTORY COURSES

SINGLE-TERM COURSES

1
INTRODUCTION TO AMERICAN LITERATURE
Carolyn Allen, with Katherine Anderson, reader
1981–82
University of Washington
Seattle, WA 98195

Course Objectives

English 267, "Introduction to American Literature," is a one quarter (ten-week) course elected by sixty first- and second-year students, many of whom are either just beginning a major in English or deciding whether they wish to do so. The official course description for my section reads:

> We'll read texts by American women and men so that we can begin to identify the various literary histories that are called American. We'll give special attention to the twists and turns of the "American dream." Class discussion, deliberation, and differences of opinion will be central to what we do. Texts will be the *Norton Anthology of American Literature*, Vol. 1; Twain, *Complete Short Stories*; Cather, *My Antonia*; Hurston, *Their Eyes Were Watching God*; Fitzgerald, *The Great Gatsby*.

The course traditionally is a standard survey of American literature from its beginnings through the early twentieth century. My section challenged the canonized idea of American literary history, indeed of American social, cultural, and political history, by demonstrating that history is a fiction written by those who wish to retain a record of their own values— values unalterably, though usually unconsciously, marked by sex, race, and class. Within this general framework I chose to explore the myth of the "American dream," especially as it begins in the conflicting Puritan notions of good works and strong faith, and ways in which those early ideas allowed

3

an American dream that later proved to be something like a nightmare for many white women, people of the working class, and people of color.

So it was important to begin with seventeenth- and eighteenth-century American literature, to include Sarah Knight and Phillis Wheatley, to point out both their uniqueness, their isolation, ways in which they shared the dominant culture and ways in which they broke, however gently, from it. From there we went on to look at nineteenth-century literary history in the context of various social and political movements. We concluded with three novels, each with a different kind of "dream." This structure allowed us not just to study the literature, but also to understand the politics of canon formation and to uncover the biases hidden by clichés like the "American dream."

Syllabus

I. Early American Literature
Class 1   William Bradford, all (*The Norton Anthology of American Literature*, Vol. 1)
       2   Mary Rowlandson and Sarah Kemble Knight, all (Norton)
       3   Cotton Mather, from *The Wonders of the Invisible World* (Norton)
       4–5   Jonathan Edwards, Letter to Coleman; Benjamin Franklin, "Information . . . America," "Remarks Concerning Savages," selections from *Autobiography* (pp. 348–60, only); Phillis Wheatley, "On Being Brought . . . ," "To His Excellency . . ." (Norton)
II. Nineteenth-Century American Literature
       6–9   Ralph Waldo Emerson, "Self-Reliance"; Henry David Thoreau, selections from *Walden*, "Where I Lived and What I Lived For," "Conclusion" (Norton)
       10–13   Edgar Allan Poe, "The Fall of the House of Usher"; Nathaniel Hawthorne, "Young Goodman Brown," "The Maypole of Merrymount," "Rappaccini's Daughter" (Norton)
       14–15   Margaret Fuller, all (Norton)
       16   Frederick Douglass, from *My Bondage and Freedom* (Norton)
       17   Mid-term exam
       18–21   Herman Melville, "Bartleby the Scrivener" (Norton); Mark Twain, "The Notorious Jumping Frog," "The Man Who Corrupted Hadleyburg" (*Complete Short Stories*)
       22–24   Walt Whitman, "When I Heard at Close of the Day," "Out of the Cradle Endlessly Rocking"; Emily Dickinson, poems #303, 435, 520, 609, 754, 1129, 1540, 1624 (Norton)

III. Twentieth-Century American Literature
    25–28 Willa Cather, *My Antonia*
    29–32 F. Scott Fitzgerald, *The Great Gatsby*
    33–36 Zora Neale Hurston, *Their Eyes Were Watching God* (paper of
              five pages due on the topic of your choice about this
              book)

2
SURVEY OF AMERICAN LITERATURE
Carolyn L. Karcher
Fall, 1981
Temple University
Philadelphia, PA 19122

Course Objectives

In most respects my Survey of American Literature is quite traditional. It begins with the Puritans and traces the development of American literature and ideology from the seventeenth through the nineteenth centuries, drawing attention to both continuities and changes from one era to the next. In three respects, however, my syllabus departs from tradition: (1) it extends to 1900, instead of 1865, because the Department was then experimenting with reducing the survey to a one-semester course; (2) it omits many minor figures in the canon and one major author (Edgar Allan Poe), in order to make room for works by Indians, Blacks, and women, hitherto excluded from the canon; (3) it is structured as a dialectic between the opposing viewpoints of white and non-white, male and female, and emphasizes the contradiction between the Anglo-American vision of a consecrated nation and the Indian and Black experience of extermination and enslavement.

    Thus my syllabus juxtaposes Mary Rowlandson's *Narrative of Captivity* and William Bradford's account of the Pequot War (*Of Plymouth Plantation*, XXVIII), both of which portray the Indians as incarnate fiends, with the orations of Chiefs Logan, Speckled Snake, and Seattle, which present the Indian view of white treachery and greed, and which articulate an antithetical value system centered around harmony with the earth. Similarly, the syllabus sets up a dialogue between Ralph Waldo Emerson and Margaret Fuller, who applies Emerson's ideas of self-reliance to women, and who ultimately discards Transcendentalism for social action (I use both

"The Great Lawsuit" and her letters analyzing the Italian revolution of 1848, in which she participated). It also invites comparison of Fuller with Henry David Thoreau, whose evolution from *Walden* to "A Plea for Captain John Brown" followed parallel lines, but did not culminate in joining a movement.

The central section of the syllabus is devoted to slavery. A session on slave songs and abolitionist poetry highlights both their common features (use of dialect, irony, typology) and their different origins, functions, and preoccupations. In addition, it fosters appreciation of the sophisticated oral literature that slaves forged out of their oppression. Frederick Douglass's *Narrative*, Harriet Beecher Stowe's *Uncle Tom's Cabin* (both read in full), and Herman Melville's "Benito Cereno" provide complementary views of slavery and opportunities to speculate about the role that race, class, and gender play in determining each writer's orientation and special concerns.

The focus on gender as a possible source of difference continues in the sessions on Walt Whitman and Emily Dickinson (the public, expansive persona of the male poet vs. the private, diminutive persona of the female poet) and Charlotte Perkins Gilman's "The Yellow Wallpaper" and Henry James's *The Turn of the Screw* (a woman's perspective on female hysteria vs. a man's). Winding up the course, the last two works on the syllabus, Mark Twain's *Huckleberry Finn* and Stephen Crane's "The Monster" assess the legacy of slavery from a post-Civil War standpoint and return to the central contradiction that American literature embodies.

Booklist

The Norton Anthology of American Literature, Vol. 1
Stephen Crane, *Maggie and Other Stories*
Frederick Douglass, *Narrative of the Life of Frederick Douglass*
Charlotte Perkins Gilman, *The Yellow Wallpaper*
Henry James, *The Turn of the Screw*
Harriet Beecher Stowe, *Uncle Tom's Cabin*
Mark Twain, *Huckleberry Finn*

Syllabus

Class 1   Introductory Lecture—The Politics of Defining American
            Literature
2   John Winthrop, "A Model of Christian Charity";
            William Bradford, *Of Plymouth Plantation*, Bk. I, Ch.
            IX, (Norton) Bk. II, Ch. XXVIII (hand-out);
            Mary Rowlandson, *Narrative of Captivity*;
            Anne Bradstreet, "Verses Upon the Burning of Our
            House";

Edward Taylor, *Preparatory Meditations*, "Prologue" (Norton)

3 Selected American Indian orations by Chiefs Logan, Speckled Snake, and Seattle (hand-out);
St. Jean de Crèvecoeur, *Letters from an American Farmer*, (Norton); Letter IX (hand-out)

4 Jonathan Edwards, "Personal Narrative";
Benjamin Franklin, *Autobiography*, Books I–II (pp. 287–360) (Norton)

5 Bradford, *Of Plymouth Plantation*, Bk. II, Ch. XIX;
Cotton Mather, *Wonders of the Invisible World* (Norton);
Thomas Morton, *New English Canaan* (hand-out);
Nathaniel Hawthorne, "Young Goodman Brown," "The Maypole of Merrymount" (Norton)

6 Hawthorne, "The Minister's Black Veil," "Roger Malvin's Burial," "My Kinsman, Major Molineux" (Norton)
Paper Due: Hawthorne and the Colonial Heritage (3–5 pp.)

7 Ralph Waldo Emerson, *Nature*, "The American Scholar," "Self-Reliance," "The Problem," "Hamatreya," "The Snow-Storm," "Ode to W.H. Channing," "Days" (Norton)

8 Margaret Fuller, "The Great Lawsuit" (Norton); Letters from Italy of Oct. 18, 1847; November, 1847; March 29 and April 1, 1848; May 7, 1848 (hand-out)

9 Henry David Thoreau, "Resistance to Civil Government," "Plea for Captain John Brown" (Norton)

10 Thoreau, *Walden*: "Economy," "Where I Lived and What I Lived For," "Higher Laws," "Conclusion" (Norton)

11 Lecture on Slavery

12 Douglass, *Narrative of the Life of Frederick Douglass*

13 Poetry by Slaves and Abolitionists (hand-out)
Paper due: Comparison and Contrast of Emerson, Thoreau, and Fuller (4–6 pp.)

14 Stowe, *Uncle Tom's Cabin*

15 Herman Melville, selections from *Typee*, "Bartleby, the Scrivener" (Norton)

16 Melville, "Benito Cereno" (Norton)

17 Discussion of Melville, Stowe, Douglass (review)

18 Lecture on Walt Whitman and Emily Dickinson
Paper due: Douglass, Stowe, and Melville (6–8 pp.)

19 Emerson, "The Poet";
Whitman, "Preface" to *Leaves of Grass*, "Out of the Cradle Endlessly Rocking," "When Lilacs Last in the Dooryard Bloom'd" (Norton)

20 Whitman, "Song of Myself" (Norton)

21 Bradstreet, "The Prologue;"

> Dickinson, "Letters to Thomas Wentworth Higginson,"
> poems # 187, 258, 280, 281, 303, 341, 348, 435, 465, 512,
> 709, 1072, 1129, 1545, 1551, 1601 (Norton)

22   Gilman, *The Yellow Wallpaper*
23   James, *The Turn of the Screw*
24   Twain, *Huckleberry Finn*, Chapters 1–16
25   Twain, *Huckleberry Finn*, Chapters 17–end
26   Crane, "The Monster," *Maggie and Other Stories*

Written Assignments

Paper #1 (3–5 pp.)

Analyze some aspect of the Colonial heritage reflected in Hawthorne's tales. You may focus on one or more of the tales, or on a theme, motif, or historical incident, or on Hawthorne's attitude toward a particular aspect of the Colonial heritage.

The purpose of this assignment is to stimulate you to draw together the first segment of readings and to think about the similarities and differences between the Puritan and eighteenth-century world view and the nineteenth-century world view. To what extent is Hawthorne an heir of Puritanism? a critic of it? a rebel against it? a victim of it? To what extent does he perceive his forefathers accurately?

Here are some possible themes or subjects:

1. The witchcraft delusion
2. The American Revolution
3. The Calvinist doctrine
   of innate depravity
4. Indian wars
5. The Founding Fathers
6. Merry Mount
7. The wilderness
8. The City on a hill
9. The devil
10. Typology
11. Sin and guilt
12. The American dream

Paper #2 (5–6 pp.)

Emerson, Thoreau, and Fuller were all major participants in the Transcendentalist movement, but each emphasized different features of the movement. Take some aspect of their thought or writing and explore the similarities and differences their works exhibit. You must discuss at least two of these writers. Where appropriate, you should relate the Transcendentalists to earlier writers. In the process, you should arrive at a clearer understanding of how Transcendentalism both breaks with earlier American religious ideas and translates them into new forms.

Here are some possible topics:

1. The theme of self-reliance in Emerson, Thoreau, and Fuller
2. Emerson's and Thoreau's visions of nature (comparisons with the
   Puritans and Edwards appropriate)

3. The theme of American destiny in Emerson and Fuller
4. The theme of individualism in Emerson and Thoreau (comparisons with Franklin appropriate)
5. The attitude toward the "fathers" in Emerson, Thoreau, and Fuller (comparison with Hawthorne perhaps useful)
6. The individual vs. society in Emerson, Thoreau, and Fuller (comparison with Winthrop possibly useful)
7. The idealized vision of America in Thoreau and Fuller
8. The critique of America in Thoreau and Fuller
9. The influence of Emerson on Fuller and Thoreau (what is Emersonian in their thinking? where has each modified his ideas?)
10. The political evolution of Thoreau and Fuller from Transcendentalism toward political activism
11. Unresolved contradictions in Emerson and Thoreau
12. The theme of "higher law," or private conscience, in Emerson, Thoreau, and Fuller (comparisons with the Puritans appropriate)
13. The attitude toward the body and sexuality in Emerson, Thoreau, and Fuller
14. Free association in the style of Emerson, Thoreau, and Fuller
15. The attitude toward philanthropy, social reform, and slavery in Emerson, Thoreau, and Fuller (this can include women's rights)
16. Mysticism in Emerson and Thoreau (this could include their attraction to Eastern religions, for those of you who have background in this area)

Paper #3 (6-8 pp.)

Frederick Douglass's *Narrative*, Harriet Beecher Stowe's *Uncle Tom's Cabin*, and Herman Melville's "Benito Cereno" all expose the evils of slavery and seek to refute or subvert the racist assumptions on which slavery and discrimination against Blacks were based. Choose some aspect of slavery that all three writers focus on, and compare and contrast their treatment of it. You may, if you wish, expand the scope of your paper to include the slave and abolitionist poems we have studied.

Here are some possible topics:
1. The issue of slave violence (can include slave and abolitionist poetry)
2. The contrast between the masters' and slaves' viewpoints (can include slave poetry, as well as the various characters in the three books)
3. Religion and slavery (can include the indictment of the churches' hypocrisy, the uses of Biblical quotations to support and condemn slavery, the authors' religious ideals, the theme of apocalyptic judgment, the slaves' use of typology)
4. A comparative analysis of Douglass's, Stowe's, and Melville's rhetorical techniques and purposes
5. The use of irony in the antislavery argument (could analyze the different types of irony we find in the slave and abolitionist poems, Douglass's *Narrative*, *Uncle Tom's Cabin*, and "Benito Cereno")
6. The refutation of racist arguments in Douglass, Stowe, and Melville

7. The master-slave relationship as pictured in slave poems, Douglass's *Narrative*, *Uncle Tom's Cabin*, and "Benito Cereno" (can explore the theme of appearance vs. reality)
8. The portrayal of Blacks and of relationships among slaves in Douglass, Stowe, and Melville
9. The effects of slavery on slaves, masters, and the nation (can compare the three authors' central metaphors for what slavery means to them)

3
THE COMPLEX FATE
Arnold Krupat
Fall, 1982–Spring, 1983
Sarah Lawrence College
Bronxville, NY 10708

Course Objectives

"The Complex Fate" is a year-long survey in American literature from the Puritan invasion to the present. In its choices of authors and texts, the course emphasizes the degree to which American writing is the product of specific historical and intellectual encounters among black, white, and red people on this continent. This emphasis inevitably questions white cultural dominance of American literary writing, and, by logical extension, questions as well traditional hierarchies of gender and region: so far as possible, we read and discuss *not only* writing by white, eastern males. In this way issues of literariness and canonicity are made explicit, e.g., what are the criteria qualifying texts for study as *literature*, how is the pedagogical *canon* of "major" texts determined, and by what authority is it sustained?

The attempt regularly is to historicize the texts we read, to see them as responses to social and historical forces and not only as the pure products of individual "genius." Thus the secondary readings perform the function of providing specific contextual material ("facts," "background"); but they are also used to provide instances of different critical approaches—the liberal idealism of Perry Miller and the mythologizing of D.H. Lawrence and Leslie Fiedler, the sociological reading of Ann Douglas and the eclecticism of Paul Goodman. In using these secondary materials to examine the inter-relations of politics/art, history/literature, we consider as well the degree to which critical commentary is also of its time and place, not some timeless meditation on fixed and immutable "classics."

With all of this, most of our time in the classroom is spent within the textual system of signification. This is an undergraduate course, and it is important to practice close and careful reading; if the distinction is important, this is a course in literature, not the sociology of literature.

We conclude with a series of angry or apocalyptic visions by and about blacks, women, Indians—the imaginative ploughing under of Plymouth Plantation—and our ongoing consideration for what, in reality, must be supported or changed.

Booklist and Articles

The Bible, King James version
The Norton Anthology of American Literature, Vol. I
Virginia I. Armstrong, ed., *I Have Spoken: American History through the Voices of the Indians*
James Baldwin, *Notes of a Native Son*
Imamu Amiri Baraka, various texts
Donald Barthelme, *Unspeakable Practices, Unnatural Acts*
Daniel Boone, The "Autobiography of Daniel Boone," in John Filson, *Discovery, Settlement, and Present State of Kentucke*
Dee Brown, *Bury My Heart at Wounded Knee*
Stanley Cavell, *The Senses of Walden*
Abraham Chapman, ed., *Literature of the American Indian*
Kate Chopin, *The Awakening*
James Cox, "Autobiography and America," in *Aspects of Narrative: Selected Papers from the English Institute, 1971*, ed., J. Hillis Miller
Ann Douglas, *The Feminization of American Culture*
Richard Drinnon, *Facing West: The Metaphysics of Indian-Hating and Empire Building*
T.S. Eliot, *Selected Poems*
Leslie Fiedler, *Return of the Vanishing American*
F. Scott Fitzgerald, *The Great Gatsby*
Emma Goldman, *Living My Life*, Vol. I
Paul Goodman, *Growing Up Absurd*
William T. Hagan, *American Indians*
Ernest Hemingway, *In Our Time*
Henry James, "Daisy Miller"
Jack Kerouac, *On the Road*
Annette Kolodny, "Some Notes on Defining a Feminist Literary Criticism," *Critical Inquiry*, Autumn, 1975
———, "A Map for Rereading: Or, Gender and the Interpretation of Literary Texts," *New Literary History*, Spring, 1980
Arnold Krupat, "American Autobiography: The Western Tradition," *The Georgia Review*, Summer, 1981
Ann Lane, ed., *The Charlotte Perkins Gilman Reader*

D.H. Lawrence, *Studies in Classic American Literature*
Perry Miller, *Errand Into the Wilderness*
Gary Nash, *Red, White, and Black: The Peoples of Early America*
Gary Nash and James Weiss, eds., *The Great Fear: Race in the Mind of America*
Howard Norman, tr. and ed., *The Wishing Bone Cycle*
Simon Ortiz, *Sand Creek*
Ezra Pound, *Selected Poems*
Philip Rahv, *Literature and the Sixth Sense*
Adrienne Rich, *On Lies, Secrets, and Silences*
————, *A Wild Patience Has Taken Me This Far*
J.D. Salinger, *The Catcher in the Rye*
Henry Nash Smith, *Virgin Land*
Frederick W. Turner, III, ed., *The Portable North American Indian Reader*
Mark Twain, *Huckleberry Finn*
Wilcomb Washburn, *The Indian in America*
William Carlos Williams, *In the American Grain*
————, *Selected Poems*
Richard Wright, *Native Son*

Syllabus, Fall Semester

(OR indicates book/article *on reserve* at the library.)

Class 1   *The Bible*, "Genesis," 1-4, 25: 20-27; William Bradford, *Of Plymouth Plantation*, Bk. I, ch. ix, Bk. II, ch. xi (Norton); Williams, "The Voyage of the Mayflower" (Williams, IAG); Fiedler, "The World Without a West" (Fiedler, RVA: OR)

2   Turner, from the Iroquois Creation story, pp. 36-42, "This Newly Created World," Winnebago, p. 238, "Emergence Song," Pima, p. 238, Powhatan, p. 242 (Turner, PNAIR); Anaquoness, letter, "Dear Miss Nurse" (Armstrong, IHS: OR); Lawrence, "Foreword," "The Spirit of Place" (Lawrence, SCAL); Hagan, ch. 1 (Hagan, AI: OR)

3   Bradstreet, "Before the Birth...," "To My Dear and Loving Husband," "A Letter to Her Husband...," "Upon the Burning of Our House...," "As Weary Pilgrim" (Norton); Bradford, Bk. II, ch. xix (Norton); Williams, "The May-Pole at Merry Mount" (Williams, IAG); Hawthorne, "The Maypole of Merry Mount" (Norton)

4   Drinnon, Introduction, chs, I, II, III (Drinnon, FW: OR); Cotton Mather, from *The Wonders of the Invisible World* (Norton); Hawthorne, "Young Goodman Brown" (Norton); Daniel Boone, "Autobiography" (Boone:

OR); Krupat, "American Autobiography: The Western Tradition" (OR); Gary Nash, Introduction (Nash, RWB: OR); Perry Miller, "Errand Into the Wilderness" (Miller, EIW: OR)

5   Franklin, "The Way to Wealth," "Remarks Concerning the Savages of North America," "Letter to Ezra Stiles" (Norton); Armstrong, Introduction to *I Have Spoken* (OR); #30, Canassatego, in *I Have Spoken* (OR); William Bradford, Bk. II, ch. xxiii (Norton); Lawrence, "Benjamin Franklin" (Lawrence, SCAL); Williams, "Notes for a Commentary on Franklin" (Williams, IAG)

6   Thomas Jefferson, Query VI from *Notes on the State of Virginia*, "The Declaration of Independence" (Norton); Hagan, ch. 2 (AI:OR); Hawthorne, "My Kinsman, Major Molineux" (Norton); Lawrence, "Nathaniel Hawthorne and 'The Scarlet Letter'" (Lawrence, SCAL); Henry Nash Smith, Prologue, ch. 1 (Smith, VL: OR)

7   Emerson, from "Nature," Introduction, ch. 1 (Norton); Miller, "Nature and the National Ego" (Miller, EIW: OR); Paula Gunn Allen, "The Sacred Hoop: A Contemporary Indian Perspective on American Indian Literature" (Chapman, LAI: OR); Turner, oratory from the Indians, pp. 243-256 (Turner, PNAIR: OR)

8   Walt Whitman, "Song of Myself" (Norton); Lawrence, "Whitman" (Lawrence, SCAL)

9   Whitman, cont.; James Cox, "Autobiography and America" (OR)

10   Thoreau, from *Walden*: "Economy," "Where I Lived and What I Lived For," "The Pond in Winter," "Spring," "Conclusion" (Norton); Stanley Cavell, "Words" (Cavell, SOW: OR)

11   Gary Nash, chs. 7, 8 (Nash RWB: OR); Phillis Wheatley, "On Being Brought from Africa to America" (Norton); Frederick Douglass, from *My Bondage and My Freedom*: "The Last Flogging," "Letter to his old master" (Norton); James Baldwin, "Notes of a Native Son" (Baldwin, NNS: OR); Thoreau, "Slavery in Massachusetts," "A Plea for Captain John Brown" (Norton)

12   John Woolman, from *The Journal* (Norton); Thoreau, "Life Without Principle" (Norton); Melville, "Benito Cereno" (Norton)

13   Thoreau, "Civil Disobedience" (Norton); Melville, "Bartleby the Scrivener" (Norton); Melville, from *The Confidence Man*, ch. XXVI, "Containing the Metaphysics of Indian-Hating...," (Turner, PNAIR)

Syllabus, Spring Semester

(OR indicates book/article *on reserve* at the library)

Class 1   Mark Twain, *Huckleberry Finn*; Ann Douglas, "Introduction: The Legacy of American Victorianism" (Douglas, FAC: OR); Joseph Boskin, "Sambo: The National Jester in the Popular Culture" (Nash and Weiss, TGF: OR)

2   Film showing: John Ford's *Cheyenne Autumn*; Dee Brown, ch. 14, "Cheyenne Exodus" (Brown, BMHWK: OR); Little Wolf's speech, #199 (Armstrong, IHS: OR); Washburn, "The Civil War and its Aftermath," "The Reservation Indian" (Washburn, IA: OR)

3   Emily Dickinson, poems 130, 187, 214, 241, 258, 303, 328, 341, 348, 465, 510, 569, 585, 709, 754, 986, 1072, 1100, 1129, 1624 (Norton); Adrienne Rich, "E" (handout), "Women and Honor: Some Notes on Lying" (Rich, OLSS: OR)

4   Charlotte Perkins Gilman, "The Yellow Wallpaper," "If I Were a Man" (Lane, CPGR); Kate Chopin, *The Awakening*

5   Chopin, cont.; Henry James, "Daisy Miller"; Emma Goldman, from *Living My Life*, vol. I: chs. 1 and 2 (OR); Annette Kolodny, "Some Notes on Defining a Feminist Literary Criticism" (OR), "A Map for Rereading: Or, Gender and the Interpretation of Literary Texts" (OR)

6   Ezra Pound, "A Pact," "The River Merchant's Wife, A Letter," "Hugh Selwyn Mauberley" (Pound, SP); T.S. Eliot, "The Waste Land" (Eliot, SP); Philip Rahv, "Paleface and Redskin" (Rahv, LSS: OR)

7   Kenneth Rexroth, "American Indian Songs" and Mary Austin, "The Path on the Rainbow" (Chapman, AIL: OR); traditional Indian songs, pp. 238-241 (Turner, PNAIR); selections from *The Wishing Bone Cycle* (Norman, WBC: OR); Williams, "Père Sebastian Rasles" (Williams, IAG); Williams, "The Red Wheel Barrow," "This is Just to Say," "The Widow's Lament in Springtime," from "Spring and All" (Williams, SP)

8   Ernest Hemingway, *In Our Time*

9   F. Scott Fitzgerald, *The Great Gatsby*

10   Richard Wright, *Native Son*; James Baldwin, "Many Thousands Gone" (Baldwin, NNS: OR)

11   J. D. Salinger, *The Catcher in the Rye*; Paul Goodman, from *Growing Up Absurd*: chs. ii and viii (OR)

12   Jack Kerouac, *On the Road*; Paul Goodman, from *Growing Up Absurd*; ch. ix, Appendix E (OR)

13   Drinnon, "The Problem of the West" (Drinnon, FW: OR); Donald Barthelme, "The Indian Uprising" (Barthelme,

UPUA: OR); Rich, "Heroines," "Self-Hatred" (Rich,
WPHTMTF: OR); Imamu Amiri Baraka (handout);
Simon Ortiz, from *Sand Creek* (handout)

4
AMERICAN VOICES
Louis Kampf
Fall, 1982
Massachusetts Institute of Technology
Cambridge, MA 02139

Course Objectives

The purpose of the course is to examine how various social groups—
Native Americans, slaves, immigrants, women, gays, etc.—have reacted to
the notion of the American Dream, and the voices through which they
expressed these reactions. Franklin's *Autobiography* is the classic expression
of the Dream. It is written in the standard English of the eighteenth-century
familiar essay, an instrument appropriate enough for this comfortably successful WASP male; one can imagine Franklin talking this way. The matter
is not so simple for a slave woman, for Black Elk, or for a contemporary
Chinese-American girl. At the end of the course, in Alice Walker's story, I
ask the students to consider why the mother speaks in Mississippi Black
English, but thinks in very literary standard English. In a number of the
readings (J.G. Neihardt, Mike Gold, for example) people are represented as
speaking English, when in reality they were speaking other languages. For
these people, the learning of English becomes part of the attainment of the
American Dream, as well as one symbol of cultural loss.

Songs, non-standard literary forms, and documentary films are used
because they so often allow the unhampered expression of people's voices.
And with such unhampered oral release, people's deepest feelings about the
American Dream emerge in often surprising ways.

Course Requirements

You are expected to do *all* the reading, attend *all* classes, and view all
the films. You will hand in informal papers discussing the reading or films as
indicated on the syllabus. In writing the papers, *begin with your own reac-*

tions. Does the work do anything to you? Or does it leave you cold? Why? Try to explain your reactions. Who is speaking to you in the work? What is s/he trying to do to you? Is a reader or viewer of your own sex, social class, race being addressed? Or someone else? In addition, if you wish to write something about what's going on in class, feel free to do so. Papers are due in class on the day assigned—not several hours or days later. Lateness will be reflected in your grade.

If the class is large enough, some of the teaching will be done by groups of students. Each group will first have a meeting to discuss the work and to outline what it wants to do in class; the group will then meet with me to discuss its plans; finally, it will meet once again to straighten out loose ends.

Booklist

Linda Brent, *Incidents in the Life of a Slave Girl*
Benjamin Franklin, *Autobiography*
Mike Gold, *Jews Without Money*
M. Goodwin, "From Memphis to Norfolk"
Maxine Hong Kingston, *The Woman Warrior*
J. G. Neihardt, *Black Elk Speaks*
Miguel Pinero, *Short Eyes*
Studs Terkel, *American Dreams*
Alice Walker, "Everyday Use"

Syllabus

Class 1	Introductory
2	Songs: Merle Haggard, "Okie From Muskogee," Bob Dylan, "Subterranean Homesick Blues"; paper: 1 page
3	Film: "The War At Home"
4	Discussion; paper: 1 page
5–6	Benjamin Franklin, *Autobiography* (pp. 15–181); "The Way To Wealth" (pp. 188–97); paper: 2 pages
7–8	J. G. Neihardt, *Black Elk Speaks*; paper: 2 pages
9–10	Linda Brent, *Incidents in the Life of a Slave Girl*; paper: 2 pages
11	Film: "Fannie Bell"
12	Songs: "Go Down Moses," "Grizzly Bear" (handout); paper: 1 page
13–14	Mike Gold, *Jews Without Money* (handout); paper: 2 pages
15–16	Maxine Hong Kingston, *The Woman Warrior*; paper: 2 pages

17-18   Studs Terkel, *American Dreams* (Castillo, Rasmussen, Fuller, O'Brien, Slabaugh, De Loria, Robinson, Fox, Edwards, Turner, Fielding, Jarrett, Rosenzweig, Scala, Duncan, Rosa, Schwarzenegger, Baylies, Kunzman, Cruz, Christianson, Nearing, Kucinich, Lopez, Campbell, Bendinger, Culbert, Lovejoy, Spencer, Johnson, Rocco); paper: 2 pages (include your own American Dream)

19   Film: "Short Eyes"; read the play, by Miguel Pinero, before you come to the movie; paper: 1 page

20   Discussion

21   Film: "Word is Out"

22   Discussion; paper: 1 page

23   Film: "Good Mornin' Blues"

24   Blues by Bessie Smith, Memphis Minnie, Blind Lemon Jefferson, Robert Johnson, Jimmie Rodgers, etc. (handout); paper: write a blues

25   Blues continued; M. Goodwin, "From Memphis to Norfolk" (handout); paper: 1 page

26   Film, "Always for Pleasure"

27   Discussion

28   Bring your favorite song to class—if you have one, and are able to do so

29   Film, "Quilts in Women's Lives"

30   Alice Walker, "Everyday Use" (handout); paper: 1 page

31   Conclusions; paper critiquing the course and suggesting changes

5
MASTERPIECES OF AMERICAN LITERATURE
Missy Dehn Kubitschek
Spring, 1979
University of Illinois
Currently at University of Nebraska/Omaha
Omaha, NB 68182

Course Objectives

This course does not attempt to survey American literature: its booklist does not include every important writer, nor does it cover a range of work by any one writer. Instead, the course attempts to delineate the political and psychic tensions characteristic of American culture. In a culture traditionally anti-historical and in a time so profoundly ahistorical that college freshmen often think that the Vietnam War ended twenty years ago, this course provides a perspective on sexism, racism, and more traditionally defined politics. The course materials embody some of the tremendous variety of historical response to these problems; they examine, deplore, and celebrate American problems, American experience, and human creativity.

I have chosen individual works for many different reasons—because they are early statements of problems that students may believe to have been discovered only in the 1960s, because they indicate complexities not present in the first discussions, because they clarify or intensify a problem or a reaction. The course uses canon writers to demonstrate the presence of ideas not usually associated with the canon and thus makes evident the political bias which often controls the presentation of literature. The class will discuss the means by which a work can be de-politicized and perceived as aesthetic object rather than as social commentary; this exercise will draw attention to the apolitical approach *as an approach* rather than as "the way literature is studied and discussed." *The House of Mirth* offers especially rich opportunities for such exploration. The novel supports, indeed invites, formalist, New Critical, Marxist, feminist, and deconstructionist readings. Students will explore these readings and their philosophical/political underpinnings in order to become more aware of their own and their professors' premises. This course will provide both specific knowledge about individual American masterpieces and alternative models for the study of all literature.

Booklist

Thomas Berger, *Little Big Man*
Kate Chopin, *The Awakening*
Ralph Ellison, *Invisible Man*
William Faulkner, *As I Lay Dying*
Nathaniel Hawthorne, *The Scarlet Letter*
Herman Melville, "Benito Cereno"
Arthur Miller, "The Crucible"
Thomas Pynchon, *The Crying of Lot Forty-Nine*
David Rabe, "The Basic Training of Pavlo Hummel"
Mark Twain, *The Adventures of Huckleberry Finn*
Edith Wharton, *The House of Mirth*
Richard Wright, *Uncle Tom's Children*
(Handouts of other material)

Syllabus

I.   American Declarations, Dreams, and Nightmares
Class 1   Declaration of Independence (original and final
                     versions)
     2   Edgar Allan Poe, "Annabel Lee," "Alone," "The
                     Raven"
     3   Walt Whitman, "There Was a Child Went Forth,"
                     "Out of the Cradle Endlessly Rocking," "I Sing
                     the Body Electric"
     4–6   Twain, *Huckleberry Finn*
II. Genteel Slavery: Women in American Culture
     7   Emily Dickinson, "Safe in Their Alabaster Chambers,"
                     "Mine—by the Right of the White Election!"
                     "Wild Nights—Wild Nights!" "Tell All the Truth but
                     Tell it Slant," "I Felt a Funeral in My Brain"
     8   E. A. Robinson, "Eros Turannos," "The Mill," "The Tree
                     in Pamela's Garden"
     9–12   Hawthorne, *The Scarlet Letter*
     13–15   Chopin, *The Awakening*
     16–18   Wharton, *The House of Mirth*
     19   Midterm
III. The Intricate Knot: Race and Identity
     20–21   Melville, "Benito Cereno"
     22–24   Wright, *Uncle Tom's Children*
     25–28   Ellison, *Invisible Man*
     29   Langston Hughes lecture
     30   Wallace Stevens, "Not Ideas about the Thing but the Thing
                     Itself," "The American Sublime"

Midterm Exam

1.   No reader has ever been in danger of confusing the heroines of *The Scarlet Letter*, *The Awakening*, and *The House of Mirth:* Are the male characters as distinct, or are Dimmesdale, Robert Lebrun, and Selden small variations on the same theme? Consider their treatment(s) of the heroines, their motivations, their self-concepts, etc.

2.   Organized religion takes a drubbing in the works that we've read thus far. What corrupts religious practice in *Huck Finn* and *The Scarlet Letter*? What does religion support? What does it, by design or accident, crush?

3.   To outraged contemporary response, Whitman and Chopin sang the body electric: compare and contrast their examinations of sensuality and sexuality. What is the place of sensuality in the healthy personality? Are there, or should there be, limits on its expression in these writers' views?

Come to class prepared to write on two of these three questions.

Final Exam Questions

The final examination questions will be drawn from those below. Consider them carefully; you may wish to outline answers when you are preparing for the exam. The exam will consist of two of the one-hour questions and two of the half-hour questions.

One-Hour questions:

1.   In three of the works that we have studied, discuss the ambiguities of silence. (Among others, "Bright and Morning Star" from *Uncle Tom's Children*, *Huck Finn*, "Benito Cereno," and "The Crucible" would work well.) When does silence protect the character? When does it force him/her into a betrayal of self or others? Under what circumstances does society require speech? Is this speech more or less often than silence a betrayal? Why?

2.   Define the concept of marginality, existing on the fringes of a social order; then examine three or more characters who choose a marginal existence, a sub-human or extra-human role. Some possibilities: Mistress Hibbins in *The Scarlet Letter*, Jack Crabb as drunkard in *Little Big Man*, Huck Finn lighting out for the territories, the persona of "I Felt a Funeral in My Brain." What do their choices stem from? What do they hope to gain? Do they in fact gain it?

3.   The private vision/public vision split in focus, which we explored through Poe and Whitman, often recurs within a single work when a character realizes that her/his personal life is determined in important respects by external forces. Compare the confrontations with the public that occur in *The Awakening* or *The House of Mirth* with those in *The Crying of Lot 49*; then indicate whether these seem fundamentally like or unlike that of a male protagonist in either *Little Big Man* or *Invisible Man*.

4.   Several of the works for this course have dealt with the quest in which a hero or heroine seeks a goal at great peril. Using *Huck Finn, Invisible Man*, and *Little Big Man* delineate the motivation for undertaking the quest, major risks faced, and the rewards (if any). Then, contrast these with their counterparts in the female quest as represented in *The Awakening* or *The Crying of Lot 49*.

Half-hour questions:

1.   Compare and contrast the parts of the Wild West legend that Berger and Cummings choose to accent through Wild Bill Hickock in *Little Big Man* and Buffalo Bill in "portrait." In what ways do the poems revise our legends and our evaluations of these heroes?

2.   Hester Prynne in *The Scarlet Letter* hopes for better, truer traditions through which men and women may interact. On the basis of *As I Lay Dying*, has American culture constructed what she hopes for? Do the men and women relate to one another in the same, similar, or quite different ways in these novels? Some possible areas for exploration—the expression(s) of sexuality, the meaning of marriage, the definitions of betrayal.

3.   *Little Big Man* explores two psychologies of warfare—white and Indian. Briefly indicate their differences and then compare the white system with that in "The Basic Training of Pavlo Hummel." Are the underlying attitudes which construct the two systems the same? Similar? Quite different?

4.   *Uncle Tom's Children* shows some characters like Big Boy destroyed by stereotypes and some like Sue able to manipulate them and triumph. Briefly list the stereotypes which come into play in *Uncle Tom's Children* and *Little Big Man*; next, discuss whether Jack Crabb manipulates them successfully or whether he is destroyed by them.

5.   It has become fashionable in the last fifteen years to link the women's movement with the civil rights movement, to see racist and sexist oppression as parts of the same matrix. Is this point of view supported or denied

implicitly by earlier black male writers, as represented by Ellison's *Invisible Man* and Wright's *Uncle Tom's Children*? How do their male protagonists relate to women of color? To white women? Does the narrative voice of *Uncle Tom's Children* indicate a different attitude from that of the characters? Are these attitudes constant or shifting?

6. Ellison's concept of social and personal invisibility, as described in the prologue of *Invisible Man*, is almost infinitely expandable as a means of discussing the simplification or oversimplification of an individual by the surrounding society. One could say, for example, that the scarlet "A" makes Hester invisible in *The Scarlet Letter*. Choosing one novel, discuss the methods for making inconvenient individuals invisible and the individual's reactions or defenses. (Since our class discussion focused on this issue in *Invisible Man*, choose another work.)

6
AMERICAN VOICES—AN INTRODUCTION TO LITERATURE IN THE UNITED STATES
Paul Lauter
Fall, 1982
State University of New York/College at Old Westbury
Old Westbury, NY 11568

Course Objectives

Originally I designed this course with two ideas in mind: I wanted students to overcome the notion that what "writers" did was one thing, but what they themselves wrote was something quite different. I wanted them to see the continuities as well as the distinctions among different kinds and qualities of writing. And I wanted them to understand that there wasn't an absolute line separating, say, letters, autobiography, fiction, but that they were somewhat differing ways of creating and recreating experience; that writers used many similar writing tactics, whatever the form; and that these tactics were available to *them* as writers. So I began with letters, which most of them wrote, proceeded to autobiographical writing, and then finally went on to fiction—using folk tales and both "folklore" and fiction by Zora Neale Hurston as the transition.

Second, I wanted students to experience at least some of the many different "voices" that constitute the literary cultures of the United States. I wanted them to hear the voice of the immigrant anarchist, the fugitive slave, the New England spinster, the Philadelphia prostitute—as well as the well-heard voices of canonical writers. And I wanted them to see that "literature" was not necessarily about people in fancy houses in Great Neck or on battlefields and bull rings. That, indeed, their own lives—the lives primarily of people of color, working-class people, white suburban women— were also the stuff out of which writing was made. At the same time, I wanted them to have at least some access to the traditional group of writers who constitute the American literary canon: Edgar Allan Poe, Nathaniel Hawthorne, Herman Melville. However, my choices from these authors generally reflected themes developed elsewhere in the course—e.g., I found it useful to think about some of Poe's stories in relation to Charlotte Perkins Gilman's portrait of madness in *The Yellow Wallpaper*.

I initially tried to do songs and poetry, but found the course too crowded. I would like to do Henry David Thoreau, but sensed from other courses that the students found him quite remote. I'd also like to put Henry James together with Maimie Pinzer, but too many of my students have reading problems to be able to do that just now. I would probably not use the Sarah Orne Jewett stories with these students if she were not in a volume with Mary Wilkins Freeman, who seems to me essential to teach. I also used to do Mike Gold's *Jews Without Money*, but it is no longer in print and I cannot have so much copied.

In short, while the course works very well, reading choices depend partly on design, partly on what happens to be available, and partly on the unique needs of Old Westbury's distinctive student body.

Booklist

Linda Brent (Harriet Jacobs), *Incidents in the Life of a Slave Girl*
Charles Chesnutt, *The Conjure Woman*
Frederick Douglass, *Narrative of the Life of Frederick Douglass*
Charlotte Perkins Gilman, *The Yellow Wallpaper*
Zora Neale Hurston, *I Love Myself When I Am Laughing*
Sarah Orne Jewett and Mary Wilkins Freeman, *Short Fiction*
The Maimie Papers, Ruth Rosen and Sue Davidson, eds.
Herman Melville, *Billy Budd and Other Stories*
Elizabeth Cady Stanton, *80 Years and More*

Syllabus

Class 1 Letters by Sacco and Vanzetti (handout)
2 Benjamin Franklin, *Autobiography*, (handout), pp. 16–82
3 Franklin, *Autobiography*, pp. 83–129, and "The Way to Wealth"
4 Douglass, *Narrative*, "Preface" and pp. 21–64
5 Douglass, *Narrative*, pp. 65–end
6 Brent, *Incidents in the Life of a Slave Girl*, pp. 3–87
7 Brent, *Incidents*, pp. 87–169
8 Stanton, *80 Years and More*, pp. 1–91
9 Stanton, *80 Years*, pp. 92–185
10 *The Maimie Papers*, pp. 1–76
11 *Maimie*, pp. 76–109, 247–320
12 Exam
13 Kentucky Mountain Stories (handout)
14 Hurston, *I Love Myself*, pp. 49–59, 82–122, 169–73
15 Hurston, *I Love Myself*, pp. 177–218; Langston Hughes, "Big
      Meeting" (library reserve)
16 Nathaniel Hawthorne, "Young Goodman Brown," "The
      Minister's Black Veil," "My Kinsman, Major Moli-
      neux" (handout)
17 Hawthorne, "The Maypole of Merrymount," "The
      Birthmark," "Rappaccini's Daughter" (handout)
18 Edgar Allan Poe, "Eleanora," "The Imp of the Perverse,"
      "The Black Cat," "Berenice," "Ligeia," "The Fall of
      the House of Usher," "Ms. Found in a Bottle" (handout)
19 Melville, "The Paradise of Bachelors" and "The Tartarus of
      Maids" (handout); "Bartleby," "The Lightning-Rod
      Man," "The Town Ho's Story" in *Billy Budd*
20 Melville, "Billy Budd"
21 Chesnutt, *The Conjure Woman*, pp. 1–131
22 Chesnutt, *Conjure Woman*, pp. 132–229
23 Jewett, "The Foreigner," "The Queen's Twin," "Miss
      Peck's Promotion," "The Passing of Sister Barsett,"
      "Aunt Cynthy Dallett"
24 Freeman, "A Mistaken Charity," "A Church Mouse," "One
      Good Time," "Gentian," "Louisa"
25 Freeman, "A Conflict Ended," "The Revolt of 'Mother,'"
      "A New England Nun," "A Village Singer," "Old Wo-
      man Magoun"
26 Gilman, *The Yellow Wallpaper*

7
AMERICAN LITERATURE:
LIBERATION AND LIMITATION
IN AMERICAN LITERARY HISTORY
John Schilb
Spring, 1982
Denison University
Currently at University of North Carolina/Wilmington
Wilmington, NC 28406

Rationale of the Course

English 230, "American Literature," has traditionally concerned a more limited span of time than its title implies. According to the description of it in the Denison University catalog, the course deals with "selected works by writers of the 19th Century, including Poe, Emerson, Thoreau, Hawthorne, Melville, Whitman, Twain, James, and Crane." In designing my own section of the course, I tended to stay within the bounds of the era invoked, trespassing them only to some extent. Moreover, I included most of the canonical figures listed, along with others of similar repute.

Yet I consider my section to be a transformation of the course as it has usually been taught, in two main respects. First, I included noncanonical writers like Charlotte Perkins Gilman, Frederick Douglass, Rebecca Harding Davis, and Maimie Pinzer, encouraging the students to juxtapose their perspectives with those of the celebrated white male writers. Second, I divided the course into units focused in turn on gender, race, and class, rather than proceeding in chronological order or through units based on conventional periodization. Such a structure, along with the comparative mode of analysis persistently applied to the readings and along with the proposed subtitle of the course ("Liberation and Limitation in American Literary History"), enabled the students to dwell on how the cultural mythologies surrounding gender, race, and class have significantly influenced both the writing of literature and the process of canon-formation. To be sure, partitioning the course in this way runs the risk of obscuring how gender, race, and class might interconnect as liberating or limiting conditions. But I tried to keep their potential links apparent to the students even as we focused on each.

Course Objectives

To read, analyze, and appreciate texts by famous American writers and by relatively unknown ones.

To reflect and build upon three premises: (1) that our designation of certain texts as "American literature" reveals our own bias as much as it reveals any objective reality, (2) that texts themselves reveal the historical conditions in which they originate, and (3) that texts and their interpreters remain subject in particular to the cultural mythologies surrounding gender, race, and class.

To develop powers of critical thinking through writing and discussion.

To develop cohesiveness as a classroom community.

Human Concerns

"I'm afraid other people in the class will be much smarter than I."
"I wonder if I can handle the workload."
"I hope it won't be too hard to read nineteenth-century language."
"Poetry makes me nervous. Will I have to figure out a bunch of symbols?"
"I'm kind of anxious about having to write things."
"I hope this course will be relevant to my life."

Booklist

The Norton Anthology of American Literature, Vol. I
Rebecca Harding Davis, *Life in the Iron Mills*
Frederick Douglass, *Narrative of the Life of Frederick Douglass*
Charlotte Perkins Gilman, *Herland*
Charlotte Perkins Gilman, *The Yellow Wallpaper*
The Maimie Papers, ed. Ruth Rosen and Sue Davidson
Mark Twain, *The Adventures of Huckleberry Finn*

Syllabus

I. Gender
Class 1–2   Edgar Allan Poe, "The Raven," "The Philosophy of Composition," "Ligeia" (Norton)
    3–4   Gilman, *The Yellow Wallpaper*
    5–6   William Bradford, selections from *Of Plymouth Plantation;* Cotton Mather, "The Trial of Martha Carrier" (Norton)
    7–10   Nathaniel Hawthorne, *The Scarlet Letter* (Norton)
    11–12   Anne Bradstreet, selected poems; Phillis Wheatley, selected poems (Norton)

        13–15   Emily Dickinson, selected poems (Norton)
        16–18   Walt Whitman, selected poems (Norton)
        19–20   Ralph Waldo Emerson, "The American Scholar" (Norton)
        21–23   Margaret Fuller, "The Great Lawsuit" (Norton)
  II.   Race
        24–27   Frederick Douglass, *Narrative*
        28–29   Henry David Thoreau, "Civil Disobedience," "Slavery in
                  Massachusetts," "John Brown" (Norton)
        30–31   Herman Melville, "Benito Cereno" (Norton)
        32–35   Mark Twain, *The Adventures of Huckleberry Finn*
 III.   Class
        36–37   Melville, "Bartleby the Scrivener" (Norton)
        38–39   Davis, *Life in the Iron Mills*
        40–45   Thoreau, selections from *Walden* (Norton)
        46–47   C. P. Gilman, *Herland*
        48–53   Selections from *The Maimie Papers*

You are also responsible for reading the biographical material connected to the texts.

Required Writing

There will be nine short writing assignments (about 500 words each), usually due on Tuesdays. Designed to assist you in your reading, they will consist of a question or two or three, which you will answer in some cases with just a few words and in other cases with whole paragraphs. These assignments will be evaluated on a numerical scale, with 1 being the lowest possible mark and 10 the highest.

There will be two longer papers (3–5 typed pages), due after classes 23 and 39. Designed to assist you in summarizing your thoughts about the first two units, they will involve topics that will be given out to you two weeks in advance. These papers will receive letter grades. They may be revised for higher grades.

There will be a final examination. It will basically be cumulative, although there will be a required question on the last unit. The test will receive a letter grade.

Short Writing Assignments
1. Due Class 3
    a. Making two columns, list as many differences between Poe's "Ligeia" and Gilman's *The Yellow Wallpaper* as you can think of, using complete sentences. For example:

      Poe   *Gilman*
      1. The narrator is a man.   1. The narrator is a woman.

b. Choose one of the most important differences from your list and, in a paragraph of at least 200 words, explain it more fully. In your explanation, be sure to indicate why the difference you have selected is, indeed, important.

2. Due Class 7
   a. For each of the following characters in *The Scarlet Letter*, explain in three or four complete sentences how he or she reacts to the adultery Prynne and Dimmesdale have committed. In preparing your explanations, think about the differences between the characters' attitudes, and consider as well if their reactions change at all:

   Prynne   Chillingworth
   Dimmesdale   Pearl

   b. In a paragraph of about 200 words, identify which of the above reactions interests you the most. More important, tell why. Although subjective feeling will probably operate here, try in your answer to make others see why they, too, should find the response you have chosen interesting. In other words, your readers should come away from your answer sensing that they have learned more about the character than about you.

3. Due Class 11
   Re-read the end of *The Scarlet Letter*—the last few pages. Then, in a paragraph of at least 250 words, identify a moral or philosophical issue that you think Hawthorne does *not* clearly resolve by the end of the book (perhaps deliberately, perhaps out of artistic clumsiness). Keep in mind that we are focusing here on a moral or philosophical issue, not a strand of the plot. In order to identify the lack of resolution, you will have to cite the evidence that Hawthorne provides which indicates he might be taking more than one stand on the issue.

4. Due Class 15
   a. Read the following poem by Emily Dickinson, paying attention in particular to the first stanza:

   I'm ceded—I've stopped being Theirs—
   The name They dropped upon my face
   With water, in the country church
   Is finished using, now,
   And They can put it with my Dolls,
   My childhood, and the string of spools,
   I've finished threading—too—

   Baptized before, without the choice
   But this time, consciously, of Grace—
   Unto supremest name—
   Called to my full—The Crescent dropped—

> Existence's whole arc, filled up,
> With one small diadem.
>
> My second Rank—too small the first—
> Crowned—Crowing—on my Father's breast—
> A half unconscious Queen—
> But this time—Adequate—Erect—
> With Will to choose, or to reject—
> and I choose, just a Crown—

Just try to get the gist of this poem—don't worry if you don't understand it thoroughly. You should, however, look up any words in it that you don't know the meaning of.

b.   Notice that in the first line, Dickinson makes a mysterious reference to "Theirs"—as if previously she had been controlled by certain people and/or forces from which she is now free. What might "They" actually be? Answer this question by making a list of people and/or forces that you think might have once restricted Dickinson's life. You can derive such a list by consulting the rest of the poem, the biographical material in the anthology, and the discussions about American culture we have already had in class. Your list need not be long, but it should consist of at least three items.

c.   Now, as a way of sensing how Dickinson's poetry can help us to think about our own lives, make a list of the people and/or forces that you feel once controlled *you* but no longer do (at least, not much). In other words, imagine that you yourself wrote the first line of Dickinson's poem. Again, your list need not be long, but it should consist of at least three items.

d.   Finally, in a paragraph of at least 200 words, compare or contrast an item from (b) with an item from (c). In other words, point out how your experience resembles or differs from Dickinson's. Note: I suspect you will be emphasizing similarity, engaging in comparison, but you can undertake a contrast if you want to.

5.   Due Class 19
a.   Make a list of at least five items (i.e., concepts, states of being, kinds of people, features of the landscape) that Whitman seems to be celebrating *throughout* his poem "Crossing Brooklyn Ferry" (and not just in one section of it).
b.   Choose one of the items from your above list and, in a paragraph of at least 200 words, explain how Whitman celebrates it in the poem. You will probably need to use quotations from it.

6.   Due Class 28
This assignment concerns your reading of Thoreau's "Resistance to Civil Government."
a.   In complete sentences, list three main ideas of the essay.
b.   Choose one of these ideas and, in a paragraph of at least 200 words, explain how Thoreau develops and supports it.

    c.   In a paragraph of at least 100 words, state whether or not you agree with the idea, and why.

7.   Due Class 32

Huckleberry Finn is a complex character—not just a boy with a singleminded desire not to be civilized. This assignment encourages you to think of his *various* characteristics in preparation for our discussion.

    a.   List at least six characteristics of Huck that you have discovered in your reading so far. Keep in mind the possibility that Huck changes during the course of the novel.

    b.   From the above list, choose a characteristic of Huck's that you think the members of the class might not have noticed as readily as they discovered others. In a paragraph of at least 250 words, explain how Huck reveals this characteristic, making specific references to the text.

8.   Due Class 44

This assignment concerns the "Higher Laws" chapter of *Walden*.

    a.   List statements and ideas contained in this chapter which lead you to feel uneasy about Thoreau (i.e., critical toward him).

    b.   List statements and ideas contained in this chapter which lead you to feel positive about him.

    c.   On the whole, does the chapter lead you to feel uneasy or positive about Thoreau? Answer this question, and defend your answer, in a paragraph of at least 250 words. Don't assume that your reader shares your assumptions.

9.   Due Class 48

    a.   List *psychological* characteristics of Maimie that you have come across during your reading of the first section of *The Maimie Papers*.

    b.   Choose one of the above characteristics and explain it more fully in a paragraph of at least 250 words, citing evidence from at least three of the letters. If you quote—a very good thing to do—make sure you use correct quotation form, identifying the page numbers.

Longer Writing Assignments

Possible topics for the paper due after Class 23:

1.   Choose Gilman's story or three poems by Dickinson or one poem by Whitman or Emerson's essay or Fuller's essay. Explain how the sentiments of this literature would be regarded by the Puritan community as it is revealed by Cotton Mather and Nathaniel Hawthorne.

2.   Gilman, Hawthorne, and Dickinson write about the isolation of a woman. Choose two of these writers and discuss, by means of comparison and contrast (although you will probably emphasize one process over the other), how they treat the theme of female isolation. Your discussion would probably confront at least one of the following ques-

tions: What causes the isolation of a woman in their respective works? How does the woman cope with the isolation? What attitude(s) toward the isolation do you think the authors wanted their readers to have? If you decide to use Dickinson, refer to at least three of her poems.

3. Choose Emerson or Fuller and, on the basis of what you know about them from their respective essays, discuss how you think one of them would respond to Poe or Gilman or Hawthorne or Dickinson or Whitman. Be sure to refer precisely to the text by Emerson or Fuller and to texts by the other author to support your speculations. If you use Dickinson, use three poems; if you use Whitman, one will suffice; if you use Poe, you may refer to "Ligeia" and/or "The Raven."

Possible topics for the paper due after Class 39:

1. In this unit, we have been examining the responses of different writers and characters to the problem of slavery. More specifically, we have been studying how they respond to two questions: (a) Is slavery moral? (b) If not, how should I act to express my disapproval of it? Compare and/or contrast the responses to the problem of slavery by two of the following, keeping in mind the two sub-questions: Douglass, Thoreau (use just one of the essays, but note its place in Thoreau's philosophical development), Captain Delano, Huckleberry Finn.

2. Douglass's autobiography, Thoreau's "Resistance to Civil Government," and Twain's novel all feature a first-person voice who inevitably creates a particular image of himself through what he says. Choose two of these works and compare and/or contrast the self-images they generate.

3. Once again, I think, we have encountered writers treating the theme of isolation, although in this unit the isolation is not centered around a woman. Consider the following list: Thoreau, Douglass, Captain Delano, Benito Cereno, Huck Finn. Choose two people from it and compare and/or contrast how they become "isolated" (whether in a physical and/or psychological sense). Your discussion would probably confront at least one of the following questions: What causes their isolation? How do they cope with it? What do the authors want their readers to think of it? If you use Thoreau, refer to just one of his essays, noting its place in Thoreau's philosophical development. Do not use both Delano and Benito Cereno.

4. Trace the development of a particular idea through Twain's novel. Do not choose one that is patently obvious.

Final Examination

This test is in two parts. You must answer the question in Part I and one of the questions in Part II, for a total of two essays. Feel free to answer the questions in any order and to jot down notes for them in your blue book. Be careful, however, to identify the numbers of the questions you answer in the book.

I. In the last unit of the course—focusing on social class—you have read the following works:

Melville, "Bartleby the Scrivener"   Gilman, *Herland*
Davis, *Life in the Iron Mills*   *The Maimie Papers*
Thoreau, *Walden* (selections)

It is fair, if a bit simplistic, to say that Melville, Davis, and Maimie tend to emphasize the *problem* of social class in American society, whereas Thoreau and Gilman focus on *solutions* to it by envisioning alternative kinds of societies. Write a unified, well-documented essay in which you identify the problem of social class as depicted by Melville or Davis or Maimie and then you identify the alternative kind of society depicted by Thoreau or Gilman. In other words, this question asks you to deal with two authors: one from a group of problem-oriented writers (Melville, Davis, and Maimie) and one from a group that imagines alternatives (Thoreau, Gilman).

II. Answer one of the following questions:
  1. In our discussions of the various works, we have noted that it is one thing to perceive that a social problem exists, another thing to do something effective about it. Discuss how a particular person perceives a social problem, and evaluate how the person acts on it, in three works you have studied—including at least one from the gender unit and one from the race unit. If you also choose a work from the social class unit, do not simply repeat what you have said in your essay for Part I.
  2. In our discussions of the various works, we have often noted how authors or characters experience a sense of conflict between their own system of values and what their society deems is right. Discuss this conflict as it appears in three works—including at least one from the gender unit and one from the race unit. If you choose a work from the social class unit, do not simply repeat what you have said in your essay for Part I.
  3. Choose one of the following pairs of authors. Compare and contrast the chief concerns and techniques of the authors within the pair:
Dickinson and Whitman
Emerson and Fuller
Hawthorne and Douglass
The Gilman who wrote *The Yellow Wallpaper* and Davis
The Thoreau who wrote "Civil Disobedience" and Twain
  4. Choose three of the works you have studied—including at least one from the gender unit and one from the race unit—and discuss the extent to which they leave certain philosophical questions unresolved. Remember the distinction we made early in the course between a philosophical question and a strand of the plot. If you use a work from the social class unit, do not simply repeat what you have said in your essay for Part I.

Multi-Term Survey Courses

8
AMERICAN LITERATURE TO 1865
Helen Jaskoski
Spring, 1973, as revised 1983
California State University
Fullerton, CA 92634

Course Objectives

The course is intended to introduce students to four major concerns of human beings as these ideas have been expressed in American literature. The focus is on the person in relation to the self, to society, to nature, and to the supernatural. The course aims to show how a variety of people of different backgrounds and philosophies have stated their thoughts and feelings on these subjects.

The course begins with poems by Edward Taylor and Anne Bradstreet partly as a practical matter: poems on handouts can be read and discussed without prior reading assignments. Puritan religious and political ideals and the tradition of self-examination are introduced. The course proper begins with *The Scarlet Letter*, which introduces all the important issues to be dealt with during the course: self-knowledge and self-deception, religion as individual and social phenomena, sources and uses of power, attitudes toward the natural world, history and the individual's relation to it. In addition, romantic beliefs and literary conventions and types of narration are mentioned. The poems by Taylor and Bradstreet are used to compare statements by real Puritans with Nathaniel Hawthorne's imaginative recreation of Puritans. Works by Jonathan Edwards and Phillis Wheatley and the Declaration of Independence and Bill of Rights document the particularly American expression of ideas of the Enlightment. Attention is given especially to the ideas of natural goodness and recovery of innocence; also discussed are eighteenth-century literary conventions and style.

The works by Philip Freneau, Washington Irving, and Frederick Goddard Tuckerman recall *The Scarlet Letter* in being imaginative and romantic recreations of a "lost" past. They are followed by the Ritual of Condolence, an actual expression of Native American culture in contrast to Freneau's romantic picture. Discussion of this work can include material on perceptions of American Indian societies that influenced Enlightenment thinkers. *Walden* sums up the first half of the course: an exercise in self-examination, a method of perceiving nature, a meditation on society—real and ideal, a reflection on the moral life.

The second half of the course begins with *Uncle Tom's Cabin*, introducing the most well-known contemporary picture of slavery. Besides the religious, moral, and political convictions it contains, the book illustrates conventions of the Victorian novel and anticipates later interest in regional and dialect literature. Unlike the two works that follow it in the reading list, Harriet Beecher Stowe's novel addresses in detail the specific hardships women endured under slavery. "Benito Cereno" follows as a completely different literary type addressing the same subject. Herman Melville's focus on the "modern" epistemological problems of documentation, testimony, and judgment, on the relation of the individual to history, and on concepts of innocence and evil invites comparison with Hawthorne especially. The Old World/New World contrast recalls themes of Puritan and Enlightenment writers and anticipates "Billy Budd," a work dealing exclusively with the Old World. Frederick Douglass's *Narrative* then presents the insider's viewpoint on slavery, by contrast with the two preceding authors. It recalls Edwards and Henry David Thoreau in being an exercise in self-examination and education; like Wheatley's verses and the Bill of Rights it is grounded in Enlightenment perceptions of the nature of man. The tradition and genre of slave narratives should also be discussed.

"Civil Disobedience" is read together with "Bartleby, the Scrivener" as both are expressions of the principle of self-reliance—the individual in opposition to society—carried to its furthest point. Jones Very's poems and "Young Goodman Brown" place the self-determined individual in a spiritual context: Very affirms in his "Enthusiasm" an absolute reliance on personal spiritual vision, while Hawthorne skeptically attacks such reliance. While "Civil Disobedience" has influenced modern political thinkers, Very's and Hawthorne's works picture tendencies that can be seen in some varieties of modern evangelical movements. "Nature" and the poems by Emily Dickinson contrast with readings from the preceding two weeks: the individual turns neither to internal nor moral principles nor to God for affirmation but to nature, either to be united with nature (Ralph Waldo Emerson) or to perceive the anguish of separation (Dickinson). The explorations of these three weeks are followed by reading the "Night Chant," an expression of perfect harmony and integration of the individual, society, nature, and God. The course ends with "Billy Budd." Once again the past is invoked, evil and the perception of evil, power and authority and their legitimation and abuse, the death of innocence. Both of the last two works are "outside" the concerns of the period proper in having been written down and published much later than 1865; both are spatially removed as well, in that the "Night Chant" is western, whereas the concerns of a course in this area rarely go west of the Mississippi, and "Billy Budd" is "about" the

British navy. However, the "Night Chant" is very old, and "Billy Budd" is very American; both are transitional works, prompting reflections on both the American-ness of American literature and what constitutes the life of a literary tradition.

Booklist

Any standard American literature anthology containing appropriate
    selections from the authors in the schedule of assigned readings
John Bierhorst, *Four Masterworks of American Indian Literature*
Frederick Douglass, *Narrative of the Life of Frederick Douglass*
Nathaniel Hawthorne, *The Scarlet Letter*
Herman Melville, "Benito Cereno," "Billy Budd," "Bartleby, the
    Scrivener"
Harriet Beecher Stowe, *Uncle Tom's Cabin*
Henry David Thoreau, *Walden*, "Civil Disobedience"
Handouts of poems by Phillis Wheatley, Jones Very, Frederick Goddard
    Tuckerman (if not in anthology)

Requirements and Mechanics

    In addition to readings, quizzes, and exams, one hour of outside reading per week is required. Outside reading may consist of any works (including introductions) not required in the assigned texts, any literary work written before 1865 by an American author, or works of criticism or literary history relevant to the literature of this period. A list of possible readings is attached.
    The class meets together once a week for three hours; credit is three semester units, upper division. Most students are not English majors but take the course as an ancillary requirement to another major (American Studies, Communications) or to fulfill a requirement in general education. Reports on outside reading are checked weekly. Besides readings, students may report on relevant theater or film productions (e.g., one semester some reported on a production of "The Crucible"). Quizzes are on content only and occur frequently. Midterm and final exam questions involve tracing thematic issues through comparison/contrast questions.

Syllabus

Class 1   Reading of selected poems by Anne Bradstreet and Edward
          Taylor
     2   Hawthorne, *The Scarlet Letter* and "The Custom House" (no
          outside reading this week)

3   Jonathan Edwards, "Personal Narrative"; Phillis Wheatley,
        poems to be assigned; Declaration of Independence and Bill
        of Rights
4   Philip Freneau, "The Indian Burying Ground"; Washington
        Irving, "The Legend of Sleepy Hollow"; Frederick Goddard
        Tuckerman, poems to be assigned
5   "Ritual of Condolence," in Bierhorst
6   Thoreau, *Walden* (no outside reading this week)
7   Midterm
8   Stowe, *Uncle Tom's Cabin* (no outside reading this week)
9   Melville, "Benito Cereno"
10 Douglass, *Narrative*
11 Thoreau, "Civil Disobedience"; Melville, "Bartleby"
12 Hawthorne, "Young Goodman Brown"; Jones Very, poems to be
        assigned
13 Ralph Waldo Emerson, *Nature*; Emily Dickinson, poems to be
        assigned
14 "The Night Chant," in Bierhorst
15 Melville, "Billy Budd" (no outside reading this week)
16 Final exam due

Supplementary Readings

Reading reports should include your name, the date the report is due, full bibliographic information on the source (see the *Chicago Manual of Style* or the *MLA Handbook* for what a bibliographical entry should look like), one sentence of synopsis, and one or two sentences of your own personal responses to what you read.

Thematic Suggestions: The Individual In Relation to the Self
Arna Bontemps, ed., *Great Slave Narratives*
Emerson, "Self-Reliance"
Charlotte Forten, *The Journal of Charlotte Forten*
Benjamin Franklin, *Autobiography*
Margaret Fuller, writings, especially on education, see Bell Gale Chevigny,
        ed. *The Woman and the Myth: Margaret Fuller's Life and Writings*
Gerda Lerner, ed., *Black Women in White America*, Part 2
Life of Olaudah Equiano, Or, Gustavus Vassa, The African
Gilbert Osofsky, ed., *Puttin' On Ole Massa*

The Individual in Relation to Nature
Poems by Longfellow, Emerson, Bryant, Freneau, Thoreau
James Fenimore Cooper, *Leatherstocking Tales*
Any chapters from A. Grove Day, *Sky Clears: Poetry of the American Indians*
Thoreau, journals

The Individual in Relation to Society
Mayflower Compact, Seneca Falls "Declaration of Sentiments"
Writings of Jefferson, Lincoln, Franklin, Adams, "The Federalist
    Papers," de Tocqueville
William Wells Brown, *Clotel, Or, The President's Daughter*
William Cullen Bryant, "The Right of Workmen to Strike" and "Freedom
    of Speech"
James Russell Lowell, "The Present Crisis"
Plays by Mercy Otis Warren

The Individual in Relation to the Supernatural
A. Grove Day, *Sky Clears*
Jonathan Edwards, "The Nature of True Virtue" and "Sinners in the
    Hands of an Angry God"
Levin, et al., eds., *What Happened in Salem?*
Cotton Mather, *Bonifacius*
Thomas Paine, *The Age of Reason*

9
MAJOR AMERICAN AUTHORS TO 1860
Kenneth Roemer
Summer, 1982
University of Texas
Arlington, TX 76019

Problems, Goals, Approaches

This course presents many of the practical and theoretical problems that frustrate teachers of surveys. It is a short-semester, summer course offered four days a week, two hours a day, for approximately six weeks, primarily to sophomore non-English majors who are required to take six hours of sophomore-level English. Such short surveys are becoming popular at universities seeking to attract as many students as possible between the "regular" semesters. Besides the restrictive length of the course, another practical problem, common to many universities, is the limited budget of the student. Most of our students work; many support families. They simply can't afford high book costs, especially in required general education courses that are not specifically required for their majors.

Appropriate responses to the shortness of the semester and the high cost of books seem relatively simple: cut back on the reading material and use an inexpensive anthology instead of a series of paperbacks. Unfortunately, besides the obvious disadvantages of these necessary concessions, such responses may aggravate certain theoretical problems relating to the selection of reading assignments. This is especially true if the English Department requires that such surveys follow a chronological presentation of "major" (i.e., "familiar" and "respected") authors, but the teacher hopes to expose the students to a variety of literary forms and viewpoints during a particular period of American history.

There are no real "solutions" to this frustrating cluster of circumstances, but one possible response is suggested in the following course outline. The reading assignments are quite short, but they do suggest the rich diversity of form and viewpoint of the oral and written literatures of early America. (There are still gaps, however; Hispanic and French travel literature, for example, are necessarily omitted.) The anthology is inexpensive, and the reserve library readings and films help to introduce a significant type of American literature—Indian literature—that is sparsely represented in most anthologies.

The organization is basically chronological, which is certainly appropriate because historical and cultural conditions shaped so much of the early American literature. Within specific divisions, however, an attempt was made to use themes or other types of connecting links (e.g., expectation/exploration, captivities, revolutionary literatures, the limitations of our ability to define "self" within natural and social settings) that would allow pairings of well-known works with other works that represent a different literary form or different viewpoint (e.g., the "Yellow Woman" oral narrative and Rowlandson's written narrative, Whitman's written songs and sung songs, Franklin's and Douglass's successful self stories, Hawthorne's and Stowe's views of the self in a village context, and the numerous provocative pairings suggested by revolutionary literatures).

Students may not walk away from such a course (actually in the summer they usually stagger away) with the neat and orderly feeling that a traditional major authors survey might offer. But they may go away with an appreciation of the exciting clashes and cross-fertilizations that characterized early American literatures and cultures.

Booklist

Texts
The American Tradition in Literature, Sculley Bradley, et al., eds.
New York: Random House, 1981. (Page references below are to this text.)
The following readings are on reserve at the library:
"Coyote and Junco," in *Finding the Center: Narrative Poetry of the Zuni*

Indians, tr. Dennis Tedlock, pp. 75-84. New York: Dial, 1972. (This is a bilingual translation.)

Excerpt from "The Night Chant," in *Four Masterworks of American Indian Literature,* ed. John Bierhorst, pp. 325-30. New York: Farrar, Straus, and Giroux, 1974.

"Yellow-Woman and Whirlwind-Man," in *Keresan Texts,* ed. Franz Boas, pp. 118-22, 260-61. *Publications of the American Ethnological Society* 8 (1928).

Excerpts from speeches by Canassatego (Iroquois) and Dragging Canoe (Cherokee) in *The Portable North American Indian Reader,* ed. Frederick W. Turner III, pp. 243-44. New York: Penguin, 1981.

Movies, Video Tapes, Slides

Navajo (BBC / Time-Life movie), approx. fifty minutes.

Iisaw: Hopi Coyote Stories with Helen Sekaquaptewa and *By This Song I Walk: Navajo Song with Andrew Natonabah.* Both are part of the *Words & Place: Native Literature from the American Southwest.* New York: Clearwater Publishing Co., both approx. twenty-five minutes in length; both are in the native languages with English subtitles.

Instructor's slides of sandpaintings relating to the Night Chant.

Syllabus

Class 1   Introduction to the Course: Why Study Early American Literature?

I. The First American Literature: Native American Oral Narratives, Songs, Ceremonies

   2-3   "Coyote and Junco," "Night Chant," "Manabozho" (pp. 621-35); Movie: *Navajo*

II. European Expectations, Explorations, and Settlements

   4-5   John Winthrop (pp. 32-42); William Bradford (pp. 14-31); Cotton Mather (pp. 114-25); Anne Bradstreet (pp. 44, 48, 56); John Woolman (pp. 204-12); William Byrd (pp. 195-201)

III. Settlement Captivities

   6   "Yellow-Woman"; Mary Rowlandson (pp. 56-86); supplementary: C. B. Brown, *Edgar Huntley* (pp. 432-49) First Examination

IV. Revolutionary Literatures

   7   Edward Taylor: Public Calm, Private Turmoil (pp. 102-14)

   8   Jonathan Edwards: Public and Private Triumph and Turmoil, "Supernatural Light" and "Sinners" (pp. 135-69)

10
PERSPECTIVES IN AMERICAN CULTURAL HISTORY
Lois Rudnick
Fall, 1983
University of Massachusetts
Boston, MA 02125

Course Objectives

English C230 explores the evolution of the "American Dream" by examining the verbal and visual expressions of men and women during three of the most fertile periods in American history before the Civil War: Puritan and Indian New England; the Age of Enlightenment and Revolution; mid-nineteenth century Romanticism and Reform. In each segment of the course, we examine the interrelationship of literary and artistic expression and the social, political, and philosophical ideas and factors that provide the historical context for understanding forms of cultural expression and conflict. The concepts that are essential to understanding how historians reconstruct and interpret the past and how analysts of culture interpret patterns of behavior and value are introduced in a variety of ways: traditional lectures, handouts, readings, definitions, texts, writing in-class and out, role-playing.

For the first segment of the course my goal is to have students begin to grapple with the roles that preconception and point of view play in historical and cultural interpretation. They begin with their own definitions of the "American Dream" which I classify and hand out. We use the handout as a contemporary context through which to view earlier versions of the dream. Students then view visual representations of America as allegorized (often as an Indian woman) in tapestry, paintings, and woodcuts and read prose and poetry excerpts of pre- and early Colonial myth-makers. In their study of Puritan and Algonquin New England in the seventeenth century, students learn to deal with new sets of preconceptions (Winthrop's "Model") and with contrasting historical points of view (Bradford and Morton on Merrymount). Students hold a trial in class to determine if Morton deserved banishment. Although the historic data is inconclusive regarding his culpability, he wins his case in England—a fact which irritates the "Puritans" in my class once they get into their roles. For their written assignment on this unit students examine how Hawthorne drew upon this minor political/historical incident to write a short story ("The Maypole of Merrymount") of much wider cultural significance. After reading about and discussing Algonquin and Seneca cultures, students write on the three versions of the Hannah Dustan captivity narrative. They are asked to interpret the meanings that each writer—Mather, Thoreau, and Hawthorne—wants the reader to derive from his story.

In the second unit of the course—Enlightenment and Revolution—we look at how economic, political, and social changes in the life of the colonies both cause and reflect shifting patterns of belief, such as the change from the seventeenth-century God-centered universe to the eighteenth-century Enlightenment's man-centered view. We view the reflection of Enlightenment ideals in architecture (the plans for Washington, D.C. and examples of neo-classical buildings) and in popular allegorizations of America in the Revolutionary and post-Revolutionary periods. We also examine these ideals through Franklin's *Autobiography* and look at the contrasting views on the human, natural, and divine held by Jonathan Edwards. Students are asked, in class, to write journal entries for a "day in the life of" Franklin and Edwards, who are presented as crossing paths on the Concord and Merrimack Rivers.

We move next to a study of "The Declaration of Independence" as a political and literary document. Students begin by exploring the overt and assumed premises on which the argument is based; they then work in teams to evaluate the document's philosophical validity and literary quality by assessing thesis, evidence, and phrasing (they have, for comparative purposes, a copy of an earlier draft). Their outside class paper asks them to draw on concepts they have studied in this period to analyze the answer to Crèvecoeur's question, "What, then, is the American, this new man?" They then read the works of those not included in the Declaration's guarantee of inalienable rights—the poetry of Phillis Wheatley, the slave narrative of Gustavus Vassa, and native American oratory.

In the final unit of the course, we examine Romantic ideals and expression. Students evalute Emerson's "American Scholar" as our "Intellectual Declaration of Independence" and examine Romantic concepts of nature in painting. (My guest lecturer takes them from the more public and "documentary" art of the Enlightenment through the more private worlds and mythic visions of Romantic artists.) When they read Thoreau, they are invited to examine metaphor as a vehicle for exploring and conveying moral and spiritual truths; when they read Hawthorne and Poe, we focus on their critique of nineteenth-century materialism and their complex dream/nightmare visions of women. Finally, we look at ways in which Romantic concepts of human nature and society affected the reform movements of the mid-nineteenth century, focusing on the Women's Rights movement, through the writings of Margaret Fuller, and on the anti-slavery movement, through the *Narrative* of Frederick Douglass.

Required Texts

David Levin and Theodore L. Gross, eds., *America in Literature* Vol.
   I (AL)

Frederick Douglass, *Narrative of the Life of Frederick Douglass*
Nathaniel Hawthorne, *The Celestial Railroad and Other Stories*
Herman Melville, *Four Short Works of Herman Melville*
Edgar Allan Poe, *Eighteen Best Short Stories*
Handouts, for which there will be a $3.00 charge

Syllabus

Class 1 Introduction
     2 "European Visions of America" handout and slides; Sykes,
         "What Do We Mean by the Study of Culture?" (handout)
     3 John Smith, "A Call to the New World" (handout); Pocahontas
         (AL, pp. 391–98)
     4 Pilgrims and Puritans (AL, pp. 3–14)
     5 William Bradford, "History of Plimouth Plantation" (AL, pp.
         22–52)
     6 Bradford (AL, pp. 52–63); Thomas Morton of Merrymount
         (handout)
     7 Hawthorne, "The Maypole of Merrymount" (*Celestial Railroad*)
         First paper due: Bradford, Morton, Hawthorne—Three
         Versions of Conflict in the New World
     8 John Winthrop, "A Model of Christian Charity" (AL, pp. 67–79),
         "On Natural and Civil Liberty" (AL, pp. 88–96)
     9 Edmund Morgan, "The Puritan Family" (handout); Anne Brad-
         street, poems (AL, pp. 15–16), "The Prologue" and "The
         Author to Her Book" (handouts)
   10 Bradstreet (AL, pp. 167–71, 172–76)
   11 Mary Rowlandson's Captivity by the Indians (AL, pp. 177–88);
        Three versions of Hannah Dustan's captivity: Cotton Math-
        er, "A Notable Exploit: *Dux Faemina Facti,*" from *Magnalia*
        Christi Americana (handout); Thoreau, from "Thursday," *A*
        Week on the Concord and Merrimack Rivers (handout);
        Hawthorne, "The Duston Family," *American Magazine of*
        Useful and Entertaining Knowledge(handout)
   12 Anthony Wallace, "Indian Life and Culture" (handout)
   13 Second paper due: Three Versions of Hannah Dustan's Captivity
        Among the Indians
   14 The Enlightenment, lecture and slides
   15 Benjamin Franklin, *Autobiography* (AL, pp. 433–37, 452–82)
   16 The Great Awakening, Jonathan Edwards, "Spiritual Narrative"
        (AL, pp. 322–34)
   17 Franklin, *Autobiography*, Part II (AL, pp. 480–92); Edwards,
        "Sinners in the Hands of an Angry God" (AL, pp. 340–46)
   18 The American Revolution, Thomas Paine, "Common Sense"
        (AL, pp. 553–68)

19 Thomas Jefferson and the Declaration of Independence (AL, pp. 586–89, 615–20); St. Jean de Crèvecoeur, "What Is An American?" (AL, pp. 537–52)
20 Phillis Wheatley, poetry (AL, pp. 710–13); Letter of Benjamin Banneker to Thomas Jefferson (AL, pp. 687–88)
21 Gustavus Vassa, excerpts from his narrative (handout); "The Indian Speaks" (AL, pp. 726–30 and handout). Third paper due: Emerson's "American Scholar"
22 Romanticism and Reform, lecture, (AL, pp. 731, 803–10); Alexis de Tocqueville, *Democracy in America* (AL, pp. 1544–49)
23 Ralph Waldo Emerson, "The American Scholar" (AL, pp. 840–45, 879–94)
24 The Romantic Aesthetic and Nature, slides and discussion Washington Allston and Thomas Cole (AL, pp. 828–32); Emerson, *Nature* (AL, pp. 845–54)
25 Henry David Thoreau, from *Walden* (AL, pp. 808–10, 962–85)
26 Thoreau, continued; Margaret Fuller, "Summer on the Lakes" (AL, pp. 1640–41)
27 Thoreau, The Life of the Imagination (AL, pp. 810–14); Nathaniel Hawthorne (AL, pp. 1182–87), "Preface to *The House of the Seven Gables*" (AL, pp. 1223–25), "Roger Malvin's Burial" (*Celestial Railroad*)
28 Hawthorne, "The Celestial Railroad" (*Celestial Railroad*), "Earth's Holocaust" (AL, pp. 1691–706)
29 Hawthorne, "Rappaccini's Daughter" and "The Birthmark" (*Celestial Railroad*). Fourth paper due: A Story by Edgar Allan Poe
30 Melville (AL, pp. 1301–07), "Bartleby, The Scrivener" (*Four Short Works*)
31 Melville, "Benito Cereno" (*Four Short Works*)
32 Edgar Allan Poe (AL, pp. 1235–39), "The Man Who Was All Used Up," "The Masque of the Red Death" (*18 Best Short Stories*)
33 Poe, "The Fall of the House of Usher" (*18 Best Short Stories*)
34 Walt Whitman (AL, pp. 989–94), "Preface to *Leaves of Grass*" (AL, pp. 995–1004); "Song of Myself," Sections 1–6 (AL, pp. 1011–16)
35 Whitman, "Song of Myself," Sections 7–10, 14–16, 19–24, 33, 38, 40–41, 49–52 (AL)
36 Women's Rights and Anti-Slavery Reforms (AL, pp. 814–19); Seneca Falls "Declaration of Sentiments" (AL, pp. 1636–40); Margaret Fuller, *Woman in the Nineteenth Century* (AL, pp. 1641–48)
37 Fuller (AL, pp. 1649–56)
38 Douglass, *Narrative of the Life of Frederick Douglass*
39 Douglass, *Narrative*
40 Douglass, *Narrative*

11
AMERICAN LITERATURE SURVEY TO 1865
A Proposed Course
Participants in the Yale Institute on
Reconstructing American Literature
Summer, 1982
Yale University

Rationale of the Course

The following syllabus was created by a group of participants in the Reconstructing American Literature Institute, which was held at Yale University in June, 1982. Their explanation of the purpose of this syllabus follows:

We realize that in the following list of headings and reading suggestions we crossed over the boundary between course syllabus and anthology table of contents. We know that in one semester teachers could not cover all of the works included with equal intensity; they would, instead, select particular emphases within each of the sections.

Our primary goal might best be expressed as two types of compromise. First, we sought to achieve some balance between the inclusion of familiar works and less familiar works—non-canonical readings that can be used to illuminate familiar texts in unfamiliar ways and to offer "new" paradigms of American literary expression. Second, we attempted to preserve a general chronological approach, but we organized this historical fiction around a series of broad headings that should encourage students to (1) consider several important developments and issues in American history and literature, and (2) juxtapose familiar and unfamiliar texts in ways that would stimulate readings of both.

We would like to include more Hispanic literature, but we were not yet aware of the sources. Most selections not otherwise noted can be found in one of the major anthologies.

Syllabus

I. Indian America
Class 1   Background lecture on Indian history, pre-European discovery.
                Possible sources: Nancy Lurie, "Historical Background," in
                Olga Hoyt, *American Indians Today*; Abraham Chapman,
                "Introduction," *Literature of the American Indian*; D'Arcy,

McNickle and Fey, *Indians and Other Americans*; Wilbur R.
Jacobs, "Native American History," *American Historical
Review* (1982)
2   Selections from the following: "Navajo Night Chant" in John
Bierhorst, ed., *Four Masterworks of American Indian Literature;* BBC movie, "Navajo"; "Zuni Creation Narratives" in
Dennis Tedlock, trans., *Finding the Center: Narrative Poetry
of the Zuni Indians;* Iroquois Ritual of Condolence in Bierhorst, *Four
Masterworks*. Bierhorst and Tedlock include notes and
introductions.
II.   European Visions of America
3   Slides of European paintings, woodcuts, tapestries on allegorizations of America as Indian woman (see, for example, Hugh
Honour, *European Visions of America*), accompanied by
excerpts from letters and narratives of European explorers—
e.g., Columbus, Cabot, Verrazzano, Rev. Samuel Purchas,
Coronado (can be found in collections of primary source
materials of early explorers), Caliban's speech in *The Tempest*
III.   Journeys
4   Tewa Migration Narrative, "Middle Place," in Alice Marriott
and Carol Rachlin, *American Indian Mythology*; excerpts
from Cabeza de Vaca, "The Seven Golden Cities of Cibola"
5   John Smith, "A Call to the New World," from *A Description of
New England Settlements* (1616) and Pocahontas legend; John
Winthrop, "A Model of Christian Charity"
6   William Bradford, excerpts from *Of Plymouth Plantation;*
Thomas Morton, excerpts from *New English Canaan*
7   Excerpts from the trial of Anne Hutchinson, in Gerda Lerner, ed.,
Female Experience: An American Documentary; poetry of
Anne Bradstreet and letter to her children; poetry of Edward
Taylor
8   Excerpts from John Woolman, *The Journal*; excerpts from
William Byrd, "The Secret History of the Dividing Line";
excerpts from "Father Dominguez' Visitation" to the Southwest (1776)
IV.   Captivities
9   Keres "Yellow Woman" story, in Franz Boas, *Keresan Texts*;
excerpts from captivity narrative of Mary Rowlandson
10   Three versions of Hannah Dustan's captivity: Cotton Mather,
from *Magnalia Christi Americana*; Nathaniel Hawthorne,
from *American Magazine of Useful and Entertaining Knowledge* (1837); Henry David Thoreau, from *A Week on the
Concord and Merrimack Rivers*
11   Excerpts from Gustavus Vassa, *The Interesting Narrative of the
Life of Olaudah Equiano, or Gustavus Vassa, The African*
V.   Literature of the Revolution
12   Jonathan Edwards, "Sinners in the Hands of an Angry God" and
"Personal Narrative"

13 Benjamin Franklin, excerpts from the *Autobiography*
14 Thomas Paine, "Common Sense"; Thomas Jefferson, unedited
    version of the "Declaration of Independence," excerpts from
    Notes on The State of Virginia
15 Letter of Benjamin Banneker to Jefferson concerning Declaration
    (1792); Phillis Wheatley, poems
16 Letters of Abigail Adams to John Adams; Indian oratory:
    Powhatan, Chief Logan, Chief Speckled Snake, Chief Black
    Hawk, Chief Seattle, Chief Cochise, Chief Tecumseh
17 Hector St. Jean de Crèvecoeur, excerpts from *Letters From an
    American Farmer*, "What is an American?" and Chapter 12
    (in which the narrator leaves the colonies during the revolu-
    tion and goes to live with Indians)
VI. Myths and Legends
18 Thomas B. Thorpe, "The Big Bear of Arkansas"; excerpts from
    Davy Crockett, *Sketches and Eccentricities of . . .* and *Almanacs*;
    excerpts from John Filson, "Narrative of Daniel Boone,"
    Discovery, Settlement, and Present State of Kentucke; first
    chapter of James Fenimore Cooper, *The Deerslayer*
19 Joel Chandler Harris, *Brer Rabbit*, tales; Winnebago trickster
    tales from Paul Radin, ed., *Trickster: A Study in American
    Indian Mythology*; Coyote tales from Jarold Ramsey, ed.,
    *Coyote Was Going There: Indian Literature of the Oregon
    Country*
20 Washington Irving, "Rip Van Winkle"; Nathaniel Hawthorne,
    "Young Goodman Brown"
VII. Songs of Experience
21 "Yankee Doodle Dandy," "Barbara Allen," "Clementine,"
    "Shenandoah"; Afro-American work songs; Irish work
    songs
22 Navajo, "By This Song I Walk," videotape and text, *Words and
    Places* (Clearwater Press, NY); Cherokee Formulas, from Å.
    Grove Day, *Sky Clears: Poetry of the American Indian*;
    Anishiwab (Chippewa) songs, from Natalie Curtis, rev. ed.,
    Indians' Book
23 Afro-American spirituals
24 Walt Whitman, "Song of Myself"
VIII. Public and Private Voices
25 Excerpts from Alexis de Tocqueville, *Democracy in America*
26 Ralph Waldo Emerson, "The American Scholar," excerpts from
    Nature and the journals
27 Edgar Allan Poe, "The Fall of the House of Usher," "The
    Masque of the Red Death"
28 Margaret Fuller, excerpts from *Woman in the Nineteenth Century*
    (or "The Great Lawsuit"); excerpts from Harriet Martineau,
    Society in America; Seneca Falls "Declaration of Senti-
    ments"
29 Hawthorne, *The Blithedale Romance*

30 Thoreau, *Walden*, first and last chapters, "Civil Disobedience"
31 Frederick Douglass, *Narrative of the Life of Frederick Douglass*;
      Linda Brent (Harriet Jacobs), *Incidents in the Life of a Slave
      Girl*, Lydia Maria Child, ed.
32 Herman Melville, "Benito Cereno," "Bartleby, The Scrivener,"
      "The Tartarus of Maids"
33 Harriet Beecher Stowe, excerpts from *Uncle Tom's Cabin*; ex-
      cerpts from *Mary Chesnut's Civil War*, ed. C. Vann Wood-
      ward
34 Rebecca Harding Davis, *Life in the Iron Mills, or, The Korl
      Woman*, ed. Tillie Olsen

12
INTRODUCTION TO AMERICAN LITERATURE: CIVIL WAR TO THE PRESENT
Joan D. Hedrick
Spring, 1978
Trinity College
Hartford, CT 06106

Course Objectives

This course centers on writers who exhibit a middle-class, as opposed to an elite or aristocratic, consciousness. Thus Mark Twain rather than Henry James is the touchstone. It also includes working-class writers like Jack London, Agnes Smedley, and Maimie Pinzer—people who aspired to middle-class status and whose writing bears the marks of both the class they came from and the class they aspired to. The central themes of the course are the shaping effect of race, class, and gender on consciousness. All of these books feature characters who are torn between conflicting value systems, whether it be Joe Christmas (in *Light in August*), who is neither white nor black, or Scarlett O'Hara, who is an unstable mixture of the Irish blood of her father and the genteel Southern ladyhood of her mother. Most of these characters struggle with an artificial set of values—exemplified by Tom Sawyer's romanticism; some of them, notably Malcolm X, see through to values that bear a direct relationship to their own experience.

Booklist

Kate Chopin, *The Awakening*
Theodore Dreiser, *Sister Carrie*
William Faulkner, *Light in August*
Harold Frederic, *The Damnation of Theron Ware*
Ernest Hemingway, *The Short Stories of Ernest Hemingway*
Jack London, *Martin Eden*
The Maimie Papers, Ruth Rosen and Sue Davidson, eds.
Margaret Mitchell, *Gone With the Wind*
Agnes Smedley, *Daughter of Earth*
Mark Twain, *The Adventures of Huckleberry Finn*
Richard Wright, *Native Son*
Malcolm X, *The Autobiography of Malcolm X*

Syllabus

Class 1	Introduction: Naturalism and Decadence. Begin reading *Huck Finn*.
2	Lecture: The Genteel Tradition
3-4	Lecture: *Huck Finn*
5	Discussion
6-7	Lecture: *The Damnation of Theron Ware*
8	Discussion
9-10	Lecture: *The Awakening*
11	Discussion
12	Lecture: Frank Norris and the Social Origins of Literary Naturalism
13	Lecture: Jack London. Paper due, 4-5 pages, on some relationship between *The Awakening* and *Martin Eden*
14	Discussion
15-16	Lecture: *Martin Eden*
17	Discussion
18-19	Lecture: *Sister Carrie*
20	Discussion
21-22	Lecture: *The Maimie Papers*
23-24	Lecture: Hemingway's Short Stories
25	Discussion
26-27	Lecture: *Light in August*
28	Discussion
29-30	Lecture: *Gone With the Wind*
31	Discussion
32-33	Lecture: *Daughter of Earth*
34	Discussion
35-36	Lecture: *Native Son*
37	Discussion
38-39	Lecture: *The Autobiography of Malcolm X*
40	Discussion

13
AMERICAN LITERATURE, 1865-1920:
THE RISE OF CRITICAL REALISM
Anne G. Jones
Fall, 1981
Allegheny College
Meadville, PA 16335

Course Objectives

English 19 normally appears on the list of courses offered at Allegheny College three times a year taught each time by a different person; the title, "The Rise of Critical Realism," has been in the catalog since before I came in 1976. Within the restrictions of period and emphasis implied in the title, we design our own, personal syllabi. In 1981, I cared most about (1) including in the content of the course as rich a diversity of voices as I could without silencing those of the traditional "mainstream" writers, and (2) offering to students as rich a variety of expressive opportunities as possible, for their feelings and their thoughts, in writing and in speech, in private and in what I hoped would eventually feel more like "community" than "public": the class.

I chose the Brooks, Lewis, Warren text less for its table of contents, however, than for its intelligent, sensitive, well-written, inevitably biased introductory essays. I hoped they, along with the Norton Critical Edition endmatter sections, would offer the students confidence in two ways: by providing models of responses to literature to choose from in addition to my own, as teacher; and by presenting analyses and interpretations of specific texts to accept, reject, and modify in developing their own. In making this choice, I reacted against the excesses of my own new critical training, and encouraged students to respond to the text solely on the basis of their individual relationship to it, thus presumably preventing the prejudice of reading others' views and at the same time developing the students' confidence in their own views. In my experience, however, the professor's voice may—in all innocence—fill the vacuum, so that students still fall into the familiar authoritarian pattern: "What does the teacher want?" I hoped the journal and personal conferences would help the students develop trust in their own responses, and I believed that offering the critical material showed respect for the students' capacity to hear other responses and to grow from dialogue as well as self-expression.

Having chosen the Brooks, Lewis, Warren text for these reasons, I then selected from its table of contents works that reflected my sense of the multiplicity of experience during the period. Dickinson introduced the traditionally taught issues of literary experience (such as realism and romanticism) as well as the issue of gender as a complex literary and cultural concern. In the second section, "Seeing New Englandly," I used the traditional section on regionalism to pursue the notion of a variety of experiences reflected in a variety of "realisms"; when we got to the "biggies," in Section III, I emphasized again the varieties of realism among Clemens, Howells, and James. Chopin, Crane, and Dreiser all transformed "realism" in ways that moved it out of its earlier limits on subject matter and treatment: into women's interiority, impressionism, and urban life "below" the bourgeoisie. Then in "Retrospective," Wharton returned us to the experiences of the period's dominant class, race, and sex: writing about Newland Archer's choices, and setting the novel when she did, Wharton offered her judgment on the period. Finally, I included Robinson as a sign of times to come; in fact, I suspected he would disappear as the realities of the term typically squeezed the syllabus. Another reality: my own training—and strengths— were such that despite my grand scheme, we spent most of each class doing close analyses of individual texts, and not very much time on history, culture, and other critics. I continue to find this a conflict, in fact.

A final note on assignments: with the "position" papers, delivered orally and copied for each person, I intended to revise some of the students' assumptions about who teaches and who learns, about written vs. oral prose, and—since the class produced several papers on most works—about the "one true and correct interpretation" of a piece of writing. Though the papers took a lot (too much) of class time, I liked them. Occasionally I divided the class into small groups to discuss the papers, and I encouraged students to revise their papers after hearing feedback and to use them as a first step toward the longer paper. Whereas the journal encouraged subjectivity, the final exam presumably ensured that all had read the material and developed their skills so that they could recognize and interpret significant short passages "new critically." Finally, to encourage the shy and discourage the jerks, I noted that the quality of class discussion is what counts.

Booklist

American Literature: The Makers and the Making, Vol. II, ed. Brooks, Lewis, and Warren (abbreviated AL/MM)
Kate Chopin, *The Awakening* (Norton Critical Edition)
Theodore Dreiser, *Sister Carrie* (Norton Critical Edition)
Mark Twain, *Adventures of Huckleberry Finn* (Norton Critical Edition)
Edith Wharton, *Age of Innocence* (Scribners)

Syllabus

I. The New Consciousness: Emily Dickinson
Class 1   Introduction: realism and romanticism. Dickinson handout

2   "The New Consciousness" (AL/MM, pp. 1197-219);
        Dickinson Introduction (AL/MM, pp. 1236-43)
3   Dickinson poetry (AL/MM)
4   No class. First 2-page paper due: taking a position and
        arguing it on Dickinson
II. Seeing New Englandly: The Various Voices of Regionalism and
     Pluralism
5   The West: Bret Harte (all in AL/MM); Twain, "Jumping
        Frog," from *Innocents Abroad*, from *Life on the
        Mississippi* (AL/MM)
6   New England: Mary Wilkins Freeman, "A New England
        Nun"; Sarah Orne Jewet, "A White Heron" (AL/MM)
7   The South: George Washington Cable, "Sieur George";
        Mary Boykin Chesnut, diary excerpts; Kate Chopin, "A
        Respectable Woman" (AL/MM)
8   Black Literature: selections from W.E.B. DuBois and Booker
        T. Washington (AL/MM)
9   Black Literature: selections from Charles Chesnutt, Paul
        Laurence Dunbar, James Weldon Johnson (AL/MM)
III. Varieties of Realism: Theory and Practice—Twain, Howells, and
      James
10   Twain, "To a Person Sitting in Darkness," "Fenimore
        Cooper's Literary Offenses" (AL/MM)
11-13   Twain, *Huckleberry Finn*
14   William Dean Howells, (all selections in AL/MM)
15   Henry James, "The New Novel," Deerfield Letter, "The
        Pupil" (AL/MM)
16   James, "The Jolly Corner" (AL/MM)
IV. Metamorphoses of Realism: Crane, Chopin, and Dreiser
17-19   Chopin, *The Awakening*
20   Stephen Crane, poems, "The Blue Hotel" (AL/MM)
21   Crane, "The Open Boat" (AL/MM)
22   No class. Long paper due: establishing interesting connec-
        tions between two or more of the works read in the course
23-25   Dreiser, *Sister Carrie*, introduction to Dreiser (AL/MM)
V.   Retrospective: Edith Wharton
26-28   Wharton, *Age of Innocence*, introduction to Wharton (AL/MM)
VI. Prospects: Edwin Arlington Robinson
29   Robinson, poems (AL/MM)

14

INTRODUCTION TO AMERICAN LITERATURE AFTER 1865
Joyce Ann Joyce
Spring, 1982
University of Maryland
College Park, MD 20742

Course Objectives

American history still reflects the struggle between Jeffersonian and Hamiltonian politics and the concomitant contradiction between theoretical equality in a classless society and real economic, social, and racial inequities. The mainstream of American literature from Thomas Paine, James Fenimore Cooper, and Ralph Waldo Emerson to John Dos Passos and John Steinbeck to more contemporary writers like William Faulkner and Robert Penn Warren manifests this duality embodied in American history. My purpose in this survey of American literature was to show how the inclusion of Black writers into the mainstream both illuminates even further the already apparent duality of American social and political thinking and more importantly enhances the depth and range of American literary thought. Such an inclusion provides examples of how the existence in this country and particular history of a group of Americans challenges the ideals upon which American history is based.

An effective way then of examining from an historical perspective this conflict between the laws of nature and the laws of man and the development of American democratic ideals is to juxtapose the major Black writers of a particular period to the major writers that represent the mainstream of American literature during that same period of time. For example, in this survey that begins with American literature after 1865, my students and I found that a clear understanding of Charles Chesnutt's characterization of Uncle Julius and his depiction of the evils of slavery in his *Conjure Woman* (1899) functioned as an indispensable litmus test for understanding the hypocrisy of the society responsible for the discrepancy between Huck Finn's (1885) affection for and dependence on Jim and his superior, paternal attitude toward a man well old enough to be his father. Huck's dilemma is rooted in the contradiction between the laws of nature, which require that he accept Jim's humanity, and the laws of man, which demand that the white man see himself as superior to the Black.

Equally stimulating class discussions resulted from the juxtaposition of Jean Toomer's *Cane* to the kinds of poetry published during the beginning years of the imagist movement and during the 1920s. We found that the poetic aspects and the naturalistic setting of Toomer's *Cane* parallel closely those of the imagist poets and white naturalistic writers respectively. Yet, the class noted that while Robert Frost and Edwin Arlington Robinson were both concerned with the effect of alienation and romantic idealism on human consciousness, Toomer helped them to understand the complexity of the concept of alienation and the provinciality of post-World War I disillusionment as expressed in the mainstream of American literature.

At the Reconstructing American Literature Conference at Yale in the summer of 1982, I realized that while most of the participants were concerned with changing the concepts behind what we call "traditional" works of the mainstream of American literature, I was more interested in what could be gained if we approached the traditional works of the existing mainstream through a thematic and stylistic analysis which focused on the similarities and differences between the works of Black and white writers. Both approaches—the one evidenced by this syllabus and the one which more overtly challenges the notion of "tradition"—have as their goals a broadening and enriching of American literary history.

Booklist

George McMichael, ed., *Anthology of American Literature*, Vol. II
Charles Chesnutt, *The Conjure Woman*
Ralph Ellison, *Invisible Man*
Zora Neale Hurston, *Their Eyes Were Watching God*
Jean Toomer, *Cane*
Richard Wright, *Native Son*

Syllabus

Class 1-3   Introduction
     3-6   Mark Twain, *Huckleberry Finn* (McMichael)
     7-9   Chesnutt, *The Conjure Woman*
    10-12   Henry James, *Daisy Miller*, "The Beast in the Jungle";
             William Dean Howells, "Editha" (McMichael)
    13-14   Stephen Crane, "The Open Boat," "The Blue Hotel"
             (McMichael)
     15   Reading day
     16   Exam
    17-19   Edwin Arlington Robinson, "Cliff Klingenhagen," "Miniver
             Cheevy," "Mr. Flood's Party"; poems by Robert Frost
             (McMichael)
     20   Reading day
     21   Wallace Stevens, "Anecdote of the Jar," "Sunday Morning,"
             "The Snow Man" (McMichael)

22-23	Countee Cullen, "Yet Do I Marvel," "Heritage" (McMichael)
24	Reading day
25-26	T.S. Eliot, "The Love Song of J. Alfred Prufrock" (McMichael)
27	Examination
28-29	Toomer, *Cane*
30-32	Hurston, *Their Eyes Were Watching God*
33-34	William Faulkner, "That Evening Sun," "Spotted Horses" (McMichael)
35-36	F. Scott Fitzgerald, "The Rich Boy"; Ernest Hemingway, "Big Two-Hearted River" (McMichael)
37-38	Wright, *Native Son*
39-41	Ellison, *Invisible Man*
42	Examination
43	Discussion

15
INTRODUCTION TO LATER AMERICAN LITERATURE
Fran Kaye
Spring, 1979
University of Nebraska
Lincoln, NB 68588

Course Description

The principles of selection and organization seem reasonably straight-forward except, perhaps, for the choice of *Surfacing*. I omitted novels by Twain, Fitzgerald, and Hemingway both because many students have already read some and because my department offers a Twain course as well as one on Fitzgerald and Hemingway. I used a popular anthology that provided many choices and that is always available used at the bookstore. All of the other texts are "classics" of American literature, although the aggre-gate list, with books by three women, two blacks, and one Native American, is probably a little unusual. I ended with *Surfacing* for a number of reasons: I like it very much; Atwood was scheduled to visit our campus that year; Americans are altogether too ignorant of Canada and Canadian literature; Atwood's outsider's view of America sums up some of the themes of imperialism and sexism that come up throughout the course. In future, I shall probably add works by contemporary black women writers—particularly Alice Walker—and some Chicano and Chicana writers.

The arrangement of the syllabus is basically chronological, although I also tried to alternate long and short works, fiction and poetry, and so forth. Additionally, I tried to group works that could shed light on one another. Thus, Harris's sentimentalized "Free Joe" is corrected by Chesnutt's incisive *The Marrow of Tradition*. Problems with nineteenth-century ideas of woman's nature and woman's role are spotlighted by juxtaposing "Editha," "Silk Stockings," and *The Yellow Wallpaper*. Hemingway is both stylistically and thematically a forerunnner of Mailer, but Mailer is more aware of the failings of the macho code in *Armies of the Night* than Hemingway is in "Francis Macomber." The Malamud and Bellow selections offer other solutions to twentieth-century questions about man's role and man's nature, solutions drawn from a different tradition. Other groupings seem clear.

Each student was required to keep a "Reader's Notebook" with an entry explaining what is important to know about each major work. Such entries were in general due on the first day the book was discussed in class. In addition, each student was required to choose a single work, poem, short story, novel, piece of non-fiction, and present a ten-to-fifteen-minute oral report focusing on one aspect of the work. There were no exams or term papers. I based evaluation on the student's ability to think independently rather than on a test of what the student had "learned."

Booklist

Bradley, et al., eds., *The American Tradition in Literature*,
  Vol. II (abbreviated as ATL)
Margaret Atwood, *Surfacing*
Willa Cather, *Death Comes for the Archbishop*
Charles W. Chesnutt, *The Marrow of Tradition*
Theodore Dreiser, *Sister Carrie*
William Faulkner, *Absalom, Absalom*
Charlotte Perkins Gilman, *The Yellow Wallpaper*
William Dean Howells, *The Rise of Silas Lapham*
N. Scott Momaday, *The Way to Rainy Mountain*
Richard Wright, *Native Son*

Syllabus

Class 1   Introduction
      2   Walt Whitman, "When Lilacs Last in the Dooryard
              Bloomed"; Emily Dickinson, poem #285, 288, 303, 328,
              341, 435, 465, 585, 712, 986, 1624 (ATL)

3   Howells, *The Rise of Silas Lapham*
4   Howells, *Silas Lapham*; Hamlin Garland, "The Return of a Private" (ATL)
5   Henry James, *Daisy Miller* (ATL); Twain, from *Innocents Abroad* (ATL)
6   Stephen Crane, "The Bride Comes to Yellow Sky," "A Man Said to the Universe"; Edwin Arlington Robinson, "Luke Havergal," "Eros Turannos," "The Man Against the Sky," "Mr. Flood's Party" (ATL)
7   Mark Twain, "The Private History of a Campaign That Failed," "The Quarles Farm," from *Autobiography*; Joel Chandler Harris, "Free Joe and the Rest of the World"; Twain, "The Man That Corrupted Hadleyburg" (ATL)
8-9 Chesnutt, *The Marrow of Tradition*
10   Robert Frost, "The Death of the Hired Man," "Home Burial"; Carl Sandburg, "Grass"; Elinor Wylie, "Wild Peaches"; Edna St. Vincent Millay, "I Shall Go Back Again to the Bleak Shore," "What Lips My Lips Have Kissed"; E.E. Cummings, "Buffalo Bill's," "my sweet old etcetera," "somewhere i have never travelled" (ATL)
11   Howells, "Editha"; Kate Chopin, "A Pair of Silk Stockings" (ATL); Gilman, *The Yellow Wallpaper*
12-13 Dreiser, *Sister Carrie*
14-15 Cather, *Death Comes for the Archbishop*
16   Ezra Pound, "Mauberly"; T.S. Eliot, "The Love Song of J. Alfred Prufrock," "Gerontion"; F. Scott Fitzgerald, "Babylon Revisited" (ATL)
17   Katherine Anne Porter, "The Jilting of Granny Weatherall"; Eudora Welty, "Death of a Traveling Salesman"; Flannery O'Connor, "The Life You Save May Be Your Own"; William H. Gass, "In the Heart of the Heart of the Country" (ATL)
18-20 Faulkner, *Absalom, Absalom*
21   Wallace Stevens, "Peter Quince at the Clavier," "Sunday Morning," "Emperor of Ice-Cream"; William Carlos Williams, "To Mark Anthony in Heaven," "This is Just to Say," "The Young Housewife" (ATL)
22-23 Wright, *Native Son*
24   Ernest Hemingway, "The Short Happy Life of Francis Macomber"; Norman Mailer, from *Armies of the Night*; Bernard Malamud, "The Mourners"; Saul Bellow, "A Father-to-Be" (ATL)
25   William Stafford, "One Home," "The Farm on the Great Plains"; James Dickey, "Cherrylog Road" (ATL); J.V. Cunningham, from "To What Strangers, What Welcome" (handout)

26–27 Momaday, *The Way to Rainy Mountain*
28   from Momaday, *Angle of Geese* (handout)
29–30 Atwood, *Surfacing*

16
AMERICAN LITERATURE: WHITMAN TO THE PRESENT
Juanita Lawhn and Sandra Mondin
1982–83
San Antonio College
San Antonio, TX 78284

Critique of Original Course

After attending the Reconstructing American Literature Institute, we saw the importance of teaching Langston Hughes's poetry because of his influence on Chicano literature. We also decided to add Toni Morrison as a result of a particularly intense session on Ralph Ellison's *Invisible Man* during which the black women present stressed not only the excellence of Morrison as a writer but also the need to teach sections of *The Bluest Eye* to "correct" Ellison's superficial depiction of women and his comic treatment of father-daughter incest. Another change we made was to substitute a chapter from Zora Neale Hurston's classic novel *Their Eyes Were Watching God* for one of her short stories, which we had originally included. A final change involved adding more Chicana writers as well as a Native American and an Asian-American writer—both women—in order to get a better balance of male and female writers.

Writing Assignment

Our major writing assignment is a thirty-page journal which is turned in three times a semester—ten pages minimum each time. The purpose of the journal is to inspire students to think; to get them to formulate their own ideas; to praise and/or condemn writers, works, periods; to find answers to questions posed for them or posed by them; to make judgments and to expand from the course, to relate the world around them to American literature and vice versa.

We grade the journals on the amount of thought and effort they show, on creativity and originality, and on the quality of insights and judgments they contain.

We urge students to make their journals personal; they can often be fun and informal in tone. They may use their journals to rave or rage as long as they relate their entries to class assignments. We give extensive suggestions, both general and specific for journal entries. We also encourage students to include a variety of lengths and kinds of entries—research, personal explications, parodies, drawings or illustrations, original poems, burlesques, and whatever else the students can think of.

Booklist

There is no particular text for this syllabus because we devised a course that ideally we would like to teach. For the minority literature, we use handouts for the most part.

Syllabus

Week 1	Walt Whitman, "Song of Myself"
2	Emily Dickinson, poem numbers 67, 76, 130, 160, 162, 182, 214, 216, 241, 249, 252, 254, 258, 280, 285, 288, 303, 324, 341, 348, 401, 435, 441, 449, 461, 465, 511, 556, 579, 636, 640, 650, 712, 732, 816, 986, 1052, 1078, 1129, 1207, 1263, 1624, 1732, 1755
3	Sarah Orne Jewett, "The Dulham Ladies"; Harriet Beecher Stowe, "Miss Asphyxia"; Mary E. Wilkins Freeman, "A New England Nun"; Charles W. Chesnutt, "The Goophered Grapevine"
4	Kate Chopin, *The Awakening*; William Dean Howells, "Editha"
5	Mark Twain, "The Man That Corrupted Hadleyburg"; Hamlin Garland, "The Return of a Private"; Charlotte Perkins Gilman, "The Yellow Wallpaper"
6	Henry James, *Daisy Miller*; Edith Wharton, "The Other Two"
7	Stephen Crane, "The Open Boat," from *The Black Riders*: "Should the world roll away," "I saw a man pursuing the horizon," from *War is Kind*: "Do not weep, maiden, for war is kind," "A newspaper is a collection of half injustices," "A slant of sun on dull brown walls," "The trees in the garden rained flowers"; Theodore Dreiser, chapters 1 and 2 from *Sister Carrie*
8	Edwin Arlington Robinson, "Luke Havergal," "Cliff

Klingenhagen," "Richard Cory," "Miniver Cheevy,"
"Mr. Flood's Party," "Credo," "Karma," "The Man
Against the Sky"; Robert Frost, "The Death of the
Hired Man," "Mending Wall," "After Apple Picking,"
"Birches," "The Road Not Taken," "Fire and Ice,"
"Nothing Gold Can Stay," "Desert Places," "Neither
out Far Nor in Deep," "Come In," "Stopping By
Woods on a Snowy Evening," "Directive"; T. S. Eliot,
"The Love Song of J. Alfred Prufrock," "Sweeny
Among the Nightingales," "A Cooking Egg"

9   Zora Neale Hurston, chapters 2 and 3 from *Their Eyes Were
        Watching God*; Jean Toomer, "Fern"; Richard Wright,
        "Big Boy Leaves Home"; Langston Hughes, "The
        Negro Speaks of Rivers," "Mother to Son," "Jazzonia,"
        "Dream Variation," "I, Too," "The Weary Blues,"
        "Cross," "Bound No'th Blues," "Brass Spittoons,"
        "Song for a Dark Girl," "Sylvester's Dying Bed,"
        "Ballad of the Landlord," "Dream Boogie," selection
        from *The Big Sea*, "Dear Dr. Butts"

10   Eugene O'Neill, *The Hairy Ape*; John Steinbeck, "Flight"

11   F. Scott Fitzgerald, "Babylon Revisited"; Ernest Heming-
        way, "The Undefeated"; William Faulkner, "The Bear"

12   Katherine Anne Porter, "Flowering Judas"; Eudora Welty,
        "Death of a Traveling Salesman"; Tillie Olsen, "Tell
        Me a Riddle"; Willa Cather, "The Sentimentality of
        William Tavener"

13   Toni Morrison, pp. 9, 127–29, 146–60 from *The Bluest Eye*
        (paperback edition); Ralph Ellison, chapter 1 from
        Invisible Man; James Baldwin, "Sonny's Blues";
        Gwendolyn Brooks, "The Mother," "Of De Witt
        Williams on His Way to Lincoln Cemetary," "Piano After
        War," "Mentors," " 'Do Not Be Afraid of No,' " "The
        Children of the Poor," "We Real Cool," "The Chicago
        Defender Sends a Man to Little Rock," "Riders to the
        Blood-Red Wrath," "Way-Out Morgan," "The Wall,"
        "Loam Norton"

14   Tomás Rivera, "It was a Silvery Night," " . . . And the Earth
        Did Not Part" from *y no se lo trago la tierra*; José
        Montoya, "El Louie"; Raul Salinas, "The Trip
        Through the Mind Jail"; Rudolfo Gonzales, "Yo Soy
        Joaquin"; Alurista, "When raza," "la caneria y el sol,"
        "the man has lost his shadow," "must be the season of
        the witch"; Bernice Zamora, "Penitents," "California,"
        "Restless Serpents"; Abelardo Delgado, "Stupid
        America"; Lorna Dee Cervantes, "Beneath the Shadow
        of the Freeway," "Refugee Ship," "Para un Revolu-
        cionario"

15   Flannery O'Conner, "A Good Man is Hard to Find"; Sylvia
      Plath, "Insomniac," "Mirror," "Words heard, by
      accident, over the phone," "Burning the Letters," "A
      Secret," "The Applicant," "Daddy," "The Jailer,"
      "Fever 103°" "Cut," "Ariel," "Nick and the
      Candlestick," "Lady Lazarus," "Death & Co.";
      Adrienne Rich, "Living in Sin," "Snapshots of a
      Daughter-in-Law," "The Demon Lover," "Planetar-
      ium," "The Burning of Paper Instead of Children,"
      "Diving into the Wreck," "When We Dead Awaken";
      Leslie Silko, "Storyteller," "Toe' Osh: A Laguna Coyote
      Story"; Maxine Hong Kingston, "No Name Woman"
      from *The Woman Warrior*; Ricardo Sanchez, "Homing";
      Oscar Zeta Acosta, chapter 1 from *The Autobiography of
      a Brown Buffalo*; Estela Portillo Trambley, "The Burn-
      ing"; Juan Bruce-Novoa, "Ann Marisse"

17
MAJOR AMERICAN AUTHORS, II
Deborah McDowell
January, 1982
Colby College
Waterville, ME 04901

Course Rationale

This course was offered in the January term and is, consequently, somewhat sketchy. Were I to offer it as a semester course, I would expand it in at least two ways: first, I would extend the selection of some of the writers already included. For example, there is considerable range in the poetry of Paul Laurence Dunbar, Langston Hughes, and Gwendolyn Brooks, both stylistically and thematically. Using work from the poets' different phases offers many interesting possibilities for studying issues like the complex relationships between writer and audience, writer and patron. Second, I would include selections from other ethnic literatures. Here, the ethnic representation is limited to Afro-American writers.

The rationale for the reading selections is simple: to expose students to literature by those who are not white and male. Because I know that by the time most students get to this sophomore survey course their notions about "major American writers" are calcified, I begin by trying to "decalcify." The first day we talk about "The Canon," who is in it and why—in other words, the politics of canonization, critical double standards, and similar issues. Students slowly come to admit that they just never thought about why they were not reading any women writers, any black writers....

The rationale for the organization of these selections is both useful and problematic, I think. First, I wanted to integrate, not simply "ghettoize," the selections by Afro-Americans and white women, for I think that approach has potentially greater and most lasting pedagogical value. Although the syllabus does not necessarily reveal it, I attempted a comparative approach in terms of race and gender. For example, James's *Daisy Miller*, Jewett's "A White Heron," and Chopin's *The Awakening* allowed us to explore the distinctions between the treatment of developing female independence and nonconformity by male and female writers. Similarly, I considered the Eliot, Toomer, Hughes, and Cullen poetry comparatively in a unit on tradition and experimentation in post-World War I American poetry.

The central weakness in the structure of the syllabus is that it reflects the familiar pre- and post-war organizing bias, the bias that we all know to be largely responsible for the underrepresentation of non-white male literature in such courses. Regrettably, the course also reflects the chronological organizational bias. In future courses, I would attempt to escape these patterns altogether or blend them with others.

Finally, courses designed to expose students to "non-canonical" literature can benefit from a wealth of secondary readings (such as those distributed at the Yale Reconstructing American Literature Institute). Such readings supplement the primary texts and, perhaps, help assure students that my efforts to "diversify" are part of a larger literary enterprise.

Syllabus

Class 1	Introduction
2–3	Mark Twain, *The Adventures of Huckleberry Finn*
4	Henry James, "The Art of Fiction," "The Real Thing"
5	James, *Daisy Miller*
6	Sarah Orne Jewett, "A White Heron"; Kate Chopin, *The Awakening*
7	Chopin, *The Awakening*
8	Paul Laurence Dunbar, selected poems; Charles Chesnutt, "The Goophered Grapevine"
9	Stephen Crane, "The Open Boat"
10	Robert Frost, selected poems
11	T.S. Eliot, "The Love Song of J. Alfred Prufrock"
12	Eliot, selected poems
13	Jean Toomer, Langston Hughes, Countee Cullen, selected poems

14   Harlem renaissance poets; Zora Neale Hurston, "The Gilded
      Six Bits"
15   Jessie Fauset, "The Sleeper Wakes"
16   Ernest Hemingway, "Big Two-Hearted River"
17   Richard Wright, "Long Black Song"; Ralph Ellison, excerpts
      from *Invisible Man*
18   Gwendolyn Brooks, selected poems
19   Toni Morrison, *Sula*

18
SURVEY OF AMERICAN LITERATURE, PART II
Linda Pannill
Spring, 1983
University of Kentucky
Lexington, KY 40506

Course Objectives

The aim of this new course is to survey literature written by Americans from 1865 to the present, in the context of American social and intellectual history. We will attempt to define the Americanness of American literature, the qualities that make it distinctive and lead us to study it apart from British literature. The unifying idea of American literature we will focus on in this course is the promise of America as a New World Garden of Eden, since writers have embraced or rejected this idea from the beginning of our history. Instead of focusing on the handful of writers usually defined as "major," we will take into account the multiplicity of viewpoints on America represented by writers of different racial and ethnic backgrounds, different regions and classes, women as well as men. The course also has as its aim improving critical vocabularies and skills in the interpretation of literary texts, so that students may formulate their own answers to the questions posed in this course.

Booklist

The Norton Anthology of American Literature, Vol. II
Richard Rodriguez, *Hunger of Memory*

Syllabus

Week 1	Introduction to the course: The New World Garden of Eden as a Theme in American Literature, Art, and Popular Culture (slide presentation)
	Joan Didion, from "Some Dreamers of the Golden Dream" (handout)
2	Mark Twain, *Adventures of Huckleberry Finn*
3–4	Edwin Arlington Robinson, "Richard Cory," "Miniver Cheevy," "Mr. Flood's Party," "The House on the Hill"; Henry James, *Daisy Miller*, "The Jolly Corner"
5	Kate Chopin, *The Awakening*
	Exam
6–7	Mary E. Wilkins Freeman, "The Revolt of 'Mother'"; Hamlin Garland, "Under the Lion's Paw"; Willa Cather, "Neighbor Rosicky"; Leslie Marmon Silko, "Lullaby," poems: "Laughing and Laughing About Something that Happened at Mesita," "Storytelling," "Toe'osh: A Laguna Coyote Story" (handouts)
8–9	Carl Sandburg, "Chicago"; T.S. Eliot, "The Waste Land" (I); Hart Crane, "The Bridge"
10	Sherwood Anderson, "A Story-Teller's Story" (Book I, Note 1); Ernest Hemingway, "Big Two-Hearted River"; F. Scott Fitzgerald, "The Rich Boy"
11	Alice Walker, "Everyday Use," "In Search of Our Mother's Gardens" (handouts); film: Alice Walker reading "Everyday Use"
	Exam
12	Joel Chandler Harris, "The Wonderful Tar Baby Story"; Charles W. Chesnutt, "The Goophered Grapevine"; Native American trickster and coyote tales (handouts); Booker T. Washington, "Atlanta Exposition Speech"; Ralph Ellison, *Invisible Man*, Prologue and Chapter 1
13	John Berryman, from "Homage to Mistress Bradstreet"; Allen Ginsberg, "A Supermarket in California"; Adrienne Rich, "The Burning of Paper Instead of Children," "For Julia in Nebraska" (handouts)
14	Richard Rodriguez, *Hunger of Memory*; Pedro Pietri, "Puerto Rican Obituary"

Sample Syllabus for American Literature 1861–1920

I compiled the syllabus that follows at the Reconstructing American Literature Project Institute in June 1982, as a model for part of an imaginary three-semester survey of American literature. I attempted to make the reading selections as varied as possible by including nontraditional forms of writing like journals and by including writers from different regions, backgrounds, and classes; different racial and ethnic groups; women as well as men. Compiling this syllabus was a useful exercise because we did not need to feel constrained by any existing textbook. We were, in effect, creating our own textbook. I did find the topical format we were to use uncongenial, since I think grouping readings under subject headings can limit students' responses to the work. Emily Dickinson seemed to belong everywhere—and nowhere.

In Spring 1983 we offered a new survey of American literature at the University of Kentucky. (See syllabus above.) The two-semester structure of our survey course (with Part II covering the period from 1865 to the present) does not correspond to the chronological breakdown of the sample syllabi we wrote at the Project Institute, but I did incorporate many of the same writers: Booker T. Washington, Charles W. Chesnutt, Willa Cather, Hamlin Garland, Kate Chopin, Mary E. Wilkins Freeman, and others. Rather than a topical approach I chose a chronological one, but the semester as a whole has a thematic focus—responses to the idea of America as a New World Garden of Eden. The most important reason for the differences between this sample syllabus and the actual syllabus is the limitation of the available textbooks.

I. Civil War: *Mary Chesnut's Civil War*, ed. C. Vann Woodward (excerpts); *Journal Of Charlotte L. Forten* (excerpts); Walt Whitman, *Drum-Taps* (excerpts)

II. Reconstruction and Reaction: Ida B. Wells (Barnett), excerpts from *On Lynching* or Charles W. Chesnutt short story "Autobiography"; W. E. B. Du Bois, "Of Mr. Booker T. Washington and Others"; Paul Laurence Dunbar, poems; Booker T. Washington, *Up From Slavery* (excerpts); Walt Whitman, *Democratic Vistas* (excerpts)

III. The West: Mary Hunter Austin, *The Land Of Little Rain* (excerpts); Willa Cather, "The Bohemian Girl" or excerpt from *My Antonia*; Hamlin Garland, *Son Of The Middle Border* (excerpts); Mark Twain, *Adventures of Huckleberry Finn*; Native American literature

IV. Urban Growth and Industrialization: Horatio Alger (excerpts); Rebecca Harding Davis, *Life In The Iron Mills*; Theodore Dreiser, *Sister Carrie*; Emma Lazarus, "The New Colossus"; Jacob Riis, *How The Other Half Lives* (excerpts); Thorstein Veblen, *The Theory of the Leisure Class* (excerpts)

V. The Changing Role of Women: Louisa May Alcott, *Little Women* (excerpts); Kate Chopin, *The Awakening* or "The Storm"; Emily Dickinson letters, poems; Mary E. Wilkins Freeman, "The Revolt of 'Mother' "; Charlotte Perkins Gilman, "The Yellow Wallpaper"; Ellen Glasgow, *The Women Within* (excerpts from early chapters); Susan Glaspell, *Trifles*; Frances E. W. Harper

poems; Henry James, *The Portrait Of A Lady*; Sarah Orne
Jewett, "A White Heron"; Elizabeth Cady Stanton, excerpts
from *Eighty Years and More*; *Correspondence, Writings And
Speeches*; or *History of Women Suffrage*; Edith Wharton, *The
House of Mirth*

19
AMERICAN LITERATURE
Aileen Chris Shafer
Fall, 1982
West Virginia University
Morgantown, WV 26506

Course Objectives

Whitman said of America, "Here is not merely a nation but a teeming
nation of nations." And yet, students, like some of us, have formed views of
American literature and life from a circumscribed literary canon. This
syllabus attempts to expand students' literary experiences by including:
celebrated writers as well as deserving but little known writers; esoteric
writers and proletarian writers; geographically diverse writers; writers of
many ethnicities; and male and female writers. The syllabus is just a beginning effort toward the goal of promoting a balanced literary view and a
representative portrait of American experience.

The assignments include varied genres: short story, novel, poetry,
essay, and biography. Specifically, when I used the syllabus, the juxtaposition of fiction and poetry with biography proved to be one of the most
fruitful approaches in the course. For example, although Emily Dickinson
and Maria Mitchell were New England contemporaries and although both
were sensitive, brilliant women who shared similar female experiences, some
of their personal views, as well as goals, differed dramatically. Specifically,
Emily thought it "dreary-to-be-Somebody!" Whereas Maria, who was,
among other honors, elected to the American Association for the Advance-
ment of Science, said the following about recognition accorded at a national
convention, "For a few days, Science reigns supreme,—we are feted and
complimented to the top of our bent ... one does enjoy acting the part of
greatness for a while!" Also, teaching *Life in the Iron Mills* prior to reading
excerpts from the life of "Mother" Mary Jones introduced students to
despair as well as hope about American poverty.

Booklist

Alan Trachtenberg and Benjamin DeMott, eds., *America in Literature*, Vol. II (T & D)
Rebecca Harding Davis, *Life in the Iron Mills*
Eve Merriam, ed., *Growing Up Female in America: Ten Lives*
Elizabeth Madox Roberts, *The Time of Man*

Syllabus

Class 1   Orientation
      2   Walt Whitman, "Preface" to *Leaves of Grass*; "Song of Myself," stanzas 1–10, 13–18 (T & D)
      3   Whitman, rest of "Song of Myself"
      4   Short paper on Whitman; in-class discussion of papers
      5   Mark Twain, "The Man That Corrupted Hadleyburg" (T & D)
      6   Twain, from *Life on the Mississippi*; Chesnutt, "The Wife of His Youth" (T & D)
      7   Joel Chandler Harris, "Free Joe and the Rest of the World"; Kate Chopin, "Desiree's Baby" (T & D); Excerpts from *Autobiography* of Susie King Taylor (*Growing Up Female*) Short paper due on Harris and Taylor
      8   "Frankie and Johnny," "Midnight Special," "Love Song—Chippewa," "A Sequence of Songs of the Ghost Dance Religion"; Sarah Orne Jewett, "A White Heron" (T & D)
      9   Emily Dickinson poems, #288, 1129, 328, 585, 130, 258 (T&D)
     10   Dickinson poems, #341, 465, 579, 401, 986 (T&D)
     11   Short paper due on Dickinson
     12   Henry James, *Daisy Miller* (T&D)
     13   James, *Daisy Miller*; Edith Wharton, "The Other Two" (T&D)
     14   Davis, *Life in the Iron Mills*
     15   Tillie Olsen, "A Biographical Interpretation" in *Life in the Iron Mills*; "'Mother' Mary Jones," *Autobiography* (*Growing Up Female*)
     16   Short paper due on Faulkner
     17   William Faulkner, "Old Man" (T&D)
     18   Introduction to Pound and Eliot; Ezra Pound, "A Pact," "Salutation," "Salutation the Second," "Salutation the Third," "The Bath Tub" (T&D)
     19   T.S. Eliot, "The Love Song of J. Alfred Prufrock" (T&D)
     20   Ernest Hemingway, "A Clean, Well-Lighted Place"; F. Scott Fitzgerald, "The Rich Boy" (T&D)
     21   Film: American Short Story version of Hemingway, "Soldier's Home"
  22-23   Roberts, *The Time of Man*
     24   Examination

25   Robert Frost, "Home Burial," "Design," "The Silken Tent,"
        "Provide Provide," "After Apple-Picking" (T&D)
26   Wallace Stevens, "Peter Quince at the Clavier," "Anecdote of the
        Jar"; William Carlos Williams, "Fine Work With Pitch and
        Copper," "The Widow's Lament in Springtime," "To
        Waken an Old Lady," "The Young Housewife" (T&D)
27   Jean Toomer, "Esther"; Langston Hughes, "Evenin' Air Blues,"
        "Harlem"; Allen Ginsberg, "Howl," Part 1; Robert Lowell,
        "For the Union Dead"; Adrienne Rich, "Living in Sin"
        (T&D)
        Short paper due on Eliot and Rich
28   Eudora Welty, "A Worn Path"; Flannery O'Connor, "Parker's
        Back"; Truman Capote, from In Cold Blood (T&D)
29-30   Saul Bellow, Seize the Day (T&D)

20
AMERICAN LITERATURE AFTER
THE CIVIL WAR
R.C. Townsend
1981
Amherst College
Amherst, MA 01002

Course Objectives

With Whitman I try to establish an appreciation of the potential of
American democracy, not only as comprised of universal "I's" but also as
reflected in and created by his experiments with language. And then more or
less explicitly I read the texts that follow against what I have set up.

I try to see what shapes the Democratic vision—or visions of
Democracy—take. I try to be responsive to how it is defended or satirized or
mourned. I try to understand how writers outside the dominant, white, male
culture view it or ignore it.

Syllabus and Booklist

Week 1   Walt Whitman, Poetry and Prose (Riverside edition), pp. 25-68,
         84-99, 116-20, 180-86, 233-40, 288-94, 297-303, 411-27,
         455-501

2   Henry James, *The American*
3   Mark Twain, *The Adventures of Huckleberry Finn*
4   Sarah Orne Jewett, *The Country of the Pointed Firs*
5   Kate Chopin, *The Awakening*
6   Theodore Dreiser, *Sister Carrie*
7   Examination
8   W.E.B. DuBois, *The Souls of Black Folk* (you could omit chapters II, VII, VIII)
9   Henry Adams, *The Education of Henry Adams* (Riverside edition), chapters I-IV, VII, X, XIV-XV, XIX-XX, XXV, XXIX-XXXI, XXXIII, p. 494-XXXV
10 Gertrude Stein, *Three Lives*
11 James Weldon Johnson, *The Autobiography of an Ex-Colored Man*
12 Sherwood Anderson, *Winesburg, Ohio*
13 Ernest Hemingway, *In Our Time*
14 F. Scott Fitzgerald, *The Great Gatsby*

Advanced Period
Courses

Nineteenth-Century Literature

21
NINETEENTH-CENTURY
AMERICAN LITERATURE
Jean Ferguson Carr
1982-83
Carnegie-Mellon University
Pittsburgh, PA 15213

Course Objectives

"Why should not we also enjoy an original relation to the universe? Why should not we have a poetry and philosophy of insight and not of tradition, and a religion of revelation to us, and not the history of theirs?" Throughout the nineteenth century American writers returned to Emerson's questions, trying to develop new language, style, forms, and ideas to express the American experience. They sought new genres and voices to include the diverse population of the new country, to respond to the range of experience of both men and women, of immigrants, slaves, Indians, children, and workers. This course will examine how writers transformed their Old World heritage as they strove to create a national voice. Despite the confident tone of such national prophets as Emerson and Whitman, the task was not easy. Many Americans had no prior place in the literature or literary production of the Old World. Writers had to form a coherent experience and audience without falsifying their diverse experiences; they had to reconcile their national goals of democracy and egalitarianism with problems of being a literary aristocracy writing within handed-down educational and cultural traditions. Above all, writers faced an unconvinced audience, who lionized British authors touring the country, who seemed to prefer Dickens or Ouida over local products, and whose school readers printed far more British selections than American.

In this course we will consider the different approaches to the problem of writing about America that are informed by authors' regional backgrounds, their race or sex, their sense of audience, and their role as writers. We will contrast, for example, the implications of portraying the artist as reformer, as preacher, as scientist, or of projecting the audience as highly literate, highly moral, or highly sheltered. We will use a popular classroom anthology of the day, *McGuffey's Sixth Eclectic Reader*, to develop a cultural context for the writing and reading of literature and to help formulate such questions as: What qualities of literature seem to be valued? What attitudes toward reading and evaluating literature does a school anthology express, and how are such attitudes reflected or criticized by authors like Emerson, Twain, or Davis? How do various writers strive to fulfill their claim of having a "new" experience or voice to express, and how do they treat the problem of literary traditions?

Requirements
Regular class participation, group oral project, two papers (four-to-six pages, topic sheets will be distributed for three possible due dates; choose two), short homework assignments, midterm and final exams.

Group Oral Projects
These projects will enable you to explore how various aspects of American culture and society affected literary issues. Topics include: American education; the popular songs, photographs, and literature of the Civil War; children's literature; newspaper thriller and dime novels; Utopian communities; melodrama and theater; abolition, temperance, and other reform movements; slave narratives.

Booklist

Rebecca Harding Davis, *Life in the Iron Mills, or the Korl Woman* (The Feminist Press)
Frederick Douglass, *Narrative of the Life of Frederick Douglass* (Signet)
Ralph Waldo Emerson, *Selected Writings* (Signet)
Nathaniel Hawthorne, *The Blithedale Romance* (Norton) and *Selected Tales and Sketches* (Rinehart); On reserve: Hawthorne's children's book, *The Wonder Book*
McGuffey's Sixth Eclectic Reader (Van Nostrand)
Herman Melville, *Great Short Works* (Harper)
Harriet Beecher Stowe, *Uncle Tom's Cabin* (Merrill); On reserve: *Key to Uncle Tom's Cabin*, handouts of hymns quoted in *UTC*, handouts of funeral poems
Mark Twain, *Adventures of Huckleberry Finn* (Riverside)

Walt Whitman, *Leaves of Grass* (Signet); On reserve: *Speciman Days*
Handouts on popular women writers: Lydia Sigourney, Fanny Fern,
    E.D.E.N. Southworth

Syllabus

Class 1   Introduction: Discussion of book production and distribu-
               tion in the nineteenth century, of bestsellers, and genres
               of books; issue of how we select what is "representative"
               of the age.
           Overview of *McGuffey Reader:* Discussion of introductory
               essay n the reading and uses of literature, the range of
               selections, the ratio of British to American selections,
               the proportion of fiction, poetry, drama, and non-
               fiction, the sense of what is "good" writing.
           Emerson, "The American Scholar": Discussion of Emerson's
               presentation of problems facing Americans (issue of
               originality vs. imitation, newness vs. the old, the "real"
               vs. tradition) and of attitudes for the American writer to
               attempt (hard work, brashness, willingness to fail,
               assertion of ambitious goal, policy of doing, exploration).
       2   Hawthorne, *The Blithdale Romance*
       3   Hawthorne, *Selected Tales and Sketches:* "The Artist of the
               Beautiful," "The Birthmark," "Sights from a Steeple,"
               Prefaces, "Rappaccini's Daughter," "Ethan Brank,"
               "Young Goodman Brown," "Feathertop, A Moralized
               Legend"
       4   Melville, "Bartleby, The Scrivener," "Benito Cereno." Paper
               I: Topics on Hawthorne
       5   Melville, "Billy Budd," and selections from "The Encantadas"
       6   Emerson, selections from journals and lectures, "Circles";
               Library assignment tracing issues from journal to essay,
               discussion of revision and of Emerson's "instructions"
               for reading as contrasted with the McGuffey lessons
       7   Emerson, "The Divinity School Address," "Self-Reliance,"
               "Experience," "Politics," "Fate"
           Midterm exam
       8   Emerson, "The Poet," and selected poems; Whitman, "Pre-
               face" to *Leaves of Grass*; Handout on Sigourney, poetry
               from *McGuffey* (Alice Cary, Samuel Woodworth, James
               Thomson, H.F. Chorley, William C. Bryant, Henry
               Wadsworth Longfellow, Sir Walter Scott, Adeline
               Whitney, E.B. Browning, Lord Byron, Felicia D.
               Hemans, Mary R. Mitford, Oliver Wendell Holmes,
               John Greenleaf Whittier, Edgar Allan Poe)

9   Whitman, *Song of Myself*, and other poems
10   Davis, *Life in the Iron Mills*; Melville, "The Tartarus of
         Maids"; Thomas Hood, "Song of the Shirt" (*McGuffey*)
         Paper II: Topics on Emerson, Whitman, Davis, poetry
11   Handouts on Fanny Fern and E.D.E.N. Southworth; Stowe,
         Uncle Tom's Cabin
12   Stowe, *Uncle Tom's Cabin*; selections in *McGuffey* on domes-
         tic virtues (e.g., Horace Greeley, "Labor," Francis
         Hopkinson, "House Cleaning," T.G. Read, "The
         Brave at Home," William Cowper, "My Mother's
         Picture")
13   Douglass, *Narrative of Frederick Douglass*. Paper III: Topics
         on Stowe, Douglass, *McGuffey*
14   Twain, *Huckleberry Finn*
15   Twain, *Huckleberry Finn*; Edward Everett, "The Dawn"
         (*McGuffey*)
Final Exam

Study Sheet for *McGuffey's Sixth Reader*

Take some time to examine the book: Look through the table of contents, look at the illustrations, read the preface, read the supplementary reading list, note the kinds of selections, the biographical notes for each author, the words that are annotated, the suggested reading questions. What qualities of style and content are praised or censured? What patterns can you see in the selection of authors, subjects, and works?

Read quickly through the introduction (pp. 11-60) to get an overview of the teaching approach being advocated. How would such a method of evaluating literature influence the selection of material? What qualities are stressed, in literature and in the process of reading? What relationship seems to be drawn between elocution and social status? between learning and patriotism? between learning and "being natural"? What is the importance of gesture and oral performance? How does this educational approach compare with the ways you have learned to read?

Examine the list of authors. Note that of the 138 items, only 66 are by American authors; of 111 authors, only 54 are Americans. Shakespeare is the most widely represented (with 9 excerpts), then Scott and Longfellow (4 each), then the Bible, Bryant, Byron, Irving, and Webster (3 each). Note that most of the authors we are reading in this course are not represented in *McGuffey's*, except for a short (and relatively unrepresentative) passage from Emerson. The following are the American authors represented (if there is more than one selection by an author, the number is given in parentheses). Look at the kind of excerpt chosen. Read several to get a sense of the range of material.

George Arnold	John P. Kennedy
Lyman Beecher (2)	Thomas S. King
William C. Bryant (3)	Henry Lee
John C. Calhoun	H.W. Longfellow (4)
Alice Cary	John Neal
W.E. Channing	Francis Parkman
Richard Henry Dana	J.G. Percival
Orville Dewey	John Pierpont
Joseph Rodman Drake	Edgar Allan Poe
Timothy Dwight	Noah Porter
Ralph Waldo Emerson	George D. Prentice
Edward Everett	William H. Prescott
James T. Fields	T.B. Read
Wilson Flagg	W.G. Simms
Benjamin Franklin	Jared Sparks
Horace Greeley	Charles Sprague
F.W.P. Greenwood	Gardiner Spring
Thomas S. Grimke	Charles Sumner
Fitz-Greene Halleck	B.F. Taylor
Robert Hayne	Henry Timrod
Patrick Henry	Daniel Webster (3)
Oliver W. Holmes (2)	Adeline Whitney
Francis Hopkinson	J.G. Whittier
W.D. Howells	John Wilson
Washington Irving (3)	R.C. Winthrop
Helen Hunt Jackson	William Wirt
Thomas Jefferson	Samuel Woodworth

Try to determine what qualities are being extolled as American, as valuable to the nation. Do you get a sense of a national character? What attitudes toward childhood and elementary education seem implicit? What cultural assumptions seem to shape selection and presentation of material? How has the *way* you react to certain pieces changed from the way a nineteenth-century reader might be expected to react? (Read an excerpt still assigned in classes and think about whether it is being presented differently; a good choice might be Shakespeare's famous play "The Folly of Intoxication," pp. 322-25). Can you find kinds of selections that seem particularly dated—either culturally or artistically? What selections still seem paticularly interesting—either culturally or artistically? What kinds of "American" experience are emphasized; what kinds are slighted or ignored? What portrait of nineteenth-century America does *McGuffey's Reader* project? Compare the selection and presentation of materials with one of the modern anthologies on reserve: what are some of the major differences?

Selected Paper Topics

Students write two four- to six-page papers, choosing from three possible due dates and from suggested topics, some of which are given below. They are also encouraged to develop their own topics.

1. Many of Hawthorne's narrators are presented as having a somewhat malevolent curiosity about other people's secrets. Coverdale (*Blithedale Romance*) is described as an eavesdropper and voyeur; Giovanni ("Rappaccini's Daughter") spies on Beatrice from the seclusion of his high tower; Aylmer ("The Birthmark") scientifically "pries" into his wife's "nature." Evaluate the problem of being an observer, focusing on one of Hawthorne's narrators.

2. In his 1842 essay "The Poet" Emerson called for a uniquely American poet. Examine his recommendations for "the poet whom I describe" and discuss how Whitman and Davis do/do not fulfill Emerson's challenge. How might they define the role? Select a specific poem or passage for focus.

3. In "The American Scholar" Emerson says: "Another sign of our times... is the new importance given to the single person... The world is nothing, the man is all; in yourself is the law of all nature... it is for you to know all; it is for you to dare all." Discuss this problematic position, comparing Emerson and either Whitman or Davis. Consider the potential conflict between private and public roles, between personal and social roles.

4. A widely read literary history of the United States makes this claim about the literature of the American "Renaissance": "American literature here, for the first time, sloughed off provincialism, and by being itself—by saying only what it wanted to say and as it wanted to say it—attained the rank and quality of world literature." Discuss the implications of this claim for one of our authors, focusing on specific problems in style, genre, subject matter, audience, or literary tradition that your author faced in making a literature that could "be itself." (Note: you will need to discuss what it might mean to have a literature "be itself" and to say "only what it wanted to say and as it wanted to say it." Are there problems with this definition of "greatness"?)

5. Huck Finn relies on various kinds of discourse to portray his world, many of which are suspect in a "rational" world (e.g., lore, magical spells, lucky charms, lies, tall tales, prayers, reveries). Discuss the challenge of such modes of communicating or articulating the world to the public discourse Huck criticizes. Focus on a particular conflict between Huck's "language" and the world's.

Group Projects

During the term each of you will work in a group preparing an oral presentation. The goal of this project is for you to supplement our more "literary" investigations by pursuing a particular cultural issue in more depth than we can in class. I'd like you to explore some of the primary documents of the age and to get a feel for material from other fields than literature (e.g., science, performing arts, history, music) or from popular culture. I would recommend, therefore, that you use some of the examining strategies we have used with the *McGuffey Reader*. Instead of reading a novel about the Civil War, examine a range of newspapers and magazines of the time; instead of preparing a report on Alcott's fiction, investigate the tables of contents of childrens' magazines or examine the instruction books for raising children. In short, do what you don't do for class assignments: skim. Be selective about what you read at length; try to find out what's available, what's "characteristic," and then read a few things more carefully.

The presentations will be about thirty minutes per group; each group of five or six students should run off a one-page outline for the class and prepare a fuller notebook of the term's investigation (the notebook should be put on reserve for the class to read). The presentations will be scheduled during our two evening sessions in weeks 11 and 14. I would like to meet with each group once early in your planning and once before the presentations. Your presentation should focus on an interesting problem for discussion; you may want to divide your group into opposing sides of an issue. Don't try to "cover" a topic, but work instead toward a useful approach to the issue.

Topics

1. *Civil War:* How did civilians perceive the Civil War? How was it different for southerners and northerners? What do we know about the reactions of slaves, of free blacks? Look at newspaper accounts, not so much for information about the battles and logistics of fighting but to get a sense of how people described the war and its aims and the conflict. Look at photographs of the war, at the illustrations in the newspapers taken from daguerreotypes. Read the sections on the war in diaries and letters. Listen to the popular way songs.

2. *Children's literature:* In class we are reading a schoolbook, full of "approved" literature for the moral and intellectual guidance of the young. Look at other literature of this sort (magazines like *St. Nicholas* or *The Youth's Companion*, fiction by Lousia May Alcott, Kate Douglas Wiggin, Frances H. Burnett, readers for younger children), but also look at what else children read. What books were most popular? What are the subjects and styles of some of the dime novels or sensation stories children devoured on the sly? A good way to find out what children were reading illicitly is to read some of the many articles of the time on what they ought *not* to read. Try to come to some conclusions about what it was like to be a child at the time, what was expected and forbidden, what qualities were praised in heroines or censured in bad boys.

3. *Melodrama:* Most Americans got their literary experiences from the

stage, not from books. Today we see few of the plays that were so wildly popular (plays like *Under the Gaslight* or *Ten Nights in a Bar-room*), although many of our popular ideas about heroes and villains, women's roles, and literary conventions are influenced by these melodramas. What plays were popular? What were their subjects and how were they presented? Who went to see plays and where? What attitudes toward representing conflict, emotion, psychological turmoil, etc. can you derive from descriptions of contemporary productions? How did play versions differ from book versions? Compare the Aiken version of *UTC* with Stowe's. Investigate how Shakespeare was produced (and experienced).

4. *The domestic ideal:* The domestic ideal ruled on both sides of the Atlantic in the nineteenth century. In England a reigning monarch enshrined the vitures of home, marriage, and family, an example that was widely eulogized in less exalted spheres. In America the idea was no less a part of the national mythology, although the harsher realities of frontier life and general domestic privations created a countermyth. Consider the myth and its counters. Compare the public assumptions with the daily lives of a range of women: read a year of letters or diaries of women in various regions and classes. Examine readings in etiquette books, household guides, fashion or domestic magazines. What implicit cultural assumptions do these how-to-do-it books reveal?

5. *Utopian communities*: Emerson wrote in 1840, "We are all a little wild here with numberless projects of social reform. Not a reading man but has a draft of a new community in his waistcoat pocket." We're reading Hawthorne's fictional account of such an experiment; explore some of the many such communities, e.g., the Shakers, Fruitlands, Brook Farm, New Harmony, Oneida, the Phalanxes, Hopedale. Read Emerson's essay "New England Reformers" and Alcott's "Transcendental Wild Oats," and other commentaries by outsiders. What attitudes toward reform and social structure inspire the communities? What threat or challenge do they seem to the general society?

22
AMERICAN ROMANTICISM
Phyllis Cole
Wellesley College Center for Research on Women
Wellesley, MA 02181

Rationale of the Course

[The following course proposal is adapted from an article by Phyllis Cole and Deborah Lambert entitled "American Literature and American Diversity: Transforming the Study of Gender and Race," Working Paper, Mellon Seminar, Wellesley College Center for Research on Women, 1983.]

Organizing a course by period can be an unsettling act if historical contemporaneity is taken with a new seriousness. American literature in its romantic phase becomes interesting in a new way when we play off against one another the well-established "romances" of white male writers, the "sentimental" poetry and fiction of white women, and the black slave narratives (mostly by men, occasionally by women.) And this picture becomes even richer when we consider private writing as well as published, when furthermore we look at the emergence into printed form (under circumstances of white cultural imperialism) of two pre-literate, non-white American folk forms of great power, black spirituals and Native American myths and legends.

To achieve such a vision in a semester-long course is not easy, especially for a historic period where the familiar male writers look so much like a pantheon. Selectivity will of course be necessary; most novels have to be sacrificed as whole texts in favor of shorter narratives, stories, poems, and chapters from novels; and these are organized so that gender and race become central issues of analysis as both theme and circumstance. Among the historical circumstances that the course tries to make clear are a commercial press relatively open to both men and women; the emergence through it of a male nationalistic romanticism and a female domestic romanticism, both secularizations of inherited Protestantism; and a national white imperialism toward blacks and Native Americans, variously sentimentalized and condemned in white texts and counter-attacked in black and Native American texts. The course does not abandon chronology, but violates it when occasion demands, and organizes reading and class-work in thematic pairs and groups. These are designed explicitly to clarify our ideas of gender and race in the texts and to avoid demeaning female or non-white subjects or forms. The traditional meanings of the term "romanticism" are used, enlarged, and questioned in the course. I keep it for its capacious ability to describe a literature of *feeling* (but now sentiment, domestic affection, religious enthusiasm as well as the much-celebrated imagination) and a literature of *nature* (but now to include the actual voices of the women, blacks, and Native Americans associated with nature in the white literature of primitivism). I teach Whitman and Dickinson at two points in the semester as a powerfully contrasting pair of romantic poets.

Here is an effort at a specific sequence. In the first six weeks of the course we discuss languages of feeling in relation to gender. Next come three weeks on Native American texts and on images of Native Americans in white texts, then a comparable unit on black texts and images. The semester ends with three weeks that come back to the end of the period, now with a fuller sense of social and political issues.

The problem of the course is to integrate the varieties of literary discourse in mid-nineteenth-century America, to see it at once as one world and as many and unbridgeable worlds. The course is both an inter-textual study and, through particular literary texts, a study of social structure. How does a text serve the needs or express the strains of its writer or readers? What are the differences of form and function between literary myths and folk myths? What is there to appreciate and criticize in "conventional" and "unconventional" forms and points of view?

Syllabus

Class 1   Literary Nationalism and Literary Domesticity. Journalistic manifestoes by William Cullen Bryant and Sarah Hale; Lydia Sigourney's domestic restlessness and sense of change in "To a Shred of Linen" and Washington Irving's legend of change and male wanderlust in "Rip Van Winkle." Here stressing the separation of spheres by gender. (See Emily Stipes Watts, *The Poetry of American Women from 1632 to 1945* [Austin: University of Texas Press, 1977], pp. 91–92 for the text of Sigourney's poem, and Judith Fetterley, *The Resisting Reader: A Feminist Approach to American Fiction* [Bloomington: Indiana University Press, 1977], chapter 1 for a feminist reading of "Rip Van Winkle.")

2   First-Person Voices and Inner Worlds. Passages from diaries, autobiographies, poems in the American Protestant traditions, including Lyman Beecher and Harriet Beecher Stowe, Phillis Wheatley and Rebecca Jackson (see *Gifts of Power: The Writings of Rebecca Jackson, Black Visionary, Quaker Eldress*, ed. Jean McMahon Humez [Amherst: University of Massachusetts Press, 1981]), Mary Moody Emerson and Ralph Waldo Emerson. Here exploring a less gender-specific world of consciousness, providing a context for analyzing the androgyny/masculinity of:

3   "Self-Reliance" as an American Ideology. Ralph Waldo Emerson, *Nature*, "Self-Reliance," "The American Scholar."

Then two challenges by women: Lidian Jackson Emerson, "The Transcendental Bible" and Margaret Fuller, *Woman in the Nineteenth Century*. (For L. J. Emerson see Ellen Tucker Emerson, *The Life of Lidian Jackson Emerson*, ed. Delores Bird Carpenter [Boston: Twayne, 1980], pp. 81–83; for Fuller, see Bell Gale Chevigny, ed. *The Woman and the Myth: Margaret Fuller's Life and Writings* [Old Westbury, N.Y.: The Feminist Press, 1976], pp. 239–78.)

4   Childhood and Death. Native elegies by Wheatley and Sigourney; then a group all influenced by Wordsworth's "Immortality Ode": Emerson, "Threnody," Henry Wadsworth Longfellow, "My Lost Youth," Harriet Beecher Stowe's scene of Little Eva's death in *Uncle Tom's Cabin*, Walt Whitman, "Out of the Cradle Endlessly Rocking," Elizabeth Oakes Smith, "The Sinless Child."

5   Women as Saints/Witches, Objects of Spiritual/Sexual Desire. "New England tales" (all concerning Puritan "goodmen" and women, all tales of good and evil): Nathaniel Hawthorne, "Young Goodman Brown"; Catharine Sedgwick, *Hope Leslie* (excerpt); Lydia Maria Child, *Hobomok* (excerpt); John Greenleaf Whittier, "Cassandra Southwick." Male destroyers: Hawthorne, "The Birthmark"; Edgar Allan Poe, "Ligeia."

6   Walt Whitman and Emily Dickinson, Selected Poems. Both inheriting the Emerson legacy, each inheriting a gender-define literary world as well.

7   Native American Legends. Female and male and social order in "The Red Swan," "The Ring in the Prairie," "Leelinau," "Manabozho." Using modern texts edited by John Bierhorst (*The Red Swan: Myths and Tales of the American Indians* [New York: Farrar, Straus and Giroux, 1976]) but examining also Henry Rowe Schoolcraft's original collection (*Algic Researches Comprising Inquiries Respecting the Mental Charac teristics of the North American Indians*, 2 vols. [New York: Harper and Bros., 1839]). Attempting to define the literary qualities of myth (cf. Bierhorst, Claude Levi-Strauss), comparing these with the "mercerized folklore" of Longfellow's adaptation from Schoolcraft, "Hiawatha" (excerpt).

8   The Noble Savage. James Fenimore Cooper, *The Last of the Mohicans*; Sedgwick, *Hope Leslie*. Male-male and male-female bonding in white primitivist romances.

9   Native and White Confrontation and Dialogue. Treaty speeches by Chief Speckled Snake and Chief Joseph (see *American Literature: The Makers and the Making*, Vol. II, Brooks, et al., eds.); Pontiac, "Paradise Opened to the Indians" (included in Schoolcraft, vol. 1, pp. 239–48), and Handsome Lake, "A Vision" (Indian millennialism before the threat of extinction: what becomes of traditional female and male roles in these new

visions of endurance?). Henry David Thoreau, "Economy" from *Walden* and passages from *Journals*—a white experiment in savagery as a means of romantic consciousness.

10 Black Spirituals. Afro-American song and millennial vision in response to enslavement by whites. Female and male singers and figures in the songs. Circumstances of gathering into print in the 1860s—cf. Schoolcraft in 1830s (see William Francis Allen, Charles Pickard Ware, and Lucy McKim Garrison, eds., *Slave Songs of the United States* [New York: A. Simpson and Co., 1867]).

11 Slave Narratives. Frederick Douglass, *Narrative of the Life of Frederick Douglass*; Linda Brent [Harriet Jacobs], *Incidents in the Life of a Slave Girl*. As autobiography and protest.

12 Anti-Slavery as Politics, Religion, Literature. Excerpts from speeches and appeals by David Walker, William Lloyd Garrison, Lydia Maria Child, Douglass. Stowe, *Uncle Tom's Cabin*.

13 Melville on Work and Slavery. "Benito Cereno," "Bartleby, the Scrivener," "The Tartarus of Maids."

14 First-Person Female and The Civil War. Julia Ward Howe, "The Battle Hymn of the Republic"; excerpts from Mary Boykin Chesnut's *Diary*, Elizabeth Stuart Phelps, *The Gates Ajar*, Charlotte Forten's *Journal*, autobiographical accounts by ex-slaves collected in George P. Rawick, ed. *The American Slave: A Composite Autobiography* (41 vols. [Westport, Conn. Greenwood Press, 1972–1979]).

15 Whitman and Dickinson, Selected Poems, Letters, Essays. Whitman's proclamation of the private as public and national, Dickinson's intensification and expansion of privacy.

23
AMERICAN ROMANTICISM
Phyllis Jones
1980–81
Oberlin College
Oberlin, OH 44074

Booklist

The American Tradition in Literature, Vol. 1, ed. Bradley, Beatty, Long, Perkins (ATL)
James Fenimore Cooper, *The Deerslayer*
Rebecca Harding Davis, *Life in the Iron Mills*
Emily Dickinson, *The Complete Poems*
Margaret Fuller, *Woman in the Nineteenth Century*
Nathaniel Hawthorne, *The Scarlet Letter*
Herman Melville, *Moby Dick*
Harriet Beecher Stowe, *Uncle Tom's Cabin*
Recommended: John Trimble, *Writing With Style*

Syllabus

Class 1–2   Introductory; Tony Tanner, "Notes for a Comparison Between American and European Romanticism" (on reserve)

I. Major Ideas and Themes of American Romanticism—Emerson as Spokesperson

    3–5   Ralph Waldo Emerson, *Nature*, "Divinity School Address," "Self-Reliance," "Experience" (read carefully); "The American Scholar," "The Poet," "Fate" (skim only) (ATL); Passages from Emerson's Journals (skim, on reserve), "Each and All," "The Sphinx," "Compensation," "Hamatreya," "Brahma," "Merlin," "Days" (ATL)

II. Romantic Responses to Nineteenth-Century Industrialization; American Uses of Pastoral

    6–9   Henry David Thoreau, *Walden*, "Civil Disobedience" (ATL)

    10   Davis, *Life in the Iron Mills*

III. Romantic Responses to Nineteenth-Century Sexism and Racism

11–12   Fuller, *Woman in the Nineteenth Century*; read closely pp.
        15–49, 62–63, 95–96, 168–79; skim the rest
13–15   Stowe, *Uncle Tom's Cabin*. Frederick Douglass, *Narrative of
        the Life of Frederick Douglass* (pp. 1659–70 ATL)
IV. New Directions in Fiction
16–17   Edgar Allan Poe, "Ligeia," "The Fall of the House of
        Usher," "The Masque of the Red Death," "The Pur-
        loined Letter," "Twice-Told Tales by Nathaniel Haw-
        thorne: A Review" (ATL)
18   Washington Irving, "Rip Van Winkle," "The Legend of
        Sleepy Hollow" (ATL)
19–20   Cooper, *The Deerslayer*; "Preface to The Leatherstocking
        Tales," "The Indian Heritage: Oratory and Poetry"
        (ATL)
21–24   Hawthorne, all tales in ATL; *The Scarlet Letter*; "Preface to
        The House of the Seven Gables" (ATL)
25–29   Melville, "Bartleby," "Hawthorne and His Mosses" (ATL);
        "Letters to Hawthorne" (on reserve); *Moby Dick*
V. New Directions in Poetry
30–33   Dickinson: (1) Begin with these poems—185, 199, 216, 241,
        258, 280, 303, 320, 341, 401, 435, 465, 508, 520, 561, 675,
        712, 765, 974, 1129, 1545
        (2) Read, on reserve, Adrienne Rich, "Vesuvius at
        Home: The Power of Emily Dickinson," and selec
        tions from the letters
        (3) It is far better to read a few poems well than to read
        too many. I will assign more poems to correlate with
        class discussion and lecture. For browsing I suggest
        the poetry of 1862, her most prolific period, often
        providing some of her best writing.
34–38   Walt Whitman, all poetry in ATL, "Preface" to 1855 edition
        of *Leaves of Grass;* for Background, Poe, "The Philo-
        sophy of Composition," "Romance," "To Science,"
        "Israfel," "To Helen," "The Raven," "Ulalume"
        (ATL)
39   The poets as early moderns

Nineteenth- to Twentieth-Century Literature

24
AMERICAN REALISM
Elizabeth Ammons
Fall, 1982
Tufts University
Medford, MA 02155

Course Objectives

This is an upper-level examination of literary realism in America between 1880 and 1920. Our study will combine standard selections with several nontraditional texts, paying special attention to the ferment of contemporary issues to which the literature responds: Social Darwinism, racism, anti-Semitism, the woman question, urban poverty, immigration and the so-called "melting pot," labor unionism, the values of *laissez-faire* capitalism.

The overall purpose of the course is to explore the ways in which art and social conscience intersect in American literature at the end of the nineteenth and the beginning of the twentieth centuries. Therefore we will examine such things as the development of narrative technique in this period during which the modern American novel was conceived, looking closely at point of view in James, the attempt to be reportorial and inclusive in Howells and Dreiser, experimentation with form in Wharton and Johnson, and borrowings from impressionism in Chopin and Crane. We will also be asking some basic, and probably unanswerable, questions about the relationship between art and life. For example, what—if any—are the limits of literary art in the service of reform? Does the very act of writing, by definition conservative in order to get published, limit rather than expand one's capacity to imagine reality? What are the differences between fiction and autobiography or fiction and discursive prose in the rendering of felt, individual reality? Can we speak of a black consciousness, a male perspective, a female point of view, that can be analyzed, rather than just sensed, in

the literature of this period? Perhaps most important: Why has the literature
of this period not received the same august institutionalization in the American literary canon as literature of the American "Renaissance" or of the
1920s?

Finally, we will be looking at major, unifying themes and contradictions
in the literature of this period—e.g., the anti-Semitism and racism of much
of the feminism in this era, or the Horatio Alger myth securely nestled in
even the most radical of the portraits of labor reform—and be asking not
only how these tensions and inconsistencies operated at the turn of the
century, but also today. We will, that is, look at the literature both in its own
time, and as it speaks to ours. We will think about the texts' social criticism as
part of history but also, when appropriate, as living, ongoing analyses of
problems with which we are still faced. Class will normally be run on a
discussion basis; requirements will include two papers and a final exam.

Booklist

Willa Cather, *O Pioneers!*
Kate Chopin, *The Awakening*
Stephen Crane, *Maggie: A Girl of the Streets*
Theodore Dreiser, *Sister Carrie*
W.E.B. DuBois, *The Souls of Black Folk*
William Dean Howells, *A Hazard of New Fortunes*
Henry James, *The Portrait of a Lady*
James Weldon Johnson, *The Autobiography of an Ex-Coloured Man*
Bert J. Loewenberg and Ruth Bogin, eds., *Black Women in 19th-Century
    American Life*
The Maimie Papers, Ruth Rosen and Sue Davidson, eds.
Upton Sinclair, *The Jungle*
Edith Wharton, *The House of Mirth*
Anzia Yezierska, *Bread Givers*

Syllabus

Class 1   Orientation
      2–4   James, *Portrait of a Lady*
      5–6   Howells, *Hazard of New Fortunes*
      7   Crane, *Maggie*
      8–9   Chopin, *The Awakening*
      10–12   Dreiser, *Sister Carrie*
      13–14   Wharton, *House of Mirth*
      15   *Maimie Papers,* selections
      16   *Black Women in 19th-Century American Life*, selections
      17   Johnson, *Autobiography of an Ex-Coloured Man*

18-19   DuBois, *Souls of Black Folk*
20-21   Sinclair, *The Jungle*
22-23   Yezierska, *Bread Givers*
24-26   Cather, *O Pioneers!*

25
AMERICAN LITERATURE: 1860-1900
John Callahan
Fall, 1979
Lewis and Clark College
Portland, OR 97219

Course Objectives

The course flows from the proposition that American literature during the Civil War and post-Civil War periods was formally and thematically preoccupied with some unresolved issues essential to the nation's democratic experiment. This approach and reading list assume that culture and politics are related to history in diverse and complex, often elusive ways. The organization of the course is intended to test out the idea that democracy, gender, race, and class are ideas and conditions bound up with one another and with the continuing evolution of American society. The choice of literature is made in a conscious effort to include substantial readings from often ignored or overlooked women and Afro-American writers. I should also note that I usually teach Melville's "Bartleby" in Part I and return to it briefly in the section on class, and that since 1979 I have built in a concluding two-hour session on the topic of convergence and divergence.

Finally, I consider the course to be in flux. For example, in fall of 1982 I included selections from Dickinson, Gilman's "The Yellow Wallpaper," and substituted *Portrait of a Lady* for *The Bostonians* in the section on "The Question of Women," and added a number of selections from Hamlin Garland to the material on class.

Booklist

Henry Adams, *The Education of Henry Adams*
Charles Chesnutt, *The Conjure Woman and Other Stories*
Kate Chopin, *The Awakening*

Stephen Crane, *Great Short Works of Stephen Crane*
Rebecca Harding Davis, *Life in the Iron Mills*
Theodore Dreiser, *Sister Carrie* (important that you have the unexpurgated
　　version, published in paper by Penguin American Library)
W.E.B. DuBois, *The Souls of Black Folk* in *Three Negro Classics*
Joel Chandler Harris, *Uncle Remus: His Songs and Sayings*
Henry James, *The Bostonians*
Mark Twain, *Huckleberry Finn*
Booker T. Washington, *Up From Slavery* in *Three Negro Classics*
Other readings, particularly those in weeks 1 and 2, will be photocopied

Syllabus

Class 1　　　　Introduction
I.　The Complexity of Democracy in American Letters
　　　2–3　　　Excerpts from Frederick Douglass, *Narrative of the Life of
　　　　　　　　Frederick Douglass, My Bondage and My Freedom, and
　　　　　　　　The Life and Times of Frederick Douglass; Abraham
　　　　　　　　Lincoln, "First Inaugural Address," "Reply to Horace
　　　　　　　　Greeley, August 22, 1862," "Emancipation Proclama-
　　　　　　　　tion," "Gettysburg Address," "Second Inaugural Ad-
　　　　　　　　dress"; Walt Whitman, "When Lilacs Last in the Door-
　　　　　　　　yard Bloomed"; Herman Melville, "Supplement" to
　　　　　　　　Battle-Pieces
II.　The Question of Women
　　　4–9　　　Davis, *Life in the Iron Mills*; Tillie Olsen, "A Biographical
　　　　　　　　Interpretation," pp. 69–115; excerpts from *The Ideas of
　　　　　　　　the Woman's Suffrage Movement, 1890–1920*; *The
　　　　　　　　Feminist Papers*; *Black Women in White America*
　　　10–15　James, *The Bostonians*
　　　16–18　Chopin, *The Awakening*
　　　19　　　Recapitulation
III.　The Question of Race
　　　20–23　Thomas Wentworth Higginson, "The Negro as Soldier,"
　　　　　　　　Life in A Black Army Regiment; Booker T. Washington,
　　　　　　　　Up From Slavery, pp. 29–40, 51–62, 145–74; DuBois,
　　　　　　　　The Souls of Black Folk, pp. 221–52, 377–87; excerpts
　　　　　　　　from Harris, *Uncle Remus*
　　　24–27　Twain, *Huckleberry Finn*
　　　28–30　Chesnutt, *The Conjure Woman*
　　　31　　　Recapitulation
IV.　The Question of Class
　　　32–33　Adams, *The Education of Henry Adams:* "The Virgin and the
　　　　　　　　Dynamo," "A Dynamic Theory of History," "A Law
　　　　　　　　of Acceleration"

34–35   Crane, *Great Short Works:*"The Monster," "Maggie: A Girl of the Streets"
36–39   Dreiser, *Sister Carrie*
40   Final Examination

26
STUDIES IN AMERICAN LITERATURE: NINETEENTH-CENTURY AMERICAN REALISM
Alfred Habegger
Spring, 1980
University of Kansas
Lawrence, KS 66045

Course Objectives

The premises of this course are: A writer's gender has a thoroughgoing effect on his/her work, and even the best literature is inescapably time- and culture-bound. Accordingly, I propose to study the development of American literary realism in the nineteenth century by stressing literary and social contexts. I believe our two best realistic novelists, William Dean Howells and Henry James, emerged in part from a tradition of women's fiction, which these two male writers both accepted and resisted. Thus, we will begin the semester by reading Susan Warner's popular *The Wide, Wide World* and Harriet Beecher Stowe's *The Minister's Wooing*, and also excerpts from recent work in Women's Studies by Ann Douglas, Nina Baym, and others. Women's fiction led to two later "movements"—Local Color as well as Realism; and both must be studied to understand either one. Local Color tended to become a female specialty in the 1870s and 80s; we will look at two of its finest practitioners, Sarah Orne Jewett and Mary Wilkins Freeman, partly to enjoy their writing, partly to grasp the contrasts between Local Color (peripheral by definition) and Realism (more central and ambitious). Realism peaked in the 1880s in the work of James and Howells; we will focus on their work during this decade. Finally, we will look forward to the explorations of masculine experience that emerged in the so-called naturalistic movement, briefly sampling the writing of Stephen Crane and Theodore Dreiser.

Booklist

Stephen Crane, *Great Short Stories*
Theodore Dreiser, *Sister Carrie*
Mary Wilkins Freeman, *The Revolt of "Mother" and Other Stories*
William Dean Howells, *A Modern Instance, The Rise of Silas Lapham,* and
    A Hazard of New Fortunes
Henry James, *Portrait of a Lady* and *The Bostonians*
Sarah Orne Jewett, *The Country of the Pointed Firs*
Harriet Beecher Stowe, *The Minister's Wooing*
Susan Warner, *The Wide, Wide World*

Other Requirements

Students are expected to have read *The Scarlet Letter* and *The Awakening*. In addition, students are urged to read some of the following novels:

E.D.E.N. Southworth, *The Hidden Hand*
Maria Cummins, *The Lamplighter*
Elizabeth Stuart Phelps, *The Story of Avis*
W.D. Howells, any of several out-of-print novels, especially *A Foregone
    Conclusion, Indian Summer, April Hopes, Annie Kilburn, The World of
    Chance*
Writing Assignments: 5,000 words of scholarly or essayistic work (by
    arrangement with instructor) and midterm and final examinations.

Course Critique

If I were to offer the course again, I would make a number of changes. Though I would still begin with Warner's novel, *The Wide, Wide World,* I would drop Stowe's novel, *The Minister's Wooing,* and this for two reasons: The book has a slick stereotyped quality I don't care for, and I think that, while Stowe contributed a great deal to local color fiction, her work doesn't really lead to realism, narrowly defined. I would replace Stowe with one of the younger women writers who wrote in the 1860s, whose fiction was reviewed by young James and Howells, and who constitute a crucial link between these two men and the earlier women's tradition of "woman's fiction" (to use Nina Baym's term). The pertinent narratives would be Lousia May Alcott's *Moods,* Elizabeth Stoddard's *Two Men,* Rebecca Harding Davis's *Margret Howth* or *Waiting for the Verdict,* or Mrs. Adeline D. T. Whitney's *The Gayworthys* (or maybe her slightly earlier *Faith Gartney's*

Girlhood). I would probably choose Whitney because she was also a mentor of Jewett's. My third novel would be *Watch and Ward*, which simply makes no sense at all unless viewed against the background of women's fiction. The remaining texts would probably be Elizabeth Stuart Phelps's *The Story of Avis*, four Howells novels (*A Foregone Conclusion, A Modern Instance, The Rise of Silas Lapham, A Hazard of New Fortunes*), three James novels (*Washington Square, The Portrait of a Lady, The Bostonians*), Jewett's *The Country of the Pointed Firs*, and Freeman's stories. I would drop Stephen Crane, simply because his work, however wonderful, represents something too removed from the continuity the course traces. Perhaps I would finish with the nicely contrasting pair of novels by Dreiser and Edith Wharton, *Jennie Gerhardt* and *The Reef*. I would also stipulate that all students are expected to have read *The Scarlet Letter, The Awakening, Madame Bovary*, and *Jane Eyre*.

27
AMERICA TRANSFORMED:
AMERICAN LITERATURE, 1865–1905
John Lowe
Spring, 1982, 1983
Saint Mary's College
Notre Dame, IN 46556

Course Objectives

When I began teaching at Saint Mary's College, I was told that my primary responsibility for teaching American Literature at the upper level would be two courses: English 341 (American Literature to 1865) and English 342 (American Literature from 1865 to 1945). The following syllabus resulted from this initial instruction and a number of other considerations: 1) I wanted to include as many works by white women and minorities as possible, while simultaneously giving continued exposure to the traditional "masters" (mostly male) in the canon. 2) Because there were so many rich texts in this field, I decided to teach mainly "realistic" novels in this course and later teach a course on literary "naturalism" and the experimental novel. 3) A colleague was teaching most early twentieth-century writers, so I decided to further limit the range by ending at 1905.

The first syllabus, which ends in 1905, was constructed prior to my involvement in the Yale Summer Institute on Reconstructing American Literature. In view of the goals I had set out in the paragraph above, I was relatively pleased with the results—the students had certainly responded enthusiastically. When I sat down with colleagues during the Yale conference to talk about teaching this period, however, I began to realize that I could better serve my students by: 1) combining both the so-called "realistic" and "naturalistic" periods in one course; 2) including more works by white women and minorities; 3) keeping most of the so-called "classic" authors, but adjusting and changing some of the texts; 4) eliminating a few of my original authors in favor of others.

I wanted to keep my organizing units, but the new material dictated some new section titles. Talking with my colleagues persuaded me to jettison some conventional phrases here too; historically relevant labels seemed more appropriate than vague literary ones such as "From Romance to Realism." New categories had to encompass the qualities of newly included writers, too, such as E. Pauline Johnson and Rebecca Harding Davis.

The new syllabus shows definite improvement in a number of areas; it has a far more accurate historical pattern, and the texts selected relate to one another in a more focused way. Although there are fine works still on the syllabus by men, most of them deal with women and/or blacks in a prominent way. The works by white women and minorities are more than token inclusions; they are important additions to a delineation of the cultural and moral development of the American nation, a nation that was truly "transformed" during this crucial epoch.

At the same time, the old syllabus had the advantage of highlighting the traumatic effect of the war more clearly; the fascinating section on "War and the Artist" has been dropped. William Dean Howells and Edith Wharton went only after a severe struggle of conscience, somewhat mitigated by the comforting thought that I would teach Wharton in the American Literature Survey course.

Booklist

Charles Chesnutt, *The Wife of His Youth* (Ann Arbor)
Harold Frederic, *The Damnation of Theron Ware* (Belknap/Harvard)
Hamlin Garland, *Main-Travelled Roads* (Signet)
William Dean Howells, *A Modern Instance* (Riverside)
Henry James, *The Portrait of a Lady* (Riverside)
Sarah Orne Jewett, *The Country of the Pointed Firs* (Norton)
Harriet Beecher Stowe, *Uncle Tom's Cabin* (Signet)
Mark Twain, *The Adventures of Huckleberry Finn* (Dell) and *Life on the Mississippi* (Signet)
Edith Wharton, *The House of Mirth* (Signet)

Poems (handouts and on reserve)

Melville, from *Battle-Pieces*: "Gettysburg," "Shiloh," "The Portent,"
   "Misgivings," "On the Photograph of a Corps Commander,"
   "The March into Virginia," "The Swamp Angel," "America,"
   "The Apparition," "Formerly a Slave"
Whitman, from *Drum-Taps*: "Beat! Beat! Drums!," "Vigil Strange I
   Kept on the Field One Night," "The Wound Dresser," "Cavalry
   Crossing a Ford," "Ethiopia Saluting the Colors"
Dickinson: "I never lost as much but twice," "Safe in their Alabaster
   Chambers," (both versions) "I like a look of Agony," "I've known
   a Heaven, like a Tent," "Hope is the thing with feathers," "To
   die—takes just a little while," "There's a certain Slant of light,"
   "Bound—a trouble," "Of Tribulation, these are They," "They
   dropped like Flakes," "The Soul has Bandaged moments," "The
   Martyr Poets—did not tell—," "The Battle fought between the
   Soul," "Pain—has an Element of Blank"

Syllabus (original course)

I. Prelude to a National Storm
Class 1–3   Stowe, *Uncle Tom's Cabin*
   4   Twain, *Life on the Mississippi*, Part I, chapters 1–21
   5–7   Twain, *The Adventures of Huckleberry Finn*
II. War and the Artist
   8   War poems: Melville and Whitman
   9   Dickinson, Poems of the 1860s
   10   Twain, *Life on the Mississippi*, Part II
III. From Romance to Realism
   11–13   James, *The Portrait of a Lady*
   14, 16–17   Howells, *A Modern Instance*
   15   Mid-term exam
   18–19   Dickinson, selected poems
IV. Transformation in the Provinces: Local Color
   20–21   Jewett, *Country of the Pointed Firs*
   22–23   Garland, *Main-Traveled Roads*
   24–25   Frederic, *The Damnation of Theron Ware*
V. Coping With the New Society: The Novel of Manners
   26–27   Chesnutt, *The Wife of His Youth*
   28–29   Wharton, *The House of Mirth*

Syllabus (revised course)

I. Reconstruction and Reaction
Class 1   Garland, "The Return of a Private"
      2   Whitman, *Democratic Vistas*
      3-5   George Washington Cable, *The Grandissimes*
      6-7   Chesnutt, *The Conjure Woman*
      8-9   James Weldon Johnson, *The Autobiography of an Ex-Colored Man*
 II. Expansion: Industrialism, Urban Growth, and Immigration
      10-11   Rebecca Harding Davis, *Life in the Iron Mills*
      12-14   Twain, *A Connecticut Yankee in King Arthur's Court*
      15-16   Theodore Dreiser, *Jennie Gerhardt*
      17   Abraham Cahan, *Yekl*
III. Rural America and Western Expansion
      18-19   Jewett, *The Country of the Pointed Firs*
      20   Mary Wilkins Freeman, "A New England Nun," "The Revolt of 'Mother'"
      21   E. Pauline Johnson, "Red Girl's Reasoning"
      22   Garland, "Up the Coulee," "Under the Lion's Paw"
 IV. Private Solutions to Public Problems
      23-25   James, *The Portrait of a Lady*
      26-27   Dickinson, selected poems
      28   Paul Laurence Dunbar, selected poems
      29-30   Kate Chopin, *The Awakening*

28
AMERICAN LITERATURE FROM THE CIVIL WAR TO WORLD WAR I
Anne Margolis
Spring, 1981
Williams College
Williamstown, MA 01267

Course Objectives

This syllabus represents an attempt to alter the conventional shape of an existing survey course in two significant respects. First, I hoped to bring to bear an American Studies approach to this period of American literature, with a special emphasis upon women as writers and central characters. Simultaneously, I was searching for a format that would enable me to demonstrate to students the link between post-bellum American literature and the emergence of international literary modernism. (Hence, the marked shift in emphasis between the first and second halves of the syllabus.) The course thus treats many of the canonized novelists of the period, but also includes fiction written by previously neglected women writers.

Given the shortness of the Williams semester (two 12-week terms separated by a January "mini-term"), this revision entailed the exclusion of poetry (Emily Dickinson comes most readily to mind) as well as black writers. Two other strictly practical considerations discouraged me from including black novelists of the period: the fact that a black colleague was currently teaching a version of the same course that focused mainly on Afro-American writers and an awareness of my own ignorance in this regard (due to conventional academic training). It should also be noted that the English department eventually voted to abolish all versions of English 208 as a survey and replaced it with multiple electives. We wanted to acknowledge explicitly our own lack of consensus over what—in fact—constitutes an acceptable literary canon for this period. (There was, however, enough overlap in the ways we all approached the teaching of English 207, the American Renaissance course, to justify retaining it in survey format.)

The first half of my 208 syllabus focused largely but not exclusively upon the ways in which fictional women (and, where applicable, their female creators) accommodated themselves to and resisted traditional expectations regarding conventional notions of woman's proper social and economic role. Questions of literary style and strategy were presented mainly in the context of how each writer came to terms with prevailing literary conventions and reader expectations (i.e., the depiction of "virtuous" characters and happy endings, the presentation of sexual relations, etc.) I included biographical information concerning the writer's career and/or excerpts from contemporaneous reviews to establish this context. At mid-semester, students read and discussed three chapters from Veblen. Then they were asked to apply his terms and ideas regarding conspicuous leisure, conspicuous consumption, and dress to the fictional destiny of the female protagonist in *Sister Carrie, The Awakening,* or *The House of Mirth.* Some semesters I assigned this as a paper topic, while at other times I administered an hour exam as indicated in the syllabus. The first half of the exam asked them to use Veblen's terms in a brief analysis of several passages and incidents from all three novels, while the second half of the exam involved a comparison of the non-conventional endings of one of the short stories and one of the novels (they were given choices of pairs).

In the remainder of the course, Henry James's *The Portrait of a Lady* (the 1881 version) and his essay "The Art of Fiction" were used, in part, as a means of "shifting gears" from our initial concern with female protagonists to an increasing stress on questions of evolving fictional technique. The relationship between stylistic experimentation and resistance to Anglo-American literary and social conventions, especially those regarding the relations between the sexes, became the central focus in lectures and discussions, thus underlining one of the implicit themes of the first half of the course. The syllabus had already been revised several times and would undoubtedly have been reworked once more had the course not been eliminated. Previous versions had included Jane Addams's autobiography, William Dean Howells's *A Hazard of New Fortunes,* and Mark Twain's *A Connecticut Yankee.* I am now at work on a new elective in nineteenth-century American literature that will focus on women's role as writers and readers of, as well as characters in, ante- and post-bellum fiction.

Booklist

Henry Adams, *The Education of Henry Adams*
Kate Chopin, *The Awakening*
Stephen Crane, *Short Stories and Tales*
Rebecca Harding Davis, *Life in the Iron Mills*
Theodore Dreiser, *Sister Carrie*
Charlotte Perkins Gilman, *The Yellow Wallpaper*
Henry James, *The Portrait of a Lady* and *The Ambassadors*
Mark Twain, *Huckleberry Finn*
Edith Wharton, *The House of Mirth*
Additional printed readings:
Thorstein Veblen, from *Theory of the Leisure Class*
Henry James, "The Art of Fiction"

Syllabus

Class 1	Introduction
2	Davis, *Life in the Iron Mills*; biographical essay by Tillie Olsen
3	Crane, "Maggie," and Crane's interview with W. D. Howells (pp. 163–66)
4–5	Dreiser, *Sister Carrie*
6–7	Chopin, *The Awakening*
8–9	Wharton, *House of Mirth*
10	Gilman, *Yellow Wallpaper*; afterword by Elaine Hedges
11	Veblen, *Theory of the Leisure Class*, Chapters 3, 4, 7
12	Midterm exam
13–15	James, *Portrait of a Lady*
16	James, *Portrait*; "The Art of Fiction"
17–19	Adams, *Education*
20–21	Twain, *Huckleberry Finn*
22–24	James, *Ambassadors*
25	Conclusion

29
AMERICAN LITERATURE—1865-1914:
IN SEARCH OF COMMUNITY
Margaret Anne O'Connor
1982
University of North Carolina
Chapel Hill, NC 27514

Course Objectives

The following course description is less a syllabus for a fifteen-week semester than it is an overview of the 1865-1914 period with important cultural developments illustrated by the group of literary works designated. In preparing specific courses, I use this overview as a visual reminder of the directions I want the course to take and the possibilities available. In such a broad survey course, I seldom have the luxury of assigning more than two novels, for instance, so my selection of these longer works dictates choices in other categories. While I cannot hope to cover all the works listed in a single semester, the list reminds me of the breadth of experience that ideally should be reflected in the individual syllabus. Too, the groupings aid me in treating the presentation of important themes of the period in a variety of genres— poetry, essays, autobiography, and fiction.

Booklist and Syllabus

I.   Reconstruction and Reaction
     Walt Whitman, from *Drum-Taps*; *Democratic Vistas*
     Mary Boykin Chesnut, from *Diary*, ed. C. Vann Woodward
     Herman Melville, from *Battle Pieces*
     Stephen Crane, *The Red Badge of Courage*
     Frances Ellen Watkins Harper, selected poems
II. Western Expansion
     Indian creation stories
     Hamlin Garland, from *Main-Travelled Roads*
     Willa Cather, "The Bohemian Girl"
     Mark Twain, from *Roughing It* or *Huckleberry Finn*
     Edgar Lee Masters, from *Spoon River Anthology*
     Sherwood Anderson, from *Winesburg, Ohio*
III. Industrialization and Urban Growth
     Walt Whitman, "To a Locomotive in Winter"
     Rebecca Harding Davis, *Life in the Iron Mills*

Crane, *Maggie: A Girl of the Streets*
Abraham Cahan, *Yekl*
Jacob Riis, from *How the Other Half Lives*
Thorstein Veblen, from *The Theory of the Leisure Class*
Charlotte Perkins Gilman, from *Women and Economics*
The Maimie Papers, ed. Davidson and Rosen
Carl Sandburg, "Chicago," "The People, Yes"
Jane Addams, from *Twenty Years at Hull House*
IV. Critiques of the New America
Mary Wilkins Freeman, "The Lumbar Poplar," "A Village Singer,"
    "A New England Nun"
Sarah Orne Jewett, "The White Heron"
Henry James, *The American*
Anderson, from *Winesburg, Ohio*
Suffragist writings: Elizabeth Cady Stanton and Susan B. Anthony
Upton Sinclair, *The Jungle*
Edwin Arlington Robinson, from *Children of the Night*, Tilbury
    Town poems
William Dean Howells, "Editha"
Mark Twain, "The War Prayer," "To the Person Sitting in
    Darkness"
Peter Finley Dunne, from *Mr. Dooley in Peace and War*
V. Between Two Worlds
Gilman, *The Yellow Wallpaper*
Paul Laurence Dunbar, "We Wear the Mask," "Sympathy" and
    other poems
James, *Daisy Miller*
Edith Wharton, *The House of Mirth*
Kate Chopin, *The Awakening*
Booker T. Washington, "Atlanta Exposition Address"; W.E.B.
    DuBois "Of Mr. Booker T. Washington and Others"; Dunbar,
    tribute to Washington
Charles Chesnutt, *The Conjure Woman* or other selected stories
VI. The New Aesthetics
Whitman, "Song of Myself"
Emily Dickinson, selected poems
Crane, poems and "The Open Boat"
Gertrude Stein, from *Tender Buttons* and *The Making of Americans*
Imagist Poetry: Hilda Doolittle, Ezra Pound, Amy Lowell

30
AMERICAN LITERATURE, 1865–1914
Robert Shulman
Spring, 1981
University of Washington
Seattle, WA 98195

Course Description

Mark Twain's cub pilot gradually learns the river and becomes a pilot. Let's take the shifting, mysterious river as an embodiment of American nature and the flux of American social reality and the cub becoming a pilot as a version of gaining an adult identity in the midst of the challenges, dangers, and instability of late nineteenth-century America. We will examine several versions of this process and its implications for American selves and society in a period when the conflict between property and human values was especially acute, when technology and racism were shaping modern America, and when women were responding independently and sometimes tragically to their situation.

Americans, Twain said, had always worshipped money, but during the Gilded Age he believed they had learned to get down in the mud and grovel after it. At the top of American society the great fortunes and their creators set a tone our writers satirized, interiorized, envied, and resisted as they shaped their own careers. The world below or outside respectable society also compelled the attention of gifted writers. Stephen Crane's probing of the underside of the city is a well-known example; Charles Chesnutt's subtle treatment of the interplay between blacks and whites is a brilliant, neglected example. Using the security of an upper-class milieu, Kate Chopin, Henry James, and Edith Wharton each deepen our insight into the situation of late nineteenth-century women. In the post-Civil War period technology and massive displacement and growth opened up immense opportunities and also intensified social and personal fragmentation. Everyday experience increasingly eroded the foundations of the traditional American religious and secular belief system at the same time that science, particularly Darwinism, sanctioned predatory practices and further undermined the orthodox structure of belief. To deal with their experiences of this rapidly changing America our writers developed the literary strategies and social psychologies that will be among our concerns. Gramsci's concept of hegemony will help us explore the consciousness of characters and creators and to relate them to the complexities of class, sex, and race in late nineteenth-century America.

Course Requirements

One requirement is to do two five-page papers and a take-home final. For the papers I've divided the class alphabetically into three groups. The papers are due the day we're scheduled to begin discussion of your book. Group 1 will do *The Financier* and *The House of Mirth*. Group 2 will do *The Conjure Woman* and *The Bostonians*. Group 3 will do *The Awakening* and *Hazard of New Fortunes*. If you would prefer to write on a book other than the one I've assigned, see me and we'll make arrangements.

For the papers, concentrate on a theme, conflict, formal achievement, or symbolic pattern; or on a moral, social, political, psychological, or racial concern and how it is brought to imaginative life. Try to define a topic that makes a difference to the novel and to you. Some topics are too general and you end up with a superficial survey. Other topics are too narrow and you end up sterile. Try to focus so that you can illuminate the work and do justice to your own intelligence and concern. I'm interested in an active exchange between your mind and feelings and the writer's. If you feel the need to consult secondary sources, be sure you have your own position worked out before you do or you will end up giving me a replay of someone else's ideas. If you use outside sources, include a list of works consulted.

Make four copies of your paper—one for me and three to pass around to others in the class. On the papers you receive, indicate what comes through clearly and what strikes you as fuzzy, raise questions when that seems appropriate, indicate what you like and dislike about it, what you agree with and disagree with and why, what seems strong and what seems weak. Please sign your name and return the paper by the next class period.

Booklist

Charles Chesnutt, *The Conjure Woman*
Kate Chopin, *The Awakening*
Stephen Crane, *Great Short Works of Stephen Crane*
Theodore Dreiser, *The Financier*
William Dean Howells, *A Hazard of New Fortunes*
Henry James, *The Bostonians*
Frederick W. Taylor, *Principles of Scientific Management*
Mark Twain, *Great Short Works of Mark Twain*
Edith Wharton, *The House of Mirth*

Syllabus

Week 1   Twain, *Great Short Works*: "Old Times on the Mississippi," "How to Tell a Story," "To the Person Sitting in Darkness"

2   Dreiser, *The Financier*
3   Taylor, *Principles of Scientific Management*
4   Chesnutt, *The Conjure Woman*
5   Chopin, *The Awakening*
6   Wharton, *The House of Mirth*
7   James, *The Bostonians*
8–9   Howells, *Hazard of New Fortunes*
10   Crane, *Great Short Works*: "An Experiment in Misery,"
       "The Open Boat," "The Monster"

31
AMERICAN LITERATURE:
FROM THE LATE NINETEENTH CENTURY
TO THE 1970s
Eleanor Q. Tignor
Albertus Magnus College
Currently at LaGuardia Community College
Long Island City, NY 11101

Critique of Original Course

English 74—American Literature from the late Nineteenth Century (after 1865) to the 1970s—was by its catalogue definition an "advanced survey course," which was to make "use of biographical and critical sources as well as original writings" (Albertus Magnus College catalogue, 1976–78). The students were English majors and other liberal arts women with good to excellent interpretive abilities. All of them had had at least one other American literature course, either English 73 or a similar less advanced prerequisite. The course was shaped by its definition, and its student population, and by other factors.

Having taught in historically black colleges where it was assumed that black literature was also American literature, I automatically included it even though it was necessary to require additional books. The Norman Foerster text (*American Poetry and Prose*), while an otherwise "solid" one, included almost no minority writers except Catholic and Jewish American; Afro-American literature was represented by a few poems and stories and two spirituals. Thus, I chose a small black-American anthology which offered enough diversity of poetry, fiction, essays, and drama to give a sense of the richness, the historical place, and the long existence of this literature. The Sterling A. Brown essay, "A Century of Negro Portraiture in American Literature" (1966), I selected to clarify these points and to underline the misrepresentations of blacks by certain white authors. Richard Wright's *Native Son*, an American landmark text illustrative of the force of environment, could not be left out any more than an Edith Wharton novel could.

Albertus Magnus College had initially hired me to teach a seminar in Afro-American literature at a time when the college seemed to be attempting to reconstruct its literature program; this circumstance supported my selection of texts. As a women's college, interest in female writers was high. *Ethan Frome*, with its New England setting and questioning themes of duty, restraint, and suffering, seemed a natural choice in a New England church-affiliated college. Flannery O'Connor, while representative of a region and a style (Southern Gothic), was already one of the popularly read, white female authors at this Catholic school. The white female poet Emily Dickinson, who had been given her much deserved place in the canon by the 1970s, and the contemporary, established white women poets Anne Sexton and Sylvia Plath were balanced against some of the black women poets whom I saw as standard: Margaret Walker and Gwendolyn Brooks, and a newer black female poet—Lucille Clifton. The visions of life offered by the standard white male fictionists of the 1920s, 1930s, and 1940s (Sherwood Anderson, Ernest Hemingway, William Faulkner, and John Steinbeck) were balanced against those of Afro-American fictionists of the same decades (Jean Toomer, Richard Wright, and Ralph Ellison). A period of intense literary and cultural achievement often ignored in American literary history, the Harlem Renaissance, was given its rightful place through teaching the writings of James Weldon Johnson, Claude McKay, Langston Hughes, Countee Cullen, and Jean Toomer.

In the final weeks of the course, I taught some works making use of similar techniques or themes but written by authors of different ethnic origins or religions. We read Edward Albee's drama *The Zoo Story* just before the equally absurd, but not as well known, black-in-white-face Douglas Turner Ward drama *Day of Absence: A Satirical Fantasy*. Inner conflict, familial differences, and spiritual paradox were some of the points of focus of works by James Baldwin (black American), James Agee and Flannery O'Connor (Catholic American), and Saul Bellow and Bernard Malamud (Jewish American).

Because of my own teaching philosophy and background, coupled with the open attitude of the department in which I taught, English 74, in retrospect, was a mini-reconstructing of American literature. Now, having been a part of the Reconstructing American Literature Institute and considering that a number of new black women writers have emerged (most notably, Toni Morrison and Alice Walker) and one has been finally recognized (Zora Neale Hurston), I would decrease the number of short works by some of the authors who are a part of the established canon or else have some of those works read for special interest essays and reports.

The other new texts which would be included in the course for more inclusive American visions of life would be the Chinese-American Maxine Hong Kingston's novel *The Woman Warrior*, the Native American Leslie Marmon Silko's novel *Ceremony*, the Puerto Rican Pedro Pietri's poem "Puerto Rican Obituary," and the Chicano Abelardo Delgado's poem "Stupid America." Because of the newness or unfamiliarity of these texts to many students, they would be excellent springboards for research projects.

A major goal of the course would be to introduce the student not to *one* American literature but to the diverse yet interrelated American literatures and the cultures and traditions they represent and interpret.

Booklist

Norman Foerster, et al., eds., *American Poetry and Prose*, 5th edition (Foerster)
James Agee, *A Death in the Family*
Leon T. Dickinson, *A Guide to Literary Study*
Robert Hayden, et al., eds., *Afro-American Literature: An Introduction*
Edith Wharton, *Ethan Frome*
Richard Wright, *Native Son*

Syllabus

I. Late Nineteenth Century to Early Twentieth Century: Realism and Naturalism

Class 1   Introduction to the Course: "Introduction" (pp. 823ff., Foerster). Also read the biographical information preceding the works of the authors studied.

2   Review of the Reading of Fiction: Dickinson, Chapter II (pp. 11ff.)

2-3   Mark Twain, "The Coyote," "Baker's Blue-jay Yarn"; Henry James, "The Real Thing," "Maud-Evelyn," "The Scarlett Letter" (Foerster)

4   Regional Writing: Bret Harte, "The Luck of Roaring Camp"; George Washington Cable, "Belles Demoiselles Plantation"; Sarah Orne Jewett, "The Dulham Ladies"; Charles Waddell Chesnutt, "The Goophered Grapevine" (Foerster); William Sydney Porter (O. Henry), "The Gift of the Magi" (on reserve) or a special interest report

5-6   Review of the Reading of Poetry: Dickinson, Chapter IV (pp. 47ff.); Emily Dickinson, poems #160, 214, 254, 258, 280, 288, 303, 328, 338, 341, 441, 448, 461, 465, 511, 536, 640, 701, 709, 712, 754, 997, 1732; Thomas Wentworth Higginson, "Emily Dickinson" (Foerster)

7   Stephen Crane, "An Experiment in Misery," "The Open
            Boat," "Do Not Weep, Maiden" (Foerster)
II. The Twentieth Century Continued—Through the 1970s
    8-10   "Introduction" (pp. 1095ff., Foerster); Sterling A. Brown,
            "A Century of Negro Portraiture in American Litera-
            ture" (Hayden); Edwin Arlington Robinson, "Luke
            Havergal," "Cliff Klingenhagen," "Flammonde," "Mr.
            Flood's Party"; Robert Frost, "The Death of the Hired
            Man," "Mending Wall," "After Apple-Picking,"
            "Birches," "The Road Not Taken," "Fire and Ice,"
            "Stopping By Woods on a Snowy Evening," "Come
            In," "The Figure a Poem Makes"; Carl Sandburg,
            "Chicago," "Fog," "Lost," "I Am the People, the
            Mob," "Cool Tombs" (Foerster)
    11-12   James Weldon Johnson, "The Creation" (Hayden); Claude
            McKay, "If We Must Die," "The White House,"
            "Harlem Shadows" (Foerster); Langston Hughes,
            "The Negro Speaks of Rivers," "I, Too, Sing America,"
            "American Heartbreak," "Song for a Dark Girl,"
            "Dream Boogie," "Harlem"; Countee Cullen, "Heri-
            tage," "Incident"; Sterling A. Brown, "Strong Men"
            (Hayden)
    13-14   T.S. Eliot, "The Love Song of J. Alfred Prufrock," *The
            Waste Land*, sections I, II, V, headnotes to III, IV;
            Cleanth Brooks, "The Waste Land: An Analysis"
            (Foerster)
    15-16   Robinson Jeffers, "To the Stone-Cutters," "Hurt Hawks,"
            "Self-Criticism in February"; E. E. Cummings, "in
            Just," "the Cambridge ladies," "Spring is like a perhaps
            hand," "next to of course god america i," "pity this busy
            monster, manunkind"; Wallace Stevens, "Domination
            of Black," "The Emperor of Ice-Cream," "Anecdote of
            the Jar"; Hart Crane, "Proem: To Brooklyn Bridge,"
            "Voyages: I" (Foerster)
    17-18   Wharton, *Ethan Frome*
    19-20   Review of the Reading of Drama: Dickinson, Chapter III
            (pp. 34ff.); A Drama of the Late 1920s: Eugene O'Neill,
            "The Hairy Ape" (Foerster)
    20-21   Jean Toomer, "Song of the Sun," "Blood-Burning Moon"
            (Hayden), "Esther" (Foerster)
    21-25   Fiction—The Twenties, Thirties, and Forties: Sherwood
            Anderson, "Hands"; Ernest Hemingway, "The Un-
            defeated"; F. Scott Fitzgerald, "The Rich Boy"; John
            Steinbeck, "Flight"; Richard Wright, "Fire and Cloud"
            (Foerster), *Native Son*; William Faulkner, "A Rose for
            Emily" (on reserve); Ralph Ellison, "King of the Bingo
            Game" (Hayden)

25-29   Poetry—The Forties to the Seventies: Robert Lowell, "New
        Year's Day," "The Drunken Fisherman," "After the
        Surprising Conversions," "Memories of West Street
        and Lepke"; Theodore Roethke, "Dolor," "I Knew a
        Woman," "What Can I Tell My Bones?"; Allen Gins
        berg, "A Supermarket in California," "In back of the
        real" (Foerster); Margaret Walker, "For My People,"
        "We Have Been Believers"; Robert Hayden, "Runagate
        Runagate," (Hayden), "The Ballad of Sue Ellen Wester
        field," "Incense of the Lucky Virgin" (Foerster);
        Gwendolyn Brooks, "Sadie and Maud," "The Chicago
        Defender Sends a Man to Little Rock, Fall, 1957,"
        "Bronzeville Man with a Belt in the Back" (Hayden);
        LeRoi Jones, "An Agony. As Now," "The Liar"
        (Foerster), "A Poem for Black Hearts," "The Dance";
        Lucille Clifton, "Good Times" (Hayden); Anne Sex
        ton's poetry (special interest reports); Sylvia Plath's
        poetry (special interest reports)

29-30   Drama—The Fifties and Sixties: Edward Albee, *The Zoo
        Story* (Foerster); LeRoi Jones, "The Revolutionary
        Theater"; Douglas Turner Ward, "Day of Absence: A
        Satirical Fantasy" (Hayden)

31-33   Fiction—The Fifties, Sixties, and Seventies: Agee, *A Death
        In the Family*; Bernard Malamud, "The Magic Barrel";
        James Baldwin, "This Morning, This Evening, So
        Soon" (Foerster), "Sonny's Blues" (Hayden); Flannery
        O'Connor, "Greenleaf" (Foerster); Ray Bradbury (spe-
        cial interest report); John Updike "Pigeon Feathers";
        Saul Bellow, "Leaving the Yellow House"; John Barth,
        "Night-Sea Journey" (Foerster)

32
REGIONALISM, REALISM, AND NATURALISM IN AMERICAN FICTION
Bette S. Weidman
Spring, 1982
Queens College/City University of New York
Flushing, NY 11367

Course Objectives

The Queens College catalog describes English 82, "Regionalism, Realism and Naturalism in American Fiction," as "Late 19th and 20th century expressions of new styles, contents and philosophies represented by these literary movements. Such writers as Mark Twain, Faulkner and O'Connor; Howells, Wharton and Lewis; and Crane, Dreiser, and Farrell." The course is an elective acceptable toward the English and American literature majors and open to other interested students, primarily juniors and seniors. In our numbering system, it follows and is more specialized than our two-semester survey of American literature or our American novel course; it is one of a series of upper-level electives that includes (English 80) "Puritanism in American Literature," (English 81) "Transcendentalism in 19th-century America," (English 83) "The American Dream," and (English 84) "Literature of the American South." Readings and course-shape vary with the instructor each semester.

My chief problem in designing this course has been including a broad representation of writers without sacrificing careful study of a few and without requiring an absurdly expensive booklist. In this semester, I solved the problem by using Barbara Solomon's anthology of thirty short stories, which includes almost all the writers the catalog suggests (as well as Mary Wilkins Freeman, Charlotte Perkins Gilman, Kate Chopin, Sarah Orne Jewett, Hamlin Garland, William Carlos Williams, and Tillie Olsen, among others) for a magnificent $2.95! For each story I asked the students to prepare a 5" x 8" index card summarizing narration, central character, action (arc of the plot as if you were graphing it), plot (summary of events), turn (a moment in the plot when the story predicts its end), significant imagery, landscape (a specialized part of the imagery), an expression of theme (a statement that takes account of the combined meaning of action and imagery) and an answer to the question of what makes the story *realistic* (regionalism and naturalism are treated as variants of realism). Although we did not use the anthology especially to examine the experience of women, we found in it a solid sample of realistic fiction, representing central writers, both men and women—a bargain these days. The students, of course, responded to the theme.

Then, having covered a range of writers, I felt more comfortable about treating four of them in closer detail. I chose two important women and two important men, who also happened to be two black writers and two white writers, two who wrote full-length novels and two who wrote novellas and short stories. All four are central to the problems of realism: Chopin shows its affinity to a region, a landscape; Crane, its attraction to reportage; Hurston, its connection to folklore; and Wright, its concern with social and economic problems. I noticed that when I kept my eye on the subject— American literary realism—and set aside chronology, I had no trouble finding the major writers. To illustrate the social and economic concerns of realism no one can deny that Richard Wright is more effective than William Dean Howells, whose work appears on the outside reading list. Why not Charles Chesnutt? He too was listed and summarized, but if you compare his use of folklore material to Zora Neale Hurston's, you can see that she makes fuller novelistic use of it. Why not do more with Henry James? Edith Wharton and Tillie Olsen, in the anthology, more than adequately represent the use of point-of-view to achieve psychological realism. In summary class sessions six and twelve (two-and-a-half hours each), I illustrated the contributions of each of the named European and American writers with short passages from the works represented on the outside reading list.

In teaching the course I began with an introduction giving a chronological account of literary developments in America since the Civil War; after that I worried more about the students' understanding of literary values *inside* the work than about the course of literary history. I trusted the students' observations, formulated on their index card records, to help me show the art of the realists. Concentrating on only four writers allowed me to introduce biography and a description of the other works of all four. In the case of Chopin and Crane, we were able to read a strong sample of additional work (Leary's edition of *The Awakening* includes 20 short stories). My reinvestigation of Stephen Crane for this course led to my teaching *Wounds in the Rain*, shockingly out-of-print, to a small graduate course in a subsequent term.

I no longer divide writers into major and minor on the grounds of my own graduate school training. For a course in realism, Chopin, Crane, Hurston, and Wright *are* major writers.

Booklist

Barbara Solomon, ed. *The Experience of the American Woman, 30 Stories*
Kate Chopin, *The Awakening and Other Stories*, ed. Lewis Leary
Stephen Crane, *Stories and Tales*, ed. R.W. Stallman
Zora Neale Hurston, *Their Eyes Were Watching God*
Richard Wright, *Native Son*

Required Writing

Two essays, with required first drafts due as indicated in the syllabus—
Essay I: Compare and contrast any two stories from the anthology; Essay II:
Choose a piece of outside reading from a European or American writer
mentioned in sessions 6, 12, or 14 and compare and contrast it to a work we
read together.

Syllabus

Week 1	Introduction
2	*The Experience of the American Woman*, pp. 31–114
3	*Experience*, pp. 115–94
4	*Experience*, pp. 195–288
5	*Experience*, pp. 289–428; Paper I draft due
6	European influences: Trollope, Flaubert, Eliot, Balzac, Tolstoy, Stendhal, Maupassant, Zola, Turgenev
7	Chopin, short stories from *The Awakening*
8	Chopin, *The Awakening*; Paper I due
9	Crane, from *Stories and Tales*
10	Crane, *The Red Badge of Courage*
11	Hurston, *Their Eyes Were Watching God*; Paper II draft due
12	American realists: Jewett, Stowe, Cable, Garland, Howells, Chesnutt, Frederic, Gale, Cather, James
13	Wright, *Native Son*
14	American naturalists: Sinclair, Glasgow, Norris, Dreiser; Paper II due

Outside Reading

European works
Anthony Trollope, *The Warden*
Gustave Flaubert, *Bouvard and Pecuchet*
George Eliot, *The Mill on the Floss; Silas Marner*
Honore de Balzac, *Eugenie Grandet; The Cure of Tours*
Leo Tolstoy, *The Cossacks; The Death of Ivan Illich; Happy Every After*
Stendhal, *The Red and the Black*
Guy de Maupassant, *Pierre et Jean; Une Vie; Our Hearts; Bel-Ami*
Emile Zola, *Therese Raquin*
Ivan Turgenev, *Home of the Gentry*

American works

Sarah Orne Jewett, *The Country of the Pointed Firs*
Harriet Beecher Stowe, *The Minister's Wooing*
George Washington Cable, *Old Creole Days*
Hamlin Garland, *Main-Travelled Roads*
John de Forest, *Miss Ravenel's Conversion from Secession to Loyalty*
William Dean Howells, *Their Wedding Journey; A Modern Instance; The Landlord at Lion's Head*
Charles Chesnutt, *The Conjure Woman; The Marrow of Tradition*
Harold Frederic, *The Damnation of Theron Ware*
Upton Sinclair, *The Jungle*
Theodore Dreiser, *Sister Carrie; An American Tragedy*
Frank Norris, *McTeague, The Octopus*
Henry James, selection of short fiction
Zona Gale, *Miss Lulu Bett*
Ellen Glasgow, *Barren Ground; Vein of Iron*
Willa Cather, *Youth and the Bright Medusa*
Mary E. Wilkins Freeman, *A New England Nun and Other Stories*
Celia Thaxter, *Among the Isles of Shoals*
Rose Terry Cooke, *Huckleberries Gathered from New England Hills*
E.W. Howe, *The Story of a Country Town*
William Carlos Williams, *The Farmers' Daughters*

Twentieth-Century Literature

33
AMERICAN LITERATURE:
1900–1940 and 1940–1980
John Callahan
Winter, Spring, 1983
Lewis and Clark College
Portland, OR 97219

Course Objectives

The courses reflect the diversity of voices and traditions in twentieth-century American literature. The topics are meant to drive home the connection between literature and history, between changes in literary form and social forms, conventions, and values. The 1980 syllabus for the latter time period included some writers (McCarthy, Salinger, Updike) who gave way, after the Yale Institute, to Anaya and Silko in order to give some representtion to Hispanic and Native American literature and to Olsen to include an American woman author's passionately effective writing about social conditions. These courses now also contain poetry, though in their original form they were fiction courses.

To complement my lectures I will suggest readings that in one way or another set the context for the work studied. For example, whenever possible I will hand out a poem whose theme converges with that of the novel under discussion (e.g., Robert Hayden's "Night Death, Mississippi" and "Tour 5" for *Intruder in the Dust*). The poems should also illustrate thematic and technical developments in recent American poetics. Other readings will be available in the library.

Booklist—American Literature, 1900–1940

American Literature: The Makers and the Making, Vol. II, eds. Brooks,
    Lewis and Warren (abbreviated in syllabus as AL:MM)
William Faulkner, *Go Down Moses*
F. Scott Fitzgerald, *Babylon Revisited and Other Stories*
Ernest Hemingway, *The Snows of Kilimanjaro and Other Stories*
Zora Neal Hurston, *Their Eyes Were Watching God*
John Steinbeck, *Of Mice and Men*
Anzia Yezierska, *Bread Givers*
Other required readings will be handed out in class

Syllabus—American Literature, 1900–1940

Class 1   Introduction
     2   "The Extraordinary in Ordinary Lives": Critical Realism
                and the Regional in American Poetry. "The Moderns:
                Founders and Beyond (1914–1945)" (AL:MM, pp.
                1803–28); E.A. Robinson, "Miniver Cheevy," "The
                Mill," "Mr. Flood's Party"; E.L. Masters, "Rutherford
             McDowell," "Lucinda Matlock," "Anne Rutledge";
                Carl Sandburg, "Chicago," "Psalm of Those Who Go
                Forth Before Daylight," "I am the People, the Mob"
                (AL:MM). Here and elsewhere I strongly recommend
                that you read the introductions to the various writers.
     3   Beyond Place: The Inner Geography of Robert Frost. Frost,
                "The Death of the Hired Man," "After Apple-Picking,"
                "Fire and Ice," "Desert Places" (AL:MM)
     4   Manners, Morals, and the Role of Place in Some American
                Fiction. Edith Wharton, "The Other Two"; Sherwood
                Anderson, "A Death in the Woods"; Willa Cather,
                "Neighbor Rosicky" (AL:MM)
     5–6   Immigrants and the American "Pursuit of Happiness": The
                Urban Jewish Idiom and Experience. Yezierska, *Bread
                Givers*
     7   Experiment and Innovation in American Poetry: Imagism.
                John Gould Fletcher, "The Skaters"; Adelaide Crapsey,
                "The Warning"; Ezra Pound, "In a Station of the
                Metro"; Marianne Moore, "To a Chameleon," "Poetry";
                E.E. Cummings, "Tumbling-hair," "i was considering
                how"; William Carlos Williams, "The Red Wheelbarrow";
                Jean Toomer, "Portrait in Georgia" (AL:MM)
     8   Imagism and Female Traditions of Sensibility. Reading:
                Amy Lowell, "Lilacs" (AL:MM)
     9   Tradition and the Contemporaniety of Individual Talent:

T.S. Eliot and Hart Crane. Eliot, "The Love Song of J. Alfred Prufrock," "Tradition and the Individual Talent"; Crane, "At Melville's Tomb," "Proem: To Brooklyn Bridge" (AL:MM), "Modern Poetry" (handout)

10–12　World War I and the American Writer. Ezra Pound, "E.P. Ode Pour L'Election de Son Sepulchre" (AL:MM); Hemingway, "A Way You'll Never Be," "In Another Country" (*The Snows of Kilimanjaro*); John Dos Passos, "The Body of an American" (handout); Fitzgerald, "May Day" (*Babylon Revisited*)

13–15　The Jazz Age: Convention and Innovation in the Twenties. Hemingway, "Hills Like White Elephants" (handout), "The Killers," "The Snows of Kilimanjaro" (*The Snows of Kilimanjaro*); Fitzgerald, "Winter Dreams," "The Rich Boy," "Babylon Revisited" (*Babylon Revisited*); Sterling Brown, "Cabaret" (handout)

16–17　In the Afro-American Grain—The Question of Idiom: American and Afro-American Idioms. Paul Laurence Dunbar, "We Wear the Mask"; James Weldon Johnson, "O Black and Unknown Bards"; Claude McKay, "If We Must Die"; Countee Cullen, "From the Dark Tower"; Langston Hughes, "The Negro Speaks of Rivers," "Young Gal's Blues," "Me and the Mule," "Dream Boogie," "Sylvester's Dying Bed," selections from *The Big Sea* (AL:MM), "Brass Spittoons" (handout)

18　Sterling Brown, "Odyssey of Big Boy," "Southern Road," "Sister Lou," "Memphis Blues," "Puttin' on Dog," "Old Lem," "Strong Men" (handouts); selections from *Jelly Roll Morton Remembers*; W.C. Handy, "St. Louis Blues" (AL:MM)

19–21　Traditions of Identity and Storytelling: Afro-American Women. Jean Toomer, "Karintha," "Fern" (AL:MM); Hurston, *Their Eyes Were Watching God*

22　William Faulkner and the Complexity of the American South. Faulkner, "A Rose for Emily," "That Evening Sun" (AL:MM)

23–25　Faulkner, *The Bear* (*Go Down Moses*)

25–26　Politics and the Writing of the Thirties. Dos Passos, selections from *The Big Money* (AL:MM); Kay Boyle, "A Communication to Nancy Cunard" (handout)

27–28　Steinbeck, *Of Mice and Men*, selections from *The Grapes of Wrath* (AL:MM)

29　Readings: Arna Bontemps, "A Summer Tragedy"; Richard Wright, "The Man Who Was Almost a Man," selections from *Black Boy* (AL:MM)

30　Convergence and Divergence: Prospects

116 RECONSTRUCTING AMERICAN LITERATURE

Booklist—American Literature, 1940–1980

Rudolfo Anaya, *Bless Me, Ultima*
E.L. Doctorow, *The Book of Daniel*
Ralph Ellison, *Invisible Man*
William Faulkner, *Intruder in the Dust*
Ernest Gaines, *The Autobigraphy of Miss Jane Pittman*
Flannery O'Connor, *Everything That Rises Must Converge*
Tillie Olsen, *Tell Me a Riddle*
Leslie Silko, *Ceremony*
Robert Stone, *A Flag for Sunrise*
Alice Walker, *Meridian*
Other readings on reserve

Syllabus—American Literature, 1940–1980

Class 1	The American Novel: State of the Art; A Canon in Flux
2–4	Race and the Issue of Craft. Faulkner, *Intruder in the Dust*; Robert Hayden, "Tour 5," "Night Death, Mississippi"
5–8	Open Fort and the American/Afro-American Vernacular. Ellison, *Invisible Man*; Robert Lowell, "For the Union Dead"; Michael Harper, "Brother John"
9–10	Olsen, "I Stand Here Ironing," "Tell Me a Riddle" (*Tell Me a Riddle*); Gwendolyn Brooks, "The Mother"
11–12	O'Connor, "Everything That Rises Must Converge," "Revelation" (*Everything That Rises*)
13–15	Afro-American Tradition: The Spoken in the Written Word. Gaines, *The Autobiography of Miss Jane Pittman*; Alice Walker, "Revolutionary Petunias," "In Search of Our Mothers' Gardens"
16–18	The Past in the Present Moment. Doctorow, *The Book of Daniel*; Morton Marcus, "Watching Your Gray Eyes"
19–21	The Emergence of Hispanic-American Literature. Anaya, *Bless Me, Ultima*; Gary Soto, "History"; Rick Casillas, "Yaqui Women: Three Generations"; Simon Ortiz, "My Mother and My Sisters"
22–24	"The Ceremony of Innocence is Drowned": Native American Landscapes of Experience. Silko, *Ceremony*; nila north Sun, "little red riding hood," "the way and the way things are"; James Welch, "The Man from Washington," "Surviving"; Meridel LeSueur, "I Light Your Streets," "Dead in the Bloody Snow"
25–27	The Radical Act: "And Could Politics Ever Be An Expression of Love?" Walker, *Meridian*; Carolyn Rodgers, "And

When the Revolution Came," "Mamma's God"
28-31   Vietnam, Vietnam, Vietnam: There is No Substitute for Pain:
        Or Is There? Stone, *A Flag for Sunrise*; LeSueur, "The
        Village"

34
MODERN AMERICAN LITERATURE
Virginia Cox
Spring, 1981 and Spring, 1983
University of Wisconsin
Oshkosh, WI 54901

Course Critique

Modern American Literature is an elective sophomore survey course designed for non-majors. It is very popular, probably because it fulfills general education requirements, and each section scheduled attracts the maximum number of students allowed (thirty-five). The students tend to be majors in business, nursing, and elementary education. Although bright and conscientious, these students usually have had little exposure to literature, and Modern American Literature may well be their only formal literary experience at the University of Wisconsin/Oshkosh.

The course is taught by nearly twenty instructors, including several whose academic specialties are not American literature, let alone twentieth-century literature.

When assigned the course after a lapse of several years, I decided to consult the syllabi on file in the English Department office in search of ideas. I was appalled to discover that only five instructors included women writers on their syllabi! Correcting that inexcusable oversight became my highest priority, and I selected texts accordingly. That task proved difficult, for the usual reason: achieving sufficient variety of authors while keeping the cost to students down.

This consideration explains the first syllabus reproduced below. I knew that my reading list was top-heavy in Hemingway and Frost, thereby excluding many important male authors, but at least, I thought, women were well represented.

After attending the Institute for Reconstructing American Literature in summer 1982, I saw that the deficiencies in Modern American Literature (or any literature course for that matter) went far beyond the exclusion of women. In order for students to appreciate the full richness of their literary heritage, they should be exposed to black, Chicano, Native American, Asian-American, blue collar, and as many regional writers as possible. I felt a strong commitment to including these writers in the course the next time I taught it. I knew that I would have to revise my syllabus extensively and that again the problem of texts would arise.

Faced with teaching the course in our fall interim (an intensive three-week course which meets for three hours daily), I chose Volume II of the *Norton Anthology* as the basic text, supplemented by two plays, two novels, and films, which offered some relief from the pressures of concentrated reading.

I was pleased by the results of the last offering of Modern American Literature and regard the revised syllabus as a major improvement. But I am still not satisfied with it and will not be until I can add even more variety, by way of Chicano, Native American, and Asian-American writers. But that will require a new text, one, to my knowledge not yet available.

Booklist (Spring, 1981)

Susan Cahill, ed., *Women and Fiction: Short Stories By and About Women*
Robert Frost, *Selected Poems*
Ernest Hemingway, *The Short Stories of Ernest Hemingway*
Carson McCullers, *Member of the Wedding*
Arthur Miller, *Death of a Salesman*
Sylvia Plath, *The Bell Jar*
J.D. Salinger, *Catcher in the Rye*
Materials not in texts will be supplied

Reading Assignments

Hemingway, "Indian Camp," "End of Something," "The Killers," "The Battler," "Now I Lay Me," "In Another Country," "Big Two-Hearted River," "A Clean Well-Lighted Place," "The Undefeated," "The Short Happy Life of Francis Macomber," "The Snows of Kilimanjaro" (*Short Stories*)
Frost, "The Figure a Poem Makes," "The Road Not Taken," "Mending Wall." *Frost's Themes—On Nature*: "The Pasture," "Prayer in Spring," "Storm Fear," "Sand Dunes," "Dust of Snow," "Design," "Spring Pools," "Stopping By Woods," "Come In," "Tree at My Window," "After Apple-Picking," "Mowing." *On Work*: "Two Tramps in Mud Time," "The Woodpile," "After Apple-Picking." *On Isolation*: "Desert Places," "Acquainted With the Night," "Vantage Point," "Tuft of Flowers," "Bereft," "An Empty Threat," "Silken

Tent." *On Reason*: "Reluctance," "Strong Are Saying Nothing,"
"There Are Roughly Zones," "Birches," "Acceptance," "Once by the
Pacific," "Neither Too Far Out," "For Once Then." *On Love*: "Fire
and Ice," "Love and a Question," "The Hill Wife," "Old Man's
Winter Night," "Revelation," "The Fear," "Home Burial," "Death of
the Hired Man." *On Transience*: "West-Running Brook," "Out,
Out—," "Nothing Gold Can Stay," "On the Need to Be Versed,"
"The Oven Bird" (*Selected Poems*)
T.S. Eliot, "The Love Song of J. Alfred Prufrock" (handout)
Miller, *Death of a Salesman*
McCullers, *Member of the Wedding*

Poetry by Women
Carolyn Kizer, "Pro Femina"
Adrienne Rich, "I am in Danger—Sir—," "Necessities of Life," "The
    Roofwalker," "Women," "Gabriel," "A Woman Mourned by
    Daughters"
Sylvia Plath, "The Colossus," "Black Rook in Rainy Weather," "Ariel,"
    "Daddy," "Kindness," "The Applicant"
Denise Levertov, "The Secret," "Hypocrite Women," "Mad Song,"
    "Night on Hatchest Cove," "The Mutes," "Stepping Westward"
Erica Jong, "Aging," "Bitter Pills for the Dark," "Ladies"
Nikki Giovanni, "For Saundra," "Woman Poem"
Anne Sexton, "You, Doctor Martin," "Housewife," "Said the Poet to the
    Analyst," "The Black Art," "Cinderella"
Gwendolyn Brooks, "We Real Cool," "Riot," "The Chicago Defender . . . "

Short Stories by Women
Eudora Welty, "A Worn Path"
Flannery O'Connor, "Revelation"
Katherine Anne Porter, "Rope"
Edith Wharton, "The Other Two"
Tillie Olsen, "I Stand Here Ironing"
Joyce Carol Oates, "In a Region of Ice"
Alice Walker, "Everyday Use"
Gertrude Stein, "Miss Furr and Miss Skeene"

Booklist (Spring, 1983)

Norton Anthology of American Literature, Vol. II
Carson McCullers, *Member of the Wedding*
Arthur Miller, *Death of a Salesman*
Sylvia Plath, *The Bell Jar*
J.D. Salinger, *Catcher in the Rye*
Materials not in texts will be supplied

Reading Assignments

The Short Story
Sherwood Anderson, "Book of the Grotesque," "Paper Pills,"
    "Departure," (Norton); Film: "I'm a Fool"
Ernest Hemingway, "In Another Country," "The Short Happy Life of
    Francis Macomber" (Norton); Film: "Soldier's Home"
F. Scott Fitzgerald, "The Rich Boy" (Norton)
William Faulkner, "A Rose for Emily" (Norton); Film: "Barn Burning"
Katherine Anne Porter, "The Jilting of Granny Weatherall" (Norton)
Eudora Welty, "Why I Live at the P.O." (Norton)
Flannery O'Connor, "Good Country People" (Norton)
Richard Wright, "Almos' a Man" (story, Norton, and film)
Saul Bellow, "Father to Be" (Norton); Film: "The Music School"
John Updike, "Separating" (Norton)
Mary McCarthy, "Cruel and Barbarous Treatment"
Tillie Olsen, "I Stand Here Ironing"

Drama
Arthur Miller, *Death of a Salesman*
Carson McCullers, *Member of the Wedding*
Tennessee Williams, *Streetcar Named Desire* (film)

Poetry
Robert Frost, "Mending Wall," "Desert Places," "Road Not Taken,"
    "Birches," "The Pasture," "Acceptance," "Design," "Once by the
    Pacific," "Stopping By Woods," "An Old Man's ...," "After Apple-
    Picking," "'Out, Out—'," "The Woodpile," "The Oven Bird"
T. S. Eliot, "Love Song of J. Alfred Prufrock"
Carl Sandburg, "Chicago," "Fog," "Cool Tombs"
William Carlos Williams, "Overture to a Dance of Locomotives," "Willow
    Poem," "Portrait of a Lady," "Shout it Jimmy!"
Wallace Stevens, "Anecdote of the Jar," "A High-Toned Old Christian
    Woman," "The Emperor of Ice-Cream"
Edna St. Vincent Millay, "What Lips My Lips Have Kissed," "Recuerdo,"
    "I Think I Should Have ...," "Loving You Less Than Life," "I Will
    Put Chaos"
Marianne Moore, "New York," "Poetry," "The Student," "The Mind Is
    An Enchanted Thing"
Jean Toomer, "Georgia Dusk"
Langston Hughes, "The Negro Speaks of Rivers," "Mother to Son," "The
    South," "Mulatto," "Song for a Dark Girl," "Young Gal's Blues"
Countee Cullen, "Yet Do I Marvel," "Incident," "Heritage," "Uncle Jim"
Imamu Amiri Baraka (LeRoi Jones), "An Agony. As Now." "I Substitute
    for the Dead Lecturer"
Gwendolyn Brooks, "Kitchenette Building," "A Song in the Front Yard,"
    "Maxie Allen," "The Lovers of the Poor"

Nikki Giovanni, "For Saundra," "Woman Poem"
Robert Lowell, "Memories of West Street and Lepke," "Man and Wife,"
  "To Speak of Woe That is in Marriage," "Eye and Tooth," "Night
  Sweat"
Allen Ginsberg, "Howl"
Anne Sexton, "All My Pretty Ones," "Flee on Your Donkey," "Sylvia's
  Death," "Cinderella"
Sylvia Plath, "Black Rook in Rainy Weather," "The Applicant," "Lady
  Lazarus," "Ariel," "Daddy"
Denise Levertov, "At the Edge," "Clouds," "The Unknown," "Olgo
  Poems"
Adrienne Rich, "Storm Warnings," "The Roofwalker," "Face to Face,"
  "The Burning of Paper...," "Diving into the Wreck," "Valediction
  Forbidding Mourning"

The Novel
Plath, *The Bell Jar*
J.D. Salinger, *Catcher in the Rye*

35
AMERICAN LITERATURE:
THE EARLY MODERN PERIOD
Sydney Janet Kaplan
Fall, 1980
University of Washington
Seattle, WA 98195

Course Objectives

In constructing a reading list for my course in American Literature,
The Early Modern Period, I try to select books that fit well with other books,
appear to ask and answer questions of each other, and open up the period in
ways that reveal its true complexity. I avoid attempting to do a survey of the
whole period—and the limitations of a ten-week quarter make that unrealis-
tic anyway. I like to use a few of the standard writers: William Faulkner,
Ernest Hemingway, F. Scott Fitzgerald, etc., but contrast them with writers
who are less known, such as Agnes Smedley and Zora Neale Hurston. In so
doing I am able to introduce into the class discussion the whole question of

"canon" building. Who is considered "great"? and why? and by whom? Most of the students have never asked why they read what they do in their classes. Once they are allowed to question the reading list, all the old assumptions are opened up for debate: race, class, and sex bias; considerations of high style versus popular taste; experimental techniques versus realism, etc.

Some of the best class discussions arise out of the differences between Hemingway's and Fitzgerald's portraits of expatriate life in the twenties and thirties and Hurston's vision of the lives of southern Black people during exactly the same time. Contrasts between Willa Cather and Smedley are useful as well. Cather's idealized West seems nearly another planet after reading Smedley. (Gertrude Stein, of course, may be used almost any way one can think of!) Although this class is not listed as a "women's studies" course, it, like all my classes, is informed by a feminist perspective. I include at least as many women authors as men, and focus much of the classwork on one of the central issues of modernism: the connections between the literary experimentation of this period and the dramatic changes in sexual roles following the first world war.

Booklist and Syllabus

Week 1	Sherwood Anderson, *Winesburg, Ohio* (Penguin)
2	Willa Cather, *My Antonia* (Houghton-Mifflin)
3	Agnes Smedley, *Daughter of Earth* (The Feminist Press)
4–5	Gertrude Stein, *Three Lives* (Vintage)
5–6	Ernest Hemingway, *The Snows of Kilimanjaro* (Scribners)
7–8	William Faulkner, *The Sound and the Fury* (Vintage)
9–10	F. Scott Fitzgerald, *Tender is the Night* (Scribners)
10–11	Zora Neale Hurston, *Their Eyes Were Watching God* (University of Illinois Press)

36
AMERICAN LITERATURE—
1914 TO THE PRESENT:
A proposed Course
Participants in the Yale Institute on
Reconstructing American Literature
June, 1982
Yale University
New Haven, CT 06520

Course Objectives

The following syllabus was designed by a group of participants at the Yale Institute held May 31–June 11, 1982 by the project on Reconstructing American Literature. It was intended more as a framework for organizing a course on modern American literature than as a definitive selection of particular readings. In some weeks, for example, the list of writers is far longer than what could reasonably by covered in an undergraduate class; some of the authors might be emphasized one term, others another term. Similarly, while particular authors and stories are listed for fiction, alternative readings are included at the end. Since different people in the group took responsibility for different sections, this syllabus, perhaps more than most, reflects the idiosyncrasies of its creators. There is, for example, little non-fictional prose, the thirties selections touch only lightly on "proletarian" fiction, while the section devoted to recent fiction does little with "modernist" writers. In other words, while the syllabus was created by a group of critics and teachers, it does not pretend to be a definitive rendering of a course on the modern period. It is meant to be suggestive, possible, useful—and replaceable.

Booklist and Syllabus

Week 1–2   Imagists and After—Poetry: Ezra Pound, essay on "Imagism"; poetry by Pound, Hilda Doolittle, Amy Lowell, Marianne Moore, William Carlos Williams, Robert Frost, Carl Sandburg, Wallace Stevens, Hart Crane, E.E. Cummings, T.S. Eliot, Edna St. Vincent Millay

2-3   Afro-American Poetry: poems by Countee Cullen, Claude
       McKay, Sterling Brown, Langston Hughes, Anne
       Spencer, Gwendolyn Bennett, Georgia Johnson, Alice
       Dunbar Nelson, James Weldon Johnson, "Preface" to
       The Book of American Negro Poetry

3-4   Harlem Renaissance and After: Alain Locke, "The New
       Negro"; selections from Jean Toomer, *Cane*; Zora Neale
       Hurston, *Their Eyes Were Watching God*

5   Fiction of the 1920s: F. Scott Fitzgerald, "May Day,"
       "Winter Dreams" (or "Rich Boy"); Ernest Hemingway,
       "Soldier's Home," "Hills Like White Elephants,"
       "The Snows of Kilimanjaro"

6   Ring Lardner, "Haircut"; Sherwood Anderson, "Death in the
       Woods"; Willa Cather, "Neighbor Rosicky"; Edith
       Wharton, *Ethan Frome*; Anzia Yezierska, "Free Vacation
       House" (or "Fat of the Land"); Gertrude Stein,
       selections from *The Autobiography of Alice B. Toklas*;
       Drama: Eugene O'Neill, *The Hairy Ape*

7-9   Fiction of the 1930s: John Dos Passos, selections from *The
       Big Money*; James T. Farrell, "The Fastest Runner on
       Sixty-First Street" (or selections from *Studs Lonigan*);
       John Steinbeck, selections from *The Grapes of Wrath*;
       Chester Himes, "The Passing . . ."; Frank Yerby,
       "Health Card"; Richard Wright, "Long Black Song,"
       "Bright and Morning Star," "Almos' a Man"; William
       Faulkner, *Go Down Moses*; Tillie Olsen, "I Stand Here
       Ironing"; Katherine Anne Porter, "The Rope" (or
       "Pale Horse"); Eudora Welty, "Why I Live at the P.O."

10   Poetry of the 1930s, 1940s, and 1950s: poetry by Gwendolyn
       Brooks, Robert Hayden, Allen Tate, Robert Lowell,
       Allen Ginsberg, Dudley Randall, Muriel Rukeyser,
       Theodore Roethke, Denise Levertov

11   Poetry of the 1960s and 1970s: poetry by Robert Bly, Sylvia
       Plath, Anne Sexton, Nikki Giovanni, Sonia Sanchez,
       Etheridge Knight, Michael Harper, John Ashbery,
       W.S. Merwin, Diane Wakoski, Adrienne Rich, Philip
       Levine, Lucille Clifton, June Jordan, Audre Lorde,
       Lawson Fusao Inada, Pedro Pietri, Sandra Estanes

12-13 Drama: Clifford Odets, *Waiting for Lefty*; Lillian Hellman,
       Little Foxes; Tennessee Williams, *A Streetcar Named
       Desire*; Edward Albee, *Zoo Story*; Imamu Amiri Baraka,
       Dutchman; Ntozake Shange, *For Colored Girls . . .*

14-16 Recent Fiction: Saul Bellow, "Looking for Mr. Green";
       Ralph Ellison, "The King of the Bingo Game," "And
       Hickman Arrives"; James Baldwin, "Sonny's Blues,"
       and "Letter to His Nephew" from *The Fire Next Time*;
       Flannery O'Connor, "Everything That Rises Must

Converge," "Revelation," "Good Country People";
John Cheever, "The Swimmer"; Joyce Carol Oates,
"House of Correction"; Leslie Marmon Silko,
"Lullabye"; Toni Cade Bambara, "My Man
Bouvanne"; Alice Walker, "Everyday Use"; James Alan
McPherson, "Solo Song: For Doc"; Philip Roth, "Eli
the Fanatic"; Estella Portillo, "The Paris Gown"

Additional Writers for Inclusion as Appropriate:

Paula Gunn Allen

Alta

John Barth

John Berryman

Ed Bullins

Joan Didion

W.E.B. DuBois

Mari Evans

Jessie Fauset

Ernest Gaines

Gail Godwin

Angelina Grimké

Jack Kerouac

Maxine Hong Kingston

Nella Larsen

Ursula LeGuin

Haki Madhubite (Don L. Lee)

Norman Mailer

Paule Marshall

Carson McCullers

Arthur Miller

N. Scott Momaday

Frank O'Hara

Simon Ortiz

Dorothy Parker

Pat Parker

Ann Petry

Ishmael Reed

Laura Riding

Carolyn Rodgers

Wendy Rose

Jane Rule

J.D. Salinger

May Sarton

George Schuyler

Isaac Bashevis Singer

Susan Sontag

Jean Stafford

Megan Terry

James Tiptree, Jr.

Melvin Tolson

John Updike

Margaret Walker

Dorothy West

John Williams

Sherley Anne Williams

Edmund Wilson

Malcolm X

Ray Young Bear

Bernice Zamora

Genre Courses

Poetry

37
AMERICAN POETRY
Betsy Erkkila
Spring, 1983
University of Pennsylvania
Philadelphia, PA 19104

Booklist

Major American Poets, Williams and Honig, eds. (abbreviated as *MAP*)
Emily Dickinson, *Final Harvest*
T.S. Eliot, *The Wasteland and Other Poems*
Allen Ginsberg, *Howl*
Nikki Giovanni, *Black Feeling, Black Talk/Black Judgment*
Langston Hughes, *Selected Poems*
Adrienne Rich, *Adrienne Rich's Poetry* (Norton Critical Edition)
Walt Whitman, *Leaves of Grass* (Norton Critical Edition)

Written assignments

Midterm, class #13
Paper I: due class #17: A textual analysis of selected poems; for example, you
might discuss a poet or compare and contrast two poets in relation to an
image (women), a theme (demons), or an ordering device (poetic masks).
Paper II: due class #24: This will be a research paper focusing upon the
relation between a poetic text and its context. For example, The Politics of
Whitman's Poetry, Pound and Modernism, Hughes and the Harlem Renaissance, Ginsberg and the Beat Aesthetics, Rich and Feminism.
Final examination

Syllabus

Class 1   Edward Taylor, "The Preface," "Housewifery," "I Kenning
           Through Astronomy Divine," "Upon a Spider Catching
           a Fly," "Oh! What a Thing Is Man? Lord, Who Am I?"
           (*MAP*); Anne Bradstreet, "The Prologue," "The
           Author to Her Book," "A Letter to Her Husband"
           (handout)
2   Henry Wadsworth Longfellow, "Hymn to Night," "The
           Day is Done," "My Lost Youth," "The Birds of
           Killingworth," "The Tide Rises, The Tide Falls," "The
           Cross of Snow," "The Bells of San Blas," "Possi-
           bilities" (*MAP*); Edgar Allan Poe, 90–115 (*MAP*),
           "The Poetic Principle" and "The Philosophy of
           Composition" (handout)
3   Ralph Waldo Emerson, "Brahma," "The Rhodora," "The
           Humblebee," "Each and All," "The Snowstorm,"
           "Days," "Saadi," "Hamatreya," "Terminus," "Ode
           Inscribed to W.H. Channing" (*MAP*), "The American
           Scholar" and "The Poet" (handout)
4   Whitman, 1855 "Preface" to *Leaves of Grass*, "Song of
           Myself"
5–6   Whitman, "Song of Myself"
7   Whitman, "The Sleepers," "There Was A Child Went
           Forth," "I Sing the Body Electric," "One's-Self I
           Sing," "Poets to Come," "Starting from Paumanok,"
           "Salut Au Monde!," "Song of the Open Road,"
           "Crossing Brooklyn Ferry," Prefatory Letter to Ralph
           Waldo Emerson (1856)
8   Whitman, "Children of Adam" and "Calamus": all poems,
           "Out of the Cradle Endlessly Rocking"
9   Whitman, "Drum-Taps": "Cavalry Crossing a Ford," "By
           the Bivouac's Fitful Flame," "Vigil Strange I Kept on
           the Field One Night," "A March in the Ranks
           Hard-Prest," "The Wound-Dresser," "When Lilacs
           Last in the Dooryard Bloom'd," "Passage to India,"
           "Prayer of Columbus," "So Long!," "Good-Bye My
           Fancy," "A Backward Glance O'er Traveled Roads"
10   Dickinson, "The Gentian weaves her fringes" (4), "I never
           lost as much but twice"(7), "Success is counted
           sweetest" (11), "Exultant is the going" (14), "One
           dignity delays for all" (16), "Bring me the sunset in a
           cup" (22), "These are the days when Birds come back"
           (23), "Just lost, when I was saved!" (27), "To learn the
           Transport by the Pain" (29), " 'Faith' is a fine invention"
           (34), "I'm 'wife'—I've finished that" (39), "Come
           slowly—Eden!" (44), "I taste a liquor never brewed"

    (46), "Safe in their Alabaster Chambers" (47), "She
    sweeps with many-colored Brooms" (49), "I like a look
    of Agony" (54), "Wild Nights—Wild Nights!" (58), "I
    can wade Grief" (61), "Hope is the Thing with feathers"
    (63), "There's a certain Slant of light" (66), "I felt a
    Funeral, in my Brain" (78), "I'm Nobody! Who are
    you?" (85)

11 Dickinson, "I reason, Earth is short" (93), "The Soul selects
    her own Society" (5), "He fumbles at your Soul" (105),
    "We play at Paste" (108), "Some keep the Sabbath
    going to Church" (112), "Before I got my eye put out"
    (115), "A Bird came down the Walk" (116), "After great
    pain, a formal feeling comes" (122), "I dreaded that first
    Robin, so" (126), "No Rack can torture me" (149),
    "There's been a Death in the Opposite House" (149),
    "Much Madness is divinest Sense" (168), "This is my
    letter to the World" (172), "This was a Poet—It is That"
    (176), "I died for Beauty—but was scarce" (177), "A
    Wife—at Daybreak I shall be" (182), "I heard a Fly
    buzz—when I died" (184), "Myself was formed—a
    Carpenter" (195), "I'm ceded—I've stopped being
    Theirs" (203), "I started Early—Took my Dog" (209),
    "Mine—by the Right of the White Election!" (212), "I
    took my Power in my Hand" (220), "I've seen a Dying
    Eye" (224), "I reckon—when I count at all" (236), "I
    had been hungry, all the Years" (240), "I like to see it
    lap the Miles" (243), "I asked no other thing" (257), "I
    dwell in Possibility" (270), "Pain—has an Element of
    Blank" (269)

12 Dickinson, "One need not be a Chamber—to be Haunted"
    (274), "Publication—is the Auction" (288), "Because I
    could not stop for Death" (290), "My Life had stood—a
    Loaded Gun" (307), "Nature—the Gentlest Mother is"
    (322), "God gave a Loaf to every Bird" (323), "A Death
    blow is a Life blow to Some" (334), "A narrow Fellow in
    the Grass" (389), "I never saw a Moor" (403), "Further
    in Summer than the Birds" (410), "Title divine—is
    mine!" (412), "Tell all the Truth but tell it slant"
    (427), Death is the supple Suitor" (504), "A Route of
    Evanescence" (508), "How happy is the little Stone"
    (519), "The Bible is an antique Volume" (525),
    "Apparently with no surprise" (542), "A Word made
    Flesh is seldom" (546), "My life closed twice before its
    close" (563), "Rearrange a 'Wife's' affection!" (565)

13 Midterm
14-15 Ezra Pound, pp. 334-71 (*MAP*)
16 Eliot, "The Love Song of J. Alfred Prufrock," "Gerontion,"

"Sweeney Among the Nightingales," "The Wasteland"; "Tradition and the Individual Talent" (handout); Paper 1 due

17 William Carlos Williams, pp. 315–33
18 Eliot, "The Wasteland"
19 Eliot, "The Wasteland," "Ash-Wednesday," "Journey of the Magi," "Marina"
20 Wallace Stevens, "Peter Quince at the Clavier," "Sunday Morning," "Anecdote of the Jar," "The Emperor of Ice Cream," "Bantams in Pine Woods," "The Idea of Order at Key West," "No Ideas About the Thing But the Thing Itself," "Crude Foyer" (*MAP*)
21 Hughes, *Afro-American Fragments*, "Spirituals," *Shadow of the Blues*, "Harlem Night Song," "Mexican Market Woman," "Love," "Border Line," "Vagabonds," "Old Walt," "Song for Billie Holliday," "Midnight Raffle," "Miss Blues'es Child," "Trumpet Player"
22 Hughes, "Me and the Mule," "Little Lyric," "Ennui," "Mama and Daughter," "S-sss-ss-sh," "Widow Woman," "Young Gal's Blues," *Magnolia Flowers*, "To Be Somebody," "Note on Commercial Theatre," "Puzzled," *Montage of a Dream Deferred, Words Like Freedom*
23 Ginsberg, *Howl and Other Poems*
24 Rich, "Storm Warnings," "Aunt Jennifer's Tigers," "An Unsaid Word," "The Middle-aged," "Living in Sin," "The Diamond Cutters," "The Knight," "Snapshots of a Daughter-in-Law," "A Marriage in the Sixties," "The Roofwalker," "Prospective Immigrants Please Note"; Paper II due
25 Rich, "Necessities of Life," "In the Woods," "Like This Together," "I Am in Danger—Sir—," "Orion," "The Demon Lover," "Planetarium," "The Burning of Paper Instead of Children," "Trying to Talk with a Man," "When We Dead Awaken," "The Stranger," "Diving Into the Wreck," "From a Survivor," "From an Old House in America"; "Poetry and Experience," "When We Dead Awaken: Writing as Re-Vision"
26 Giovanni, *Black Feeling, Black Talk/Black Judgment*

Autobiography

38
AMERICAN AUTOBIOGRAPHY
William Andrews
Spring, 1981
University of Wisconsin
Madison, WI 53706

Course Objectives

American autobiography tells the story of what it means to be an American. The study of American autobiography in this course will focus on this issue. Since America is a multi-ethnic society, the texts to be read represent not only this country's "classic" autobiographical tradition but also the first-person narratives of many outside the so-called literary and social mainstream, including white women, Afro-Americans, Asian-Americans, Jews, and Hispanic-Americans. Besides being socially and historically representative (in varying degrees), the texts to be used in this course also illustrate the experimental nature of much first-person writing in our literature. The course will try to come to terms with the texts both as creative acts of self-definition and as documents of the social and historical experience of groups and classes in America.

Booklist

Henry Adams, *The Education of Henry Adams*
Frank Conroy, *Stop-Time*
Frederick Douglass, *My Bondage and My Freedom*
Benjamin Franklin, *The Autobiography and Other Writings*
Ellen Glasgow, *The Woman Within*
Maxine Hong Kingston, *The Woman Warrior*

Norman Mailer, *The Armies of the Night*
Piri Thomas, *Down These Mean Streets*
Henry David Thoreau, *Walden and Civil Disobedience*
Great Short Works of Mark Twain, ed. Justin Kaplan
John Woolman, *The Journal of John Woolman*
Richard Wright, *American Hunger*
————, *Black Boy*

Syllabus

Class 1   Introduction
2–4   *Journal of John Woolman*
5–7   *Autobiography of Benjamin Franklin*
8–10   Thoreau, *Walden*
11–13   Douglass, *My Bondage and My Freedom*
14–15   Twain, "Old Times on the Mississippi"
16–19   *Education of Henry Adams*
20–24   Glasgow, *The Woman Within*
25–27   Wright, *Black Boy*
28–29   Wright, *American Hunger*
30–32   Thomas, *Down These Mean Streets*
33–35   Conroy, *Stop-Time*
36–39   Mailer, *The Armies of the Night*
40–43   Kingston, *Woman Warrior*

Supplement: Readings for Graduate-Level Course in American Autobiography

The following are the primary texts for the course, taught in Fall, 1982, by Professor Andrews:

The Journal of John Woolman (1774)
The Autobiography of Benjamin Franklin (1818)
H.D. Thoreau, *Walden* (1854)
Frederick Douglass, *My Bondage and My Freedom* (1885)
Linda Brent, *Incidents in the Life of a Slave Girl* (1861)
Mark Twain, *Old Times on the Mississippi* (1875)
The Diary of Alice James (1894)
Elizabeth Cady Stanton, *Eighty Years and More* (1898)
Booker T. Washington, *Up From Slavery* (1901)
Jack London, *The Road* (1907)
Henry Adams, *The Education of Henry Adams* (1907)
James Olney, ed., *Autobiography: Essays Theoretical and Critical*

Text Options for Oral Reports

Narrative of the Captivity . . . of Mrs. Mary Rowlandson (1682)
Jonathan Edwards, *Personal Narrative* (1737)
Interesting Narrative of . . . Olaudah Equiano (Gustavus Vassa) (1789)
Narrative of David Crockett (1834)
P.T. Barnum, *Struggles and Triumphs* (1869)
Narrative of . . . Henry Bibb (1849)
Austin Steward, *22 Years a Slave and 40 Years a Freeman* (1857)
Journal of Charlotte Forten (1864)
Mary Chesnut's *Diary* (1865)
William Dean Howells, *A Boy's Town* (1890)
Hamlin Garland, *Son of the Middle Border* (1917)
Elaine G. Eastman, *Sister to the Sioux* (1891)
R. Rosen and S. Davidson, eds., *The Maimie Papers* (1977)
Elizabeth Blackwell, *Opening the Medical Profession to Women* (1895)
The Living of Charlotte Perkins Gilman (1935)
Jane Addams, *Twenty Years at Hull House* (1910)
William Pickens, *Bursting Bonds* (1923)
Jacob Riis, *The Making of an American* (1901)
Josiah Flynt, *My Life* (1908)
Autobiography of Theodore Roosevelt (1913)
Alexander Berkman, *Prison Memoirs of an Anarchist* (1912)

39
AMERICAN AUTOBIOGRAPHY
Judith E. Fryer
1981
Miami University
Oxford, OH 45056

Course Objectives and Critique

The autobiography is an ideal text to use for an interdisciplinary course because it is a genre in which disciplinary lines disappear. The autobiography is at one and the same time a special kind of fiction, history, social commentary; it can be science or philosophy, theology, poetry, or even literary criticism. The autobiography—be it letters, memoirs, story, confessions, interpretation, or translation—is also an ideal text for an interdisciplinary class because it is a statement about culture; it speaks of and for a particular time and place. Studying autobiographies, then, is a way of studying history, not the history of political and military events, but rather the history of personal observation. Thus, the study of autobiography resembles in some ways the study of oral history, or the history of the inarticulate in that it offers stories otherwise unrecorded.

Autobiography is also an ideal text for freshman writers. Most entering freshmen and women are at a point in their lives of questioning themselves, their values, the purpose of education, the meaning of life. Trite as that sounds, it is true. Autobiography makes them anxious; it seems to be about them. It generates questions for them that are provoking and give them much to write about.

The autobiographies on this list are for the most part rather obvious. They are meant to be representative—representative of historical periods in America, of regions, of country and city, rich and poor, male and female, black, Indian, and white. Connections among the volumes are left for the teacher and students to find together. Many of these connections were, in my case, expected, and some were wonderfully surprising. Probably the implied thesis—and one that surprises my white, middle-class Midwestern students when they discover it—is that there is no American culture, rather there are cultures.

Students are encouraged both to read carefully and deeply—I had papers, for example, that concentrated on a single sentence or image in *Walden*— and to do outside reading—in, for example, theory of autobiography, architecture of Louis Sullivan, poetry of Nikki Giovanni, Cubism in relation to Gertrude Stein. I gave a number of supplementary lectures, using audiovisual materials when appropriate. Honors students were also given supplementary autobiographies to read: Sylvia Plath's *Bell Jar* and May Sarton's *Journal of a Solitude*; Eldridge Cleaver's *Soul on Ice*; autobiographies of Frank Lloyd Wright and Willam Carlos Williams to go along with Sullivan; Alice B. Toklas's *Staying On Alone*, and so on. I vary the list from time to time; from the list given here, the most successful texts are Stein and John Neihardt; the least successful was *Gemini* (I have much better luck with Maya Angelou's *I Know Why the Caged Bird Sings*).

Booklist

Henry Adams, *The Education of Henry Adams*
Jane Addams, *Twenty Years at Hull House*
Benjamin Franklin, *Autobiography*
Nikki Giovanni, *Gemini*
John Neihardt, *Black Elk Speaks*
Gertrude Stein, *The Autobiography of Alice B. Toklas*
Louis Sullivan, *The Autobiography of an Idea*
Henry David Thoreau, *Walden*

Syllabus

Class 1   Introduction to the course
      2   Franklin, *Autobiography* pp. 16–72
      3   Franklin, pp. 72–157
      4   Continue discussion of Franklin and of writing criteria
    5–8   Thoreau, *Walden*; paper 1 due
   9–12   Henry Adams, *Education*; paper 2 due
  13–15   Jane Addams, *Hull House*; paper 3 due
  16–18   Stein, *Alice B. Toklas*; paper 4 due
     19   Slide lecture on Gertrude Stein and Cubism
  20–22   Neihardt, *Black Elk Speaks*; paper 5 due
     23   Slide lecture on Louis Sullivan's architecture; paper 6 due
  24–26   Sullivan, *Idea*
  27–30   Giovanni, *Gemini*; paper 7 due

40
AMERICAN LIVES
Marcia Jacobson and Margaret Kouidis
Winter, 1981
Auburn University
Auburn, AL 36849

Course Objectives

English 106 is the second and final quarter of freshman composition for honors students at Auburn University. It is a theme course designed by each instructor in accord with his or her particular interests. Because Auburn is not oriented toward the liberal arts, few of our students are humanities majors. Most of the students in this course are in the sciences, many are in engineering. They will probably not take another literature course in their four years at Auburn.

Margaret Kouidis designed this syllabus; I made some changes, and I taught the course. Both of us wanted to introduce the students to some American classics, we wanted them to look carefully at the experience of Black Americans (something many white Southern students have not done), and we wanted them to read material that would make them ask questions about their own aspirations and values. We also thought a chronological survey would be useful in allowing the class to see which values have persisted in American culture and which have changed.

In the course itself, my students and I looked at themes that our authors had in common: we considered the different ways Benjamin Franklin, Henry David Thoreau, Mark Twain, and Margaret Mead view work; and we talked about the different meanings of spiritual growth in Jonathan Edwards, Thoreau, Frederick Douglass, and Malcolm X, for example. We also considered the different emphases in autobiographies written in different periods—Malcolm X and Mead both deal with their childhoods, while earlier writers do not—and we tried to account for the differences we saw. Finally, we looked for the apparently standard features of the American autobiography and then asked how many of these features were to be found in Joan Didion's work, in which the self is so overwhelmed by contemporary social and political chaos. I found my students least responsive to Edwards and Thoreau. Were I to do the course again, I would omit these two and add something like Maxine Hong Kingston's *The Woman Warrior*, which would allow us to consider an additional American ethnic experience and to do more with the question of female identity than we did.

Because the course is a composition course, the essay assignments were designed to make the students solve basic writing problems: relating a part to the whole of a work, comparing and contrasting ideas, tracing the development of a theme. The final paper allowed the students to work with something of personal interest and to gain some experience using outside material.

Booklist

Joan Didion, *The White Album*
Frederick Douglass, *Narrative of the Life of Frederick Douglass*
Jonathan Edwards, *Spiritual Autobiography* (handout)
Benjamin Franklin, *Autobiography*
Margaret Mead, *Blackberry Winter*
Henry David Thoreau, *Walden*
Mark Twain, *Roughing It*
Malcolm X, *Autobiography*

Syllabus

Class 1	Introduction
2	Edwards, *Spiritual Autobiography*
3–5	Franklin, *Autobiography*; paper 1 due
6–7	Douglass, *Narrative*
8–11	Thoreau, *Walden*; paper 2 due

12–17   Twain, *Roughing It*; paper 3 due
18–22   Malcolm X, *Autobiography*
23–26   Mead, *Blackberry Winter*
27   Final paper due
28   Mead
29   Final examination: read Didion, *White Album*

Paper Assignments

Paper 1 (500–600 words):
    Pick a short episode from Edwards's "Personal Narrative" or Franklin's *Autobiography* and explain what that episode contributes to the work it comes from.
    You may approach this any way you choose. Some possible considerations: What theme(s) does the episode illustrate? What aspects of the author's character does the episode reveal? What does the episode contribute to his development?

Paper 2 (500–600 words):
    Like Franklin, Thoreau has very definite ideas about frugality, industry, and humility. Write a paper in which you compare Franklin's and Thoreau's ideas on *one* of these subjects.

Paper 3 (500–600 words):
    Trace a theme or concern through **three** of the autobiographies we have read so far. Since this is another short paper, you cannot do detailed analyses of the three works you discuss, but support what you have to say by quotations and references to specific events in the works you discuss. Your paper should have a thesis; try to do more than simply list three occurrences of the same concern.

Paper 4 (1500 words):
    Write on one of the following:
    1. Read another book by one of the authors we've read this term and write a paper in which you explain how the autobiography enhances our understanding of that other book.
    2. Read an American autobiography that was not assigned for our class and write a paper in which you relate your book to (some of) the books we have read. Explain what traditions it carries on, what themes it develops, etc.
    3. Read a fictionalized autobiography/autobiographical novel by an American author and write a paper in which you explain what the author gained by fictionalizing his or her experience.
    This paper is a critical paper in which your own ideas will be central to your writing. However, so that you will gain some experience doing outside

reading and using it in your writing, you are required to look at three or four books and/or articles (that is, total number = three or four) and refer to them in your final paper.

Final Exam

Answer both of the following questions. Spend about an hour on each.

1. Is Joan Didion's essay, "The White Album," a fitting conclusion to a course in American autobiography?

    In answering this question, you will need to decide whether or not the essay is an autobiography in any meaningful sense. You can do this by considering some of the other autobiographies we've read and by evaluating "The White Album" against the definition of autobiography that you arrive at.

2. In both *The Autobiography of Malcolm X* and Margaret Mead's *Blackberry Winter* the protagonist searches for a family, a biological family or non-related group that serves the functions of a family. Write an essay in which you compare the two searches. Consider why each character seeks a family, what each finds in the course of the search, and how successful each finally is.

Fiction

41
THE AMERICAN STORY-CHRONICLE
Warner Berthoff
Fall, 1982
Harvard University
Cambridge, MA 02138

Course Objectives

The course is designed for students who have already read main works by the novelists who normally appear in American survey courses. The idea is (1) to introduce students to a broad range of American narrative writing that takes as one of its main purposes the documentation of actual American life, and (2) to emphasize in particular a set of works that have the coherence (design, theme, setting) of a first-rate novel, yet are not novels (or are very irregular novels, like *The Confidence-Man*), and which appear to have taken the compositional form they have—a sequence of related stories or narrated episodes—out of their authors' concern to reproduce certain effects normal to *historical* writing: in particular a documentary truthfulness and a documentary comprehensiveness. Every title on the reading list is a work of fictional, fictionalized, or autobiographical narrative which is also in some sense a chronicle , an imaginative representation of some important circumstance of American life and history.

The foregoing paragraph should explain both choices and omissions—the omission, for example, of major figures like Edgar Allan Poe and Henry James, and the choice, with Nathaniel Hawthorne, of some relatively minor sketches. The double-starred titles are to be read by all students in the course: six classics of our literature which are, first of all, *not* novels (though by authors who did write, or try to write, proper novels), yet which represent each author pretty much at her/his best. These titles give us, in addition, some common points of reference for the course as a whole. Students make up the rest of their reading (fifteen to twenty titles in all, depending on length, difficulty, etc.) according to their own interests and major-field needs. The single-starred titles represent works that seem to the instructor of particular value in one way or another and that also make (experience shows) good class reports—*The Company She Keeps*, for example, invariably results in a lively and controversial class session.

The course, along with its three-page reading list, is meant to serve a number of purposes and constituencies. The very large number of names is not meant to be intimidating but to suggest that a living literature is a good deal more than what can be represented in anthologies and syllabi. Certain chronological clusters point to historically significant developments: the concern of a whole group of writers around 1830–40, for example, with the American past and the ongoing process of American settlement, or the convergence of some exceptionally gifted writers around 1910–20 on a modernist and experimental mode of serial regionalism (Robert Frost, Edgar Lee Masters, Sherwood Anderson). Some of my best students in this course—those who have got most out of it—have been students primarily interested in writing, who have found somewhere in their choice of readings fresh models for their own work, alternatives to the prematurely demanding form of the big, compositionally perfected novel. Otherwise those who thrive in the course are usually students in History and Literature or in American Civilization, some of whom find themselves tracing grand organizing sociological themes through all their reading.

Booklist

*recommended; historically important; etc.
**required of all students

1790–1880

*Hugh Henry Brackenridge, *Modern Chivalry* (1792–1815)
Washington Irving, *The Sketch Book* (1819)
John Greenleaf Whittier, *Legends of New England* (1831)
*James Hall, *Legends of the West* (1832)
*John Pendleton Kennedy, *Swallow Barn* (1832)
James Kirke Paulding, *The Banks of the Ohio, or, Westward Ho!* (1832)
Henry Wadsworth Longfellow, *Outre-Mer* (1833), *Tales of a Wayside Inn* (1863)
*Augustus Baldwin Longstreet, *Georgia Scenes* (1835)
*Nathaniel Hawthorne, "Legends of the Province House" (1838–39)
*Caroline M. Kirkland, *A New Home—Who'll Follow?* (1839)
Johnson J. Hooper, *Some Adventures of Captain Simon Suggs*
William T. Thompson, *Chronicles of Pineville* (1845)
Thomas B. Thorpe, *Mysteries of the Backwoods* (1846)
Joseph G. Baldwin, *The Flush Times of Alabama and Mississippi* (1846)
*Charles F. Browne, *Artemus Ward His Book* (1862)

*George Washington Harris, *Sut Lovingood Yarns* (1867)
*Harriet Beecher Stowe, *Oldtown Folks* (1869)
*Mark Twain, *Roughing It* (1872), *Life on the Mississippi* (1875, 1883)
*George Washington Cable, *Old Creole Days* (1879), *Dr. Sevier* (1884),
    Bonaventure (1883)
Novels: William Gilmore Simms, *Guy Rivers* (1835); James Fenimore
    Cooper, *Home as Found* (1838); Harriet Beecher Stowe, *Uncle Tom's
    Cabin* (1852); Walt Whitman, *Leaves of Grass* (1855); Herman Melville,
    Israel Potter (1855), *The Confidence-Man* (1857), *Clarel* (1876); John
    William DeForest, *Miss Ravenel's Conversion* (1867); Mark Twain and
    Charles Dudley Warner, *The Gilded Age* (1873); Edward Eggleston,
    The End of the World (1872)

1880-1920

**Sarah Orne Jewett, *The Country of the Pointed Firs* (1896)
**Willa Cather, *My Antonia* (1918)
**Sherwood Anderson, *Winesburg, Ohio* (1919)
  E.W. Howe, *The Story of a Country Town* (1883)
 *Hamlin Garland, *Main-Travelled Roads* (1891)
  Ambrose Bierce, *In the Midst of Life* (1891; also called *Tales of Soldiers and
    Civilians*)
 *George Ade, *Fables in Slang* (1899)
 *Stephen Crane, *Whilomville Stories* (1900)
  Zona Gale, *Friendship Village* (1908)
 *Gertrude Stein, *Three Lives* (1909), *The Making of Americans* (1925)
  O. Henry, *The Four Million* (1906)
  Edwin Arlington Robinson, *The Children of the Night* (1897), *The Town
    Down the River* (1910)
 *Robert Frost, *A Boy's Will* (1913)
 *Edgar Lee Masters, *Spoon River Anthology* (1915)
 *Theodore Dreiser, *Twelve Men* (1919), *A Hoosier Holiday* (1916)
  Novels: Henry Blake Fuller, *The Cliff-Dwellers (1893), With the
    Procession* (1895); Hjalmar H. Boyesen, *Social Strugglers* (1895);
    Edward Eggleston, *The Faith Doctor* (1891); Frank Norris, *The
    Octopus* (1901); Robert Herrick, *Together* (1908); William Dean
    Howells, *New Leaf Mills: A Chronicle* (1913); Edith Wharton, *The
    Custom of the Country* (1913); Ring Lardner, *You Know Me Al* (1916)

1920-1980

**Ernest Hemingway, *In Our Time* (1925)
**William Faulkner, *Go Down Moses* (1942)
**Eudora Welty, *The Golden Apples* (1949)
 *John Dos Passos, *The Three Soldiers* (1921), *Manhattan Transfer* (1925),
    U.S.A. (1930-36)
 *E. E. Cummings, *The Enormous Room* (1922)
 *Jean Toomer, *Cane* (1923)
  Sherwood Anderson, *A Story-Teller's Story* (1924), *Tar* (1926)

*William Carlos Williams, *In the American Grain* (1925)
F. Scott Fitzgerald, *All the Sad Young Men* (1927)
Glenway Wescott, *The Grandmothers* (1927)
Thornton Wilder, *The Bridge of San Luis Rey* (1927)
*Edmund Wilson, *I Thought of Daisy* (1929), *The American Jitters* (1931),
    Memoirs of Hecate County (1946), *Upstate* (1971)
*Mike Gold, *Jews Without Money* (1930)
*Nathaniel West, *Miss Lonelyhearts* (1933), *The Day of the Locust* (1939)
  George Weller, *Not to Eat Not for Love* (1933), *Clutch and Differential*
    (1936)
James Thurber, *My Life and Hard Times* (1933)
*Henry Miller, *Tropic of Cancer* (1934)
Daniel Fuchs, *The Williamsburg Trilogy* (1934–37)
John Steinbeck, *Tortilla Flat* (1935)
*William Faulkner, *Absalom, Absalom!* (1936), *The Hamlet* (1940)
  Katherine Anne Porter, *The Old Order* (1930s–40s), *Ship of Fools* (1962)
  Allen Tate, *The Fathers* (1938)
*Richard Wright, *Uncle Tom's Children* (1938), *Eight Men* (1961)
  Thomas Wolfe, *The Hills Beyond* (1941)
*James Agee, *Let Us Now Praise Famous Men* (1941)
*Mary McCarthy, *The Company She Keeps* (1942), *The Group* (1963)
  James Michener, *Tales of the South Pacific* (1947)
  Ross Lockridge, Jr., *Raintree County* (1948)
  Delmore Schwartz, *The World Is a Wedding* (1948)
  Ray Bradbury, *The Martian Chronicles* (1950)
  Robert Penn Warren, *Brother to Dragons* (1953)
  John Cheever, *The Wapshot Chronicle* (1957), *The Wapshot Scandal*
    (1959)
  Terry Southern, *The Magic Christian* (1959)
  Clancy Sigal, *Weekend in Dinlock* (1960), *Going Away* (1962), *Zone of*
    the Interior (1975)
*J. D. Salinger, *Franny and Zooey* (1961), *Raise High the Roofbeam,*
    Carpenters (1963)
  Paul Goodman, *Empire City* (1959)
  Truman Capote, *In Cold Blood* (1965)
*[Malcolm Little], *The Autobiography of Malcolm X* (1965)
  William H. Gass, *Omensetter's Luck* (1966), *In the Heart*
    of the Heart of the Country (1968)
  Robert Coover, *The Origin of the Brunists* (1967), *The Public Burning*
    (1977)
  Richard Brautigan, *Trout Fishing in America* (1967)
*Norman Mailer, *The Armies of the Night* (1968), *The Executioner's Song*
    (1979)
  Tom Wolfe, *The Electric Kool-Aid Acid Test* (1968)
  John Berryman, *The Dream Songs* (1969), *Love & Fame* (1970)
  Robert Lowell, *History* (1973), *Day by Day* (1977)
  Albert Murray, *South To a Very Old Place* (1971)

*Theodore Rosengarten, *All God's Dangers: The Life of Nate Shaw* (1974)
Paul Zweig, *Three Journeys* (1975)
Maxine Hong Kingston, *The Woman Warrior* (1976)
Donald Barthelme, *The Dead Father* (1975)
*Renata Adler, *Speedboat* (1976)
Novels: George Santayana, *The Last Puritan* (1935); J.P. Marquand, *The Late George Apley* (1937); Ralph Ellison, *Invisible Man* (1953); Harriette Arnow, *The Dollmaker* (1954); William Gaddis, *The Recognitions* (1955); Jack Kerouac, *On the Road* (1957); Saul Bellow, *The Adventures of Augie March* (1953); Langston Hughes, the *Simple* novels (1950s); James Baldwin, *Another Country* (1962); Walker Percy, *The Moviegoer* (1961); John A. Williams, *Sissie* (1963); John Updike, the *Rabbit* novels (1960, 1971, 1981), *Couples* (1966); Joyce Carol Oates, *Them* (1970), *Wonderland* (1973); Ishmael Reed, *The Last Days of Louisiana Red* (1973), *Flight to Canada* (1976); Robert M. Pirsig, *Zen and the Art of Motorcycle Maintenance* (1974); E.L. Doctorow, *Ragtime* (1975); Larry Woiwode, *Beyond the Bedroom Wall* (1975).

Collateral Suggestions

T. G. Smollett, *The Expedition of Humphrey Clinker* (1771); Maria Edgeworth, *Castle Rackrent* (1801), *The Absentee* (1812); George Crabbe, *Tales in Verse* (1812); Walter Scott, *The Antiquary* (1816); Miss Mitford, *Our Village* (1819); John Galt, *Annals of the Parish* (1821); Mrs. Gaskell, *Cranford* (1853), *Wives and Daughters* (1866); Charles Dickens, *Little Dorrit* (1857), *Our Mutual Friend* (1865); George Eliot, *Middlemarch* (1871); Anthony Trollope, *The Way We Live Now* (1875); George Borrow, *The Bible in Spain* (1843); W. H. Davies, *The Autobiography of a Supertramp* (1908); Nikolai Gogol, *Dead Souls* (1942); M. Lermontov, *A Hero of Our Time* (1840); Ivan Turgenev, *Sketches from a Hunter's Album* (1855; also translated as *A Sportsman's Notebook*); Giovanni Verga, *Little Novels of Sicily* (1883); Ignazio Silone, *Fontamara* (1935); Gunter Grass, *The Tin Drum* (1960), *The Flounder* (1978); Gabriel Garcia Marquez, *A Hundred Years of Solitude* (1969); Peter Handke, *A Sorrow Beyond Dreams* (1972), *Short Letter, Long Farewell* (1972), *The Left-Handed Woman* (1977)

42
INTRODUCTION TO THE NOVEL
Carol Burr
Fall, 1982
California State University
Chico, CA 95929

Course Objectives

Goal: To examine the thematic and formal elements of the novel through analysis of text, periodicity, and cultural context in American social protest fiction.

The rationale for the course is based on its inclusion in General Studies. The students are often non-majors with little reading background. Therefore, I want to introduce them to works that tackle broad social issues. Protest novels make themselves as accessible as possible because they wish to move readers to action. Focusing on American protest allows students to re-evaluate their own heritage from a vantage point rarely emphasized in basic history texts. Finally, the movement from mid-nineteenth century to the present shows the changes that have occurred in the belief structures of protest (for example, the efficacy of religion, the effectiveness of nonviolence, and the connection of the individual to the society) and the literary approaches (narrative viewpoint, character development, tone, etc.). The text selection changes regularly, but the issues of class, gender, and race are common to all, and every effort is made to balance male and female, black and white perspectives. I am presently interested in incorporating more work by "ethnic," and especially Hispanic writers, like Rodolfo Anaya.

The analytical journals have a number of important uses in the course: first, they encourage writing one's perceptions when they occur; second, guided by the sample questions in the course outline, they give a forum for connecting the experience of the work with its analysis; third, they help provide ideas and even drafts for the formal analytical essays; and, finally, they are difficult to fake—one either does the reading and explores facets that catch his/her attention or one skims the text and does poorly on the journal.

If students take full advantage of the journal the final assignment seems a logical progression. The class novel uses the tools we have discovered and written about during the semester to create our own protest novel. The class as a group formulates characters, plot, climax, sample incidents; then each student writes a chapter that fits into the frame. The final examination is a critical review of the novel—its successes and failures—by the class.

Booklist

Rebecca Harding Davis, *Life in the Iron Mills*
Norman Mailer, *The Armies of the Night*, or Ayn Rand, *The Fountainhead*
Frank Norris, *McTeague*, or Upton Sinclair, *The Jungle*
Tillie Olsen, *Yonnondio*
Harriet Beecher Stowe, *Uncle Tom's Cabin*
Alice Walker, *The Color Purple*, or Toni Morrison, *Sula*
Richard Wright, *Native Son*

Course Requirements

1. Journal entries on all assigned novels: select and analyze formal (e.g., characterization, setting, modes of persuasion, structure) and thematic elements (author's purpose as reflective of period, personal and social values, etc.). Journal to be collected three times during semester: after first three novels, after next two novels, after final two novels.

2. Analytic essay on one of the novels (4–6 pages typed) and oral report (15–20 minutes) based on the essay. Both due during discussion of the novel you select.

3. Chapter of a novel to be written by the class; due for distribution to class at the end of class 15. Chapter must be a vivid dramatization of character and a logical link in the thematic and structural chain of the novel.

Syllabus

Week 1	Topics for discussion: What makes a novel? What disqualifies it? What is a protest novel?
2	Stowe, *Uncle Tom's Cabin*. Topics for journal: Who or what is Stowe attacking? How do the characters of Uncle Tom and George function together in the novel? How does *UTC* persuade us to Stowe's viewpoint? How dated is the novel?
3	*Uncle Tom's Cabin*. Topics for journal: Analyze what you consider to be the most important scene in the novel; consider it as literature and as propaganda. Can a novel be both?
4	Davis, *Life in the Iron Mills*. Topics for journal: How does this novel compare with *UTC* (consider plot development and theme)? What is Davis protesting against? How does she go about that protest? Is this great literature?

5   Norris, *McTeague*. Topics for journal: Why does the novel
        begin as it does? Do you see any social Darwinism at
        work?

6   *McTeague*. Topics for journal: What does the canary
        represent and how does it function? Journals due

7   Olsen, *Yonnondio*. Topics for journal: Why is Mazie the
        narrator? What is Olsen protesting? What if any solution
        does she offer?

8   Wright, *Native Son*. Topics for journal: How does Wright's
        view of the racial problem differ from Stowe's? Why?
        What does the rat represent? Compare its function to
        that of the canary in *McTeague*. Why did Wright write
        Native Son? Is it dated?

9   *Native Son*. Topics for journal: Explain what Bigger means in
        his final declaration, " 'What I killed for must've been
        good!' " Is he right? Journals due

10   Mailer, *Armies of the Night*. Topics for journal: Is this a novel?
        In what way? What kind of character is Mailer? What is
        he protesting?

11   *Armies of the Night*. Topics for journal: Analyze a passage:
        what journalistic devices are used—tone, persona,
        sentence structure?

12   Walker, *The Color Purple*. Topics for journal: What has
        happened to the protest novel? The black protest novel?
        Have the issues changed? The modes of persuasion?
        The use of dialect? Explain your answers.

13   *The Color Purple*. Topics for journal: What has happened to
        the society of earlier novels? Make some summarizing
        statements about the novels we have read. Journals due

14–15   Preparation and writing of class novel

16   Final: Reading of class novel; review of novel

43
AMERICAN NOVEL
SINCE THE MODERN AGE
Chester J. Fontenot
1982–83
University of Illinois at Urbana-Champaign
Urbana, IL 61801

Course Objectives

Theme: evaluating some representative texts in American literature in light of Robert Spillers's essay, "Cycle and Roots." Spillers posits a theory of American literature which endeavors to justify the exclusion of minority writers, especially Afro-Americans. He proposes that there is such a thing as an American myth, but the structure of the myth leaves out the experiences of Afro-Americans. Spillers offers a myth of Westward movement as the metaphor for the American experience, of settlement and expansion of hostile territory. The myth is completed with a cyclic return to the East Coast as a cultural and intellectual center for America.

For Spillers, minorities were not central to the settlement of the West, or to the development of American civilization as we know it. But Spillers's argument neglects some very important interchanges between Afro-Americans and "traditional" Americans which, when considered, demonstrate that the growth of America was much more of a dialectical process than of a singularly directed ethnic mythos. This graduate level course will explore that dialectic.

Booklist

Charles Chesnutt, *The House Behind the Cedars*
Kate Chopin, *The Awakening*
Ralph Ellison, *The Invisible Man*
William Faulkner, *Light in August*
F. Scott Fitzgerald, *The Great Gatsby*
Nathaniel Hawthorne, *The Scarlet Letter*
Ernest Hemingway, *The Sun Also Rises*
Zora Neale Hurston, *Their Eyes Were Watching God*
Toni Morrison, *Song of Solomon*
Mark Twain, *The Adventures of Huckleberry Finn*
Richard Wright, *Native Son*

44
MAJOR AUTHORS:
TWENTIETH-CENTURY
AMERICAN FICTION
MEN AND WOMEN WRITERS
Rita K. Gollin
Fall, 1977
State University of New York/College at Geneseo
Geneseo, NY 14454

Course Objectives

This course concentrates on three pairs of twentieth-century American men and women writers, a man and a woman in each pair, with each pair differing from the other two in such matters as their regional identities and concerns, the social classes at the center of their writings, and their narrative methods. We will see how James and Wharton anatomize the upper class society of old New York; how Dreiser and Cather write about the midwest, its pioneers and upwardly mobile individuals; and how Faulkner and Porter write about the south of their immediate experience, the southern past, and the past locked in each individual consciousness. We will study each author separately, and examine each novel, novella, and short story as a separate and unique achievement. But we will also ask whether any of the differences in the fictions of each pair seem related to the author's gender, and which similarities cut across gender. We will consider such issues as the main characters' identities (sexual, social, familial, professional) and their capacity for self-knowledge and self-fulfillment; the author's style, tone, point of view, symbols, and plotting; the central or subordinate role of setting; the date of a story's composition in the context of period taste and the author's career; and the extent to which characters and events seem ordinary or extraordinary. Finally, we will ask to what extent each work—and each writer—transcends the limits of time, place, and gender.

Booklist

Willa Cather, *My Antonia*; *Five Stories*
Theodore Dreiser, *Sister Carrie*; short stories
William Faulkner, *Viking Portable Faulkner*; *As I Lay Dying*
Henry James, *Great Short Works*
Katherine Anne Porter, *Collected Stories*
Edith Wharton, *The Age of Innocence*; *Roman Fever and Other Stories*

Syllabus

Week 1-2   Introduction; Henry James
    3-4   Wharton; exam 1
    5-6   Dreiser; reports on paper 1
    7-8   Cather; exam 2
    9-10   Faulkner
    11-12   Porter
    13   Report on paper 2; conclusions

Papers

There will be two critical/analytical papers, about five to seven type-written pages each (ca. 1200-1500 words), the first at the end of the sixth and the second at the end of the eleventh week of classes. Students will present the central conclusions of their papers to the class (taking about five minutes for each presentation).

Paper I

Choose a volume by a major twentieth-century American writer not on our syllabus—e.g., Saul Bellow, Bernard Malamud, John Updike, Toni Morrison, Anne Tyler, Eudora Welty—and discuss the way each author develops male as contrasted to female characters. Consider, e.g., whether the major characters are male or female, and whether there seems to be a difference in the way authors treat characters of their own gender. You might ask about the characters' goals and attainments, the range of their inner and outer lives, whether they seem nurturing or predatory, innovative or conformist, rebels or victims, what we are asked to admire or condemn, and with whom we are invited to identify.

Paper II

Take a pair of fictions (either two novels or two groups of short stories)—one written by a man and one by a woman—and compare and contrast them, asking (among other questions) whether any differences seem gender related. Suggestions:

Isaac Bashevis Singer and Cynthia Ozick, centering on Jewish traditions and American values; N. Scott Momaday and Leslie Marmon Silko, centering on Native American traditions and "American" values;

F. Scott Fitzgerald's *Tender is the Night* and Zelda Fitzgerald's *Save Me the Waltz*, centering on self-fulfillment and the demands of marriage;

A novel by Caroline Gordon and one by Robert Penn Warren or Allen Tate, centering on individual fulfillment as it conflicts with southern tradition;

Mary McCarthy's *Groves of Academe* and Randall Jarrell's *Pictures from an Institution*, centering on targets of satire;

Ernest Hemingway and Martha Gellhorn, centering on definitions of
  integrity;
James Baldwin's *Go Tell it on the Mountain* and Ann Petry's *The Street*,
  centering on conflicting values within the communities of Harlem.

45
THE AMERICAN NOVEL
June Howard
Fall, 1981
University of Michigan
Ann Arbor, MI 48109

Course Objectives

The novels on this reading list have been chosen to acquaint students
with the tremendous diversity of American novels, including both works
from the canon and works that are less frequently taught and represent a
somewhat greater range of American experience. (My assumption is that
"reconstructing the canon" entails not only adding new works but
approaching the established works from a new perspective.) Despite their
diversity these novels do raise some common concerns; the twentieth-
century works, particularly, have been chosen not only because they are
interesting and important in themselves but because they lend themselves to
provocative thematic and formal comparisons.

The question most persistently raised is the novels' definition of
"America" and what it means to be "American." This is a question that can
engage students very deeply, for it bears on their own beliefs and values.
This class enrolls students with widely varying amounts of experience
reading literature, including some with relatively little preparation, and a
considerable amount of class time is spent discussing fundamental, fairly
traditional questions about how to read the texts; but we also engage the
works as contributions to a living, lively tradition which is our own. On the
basis of this list one can discuss the familiar yet still fruitful topics of the
American aspiration toward community and its frequent frustration, the
utopian impulse, social criticism, ambivalence toward the machine, the
metaphysical and social implications of selfhood and freedom, the American
dream and its betrayal. One can also discuss how these topics are seen
differently from the perspectives of Black Americans and white women, the
significance of dissonant elements in the novels, the effects of innovative
forms—and many other specific, sometimes startling similarities and oppo-

sitions which emerge from examining the novels (for example, it proves fascinating to juxtapose *Moby-Dick* and *Surfacing*).

The class enrolls fifty to sixty students. One of the three weekly class meetings is a lecture; the rest are discussions, including some meetings in which about twenty minutes are spent in groups of four to five students discussing a particular question (groups' conclusions are then reported back to the whole class). The written assignments are ten one-page papers on assigned topics, a five- to six-page paper on a topic of the students' choice, and a final. The brief papers are assigned orally in class and are due during discussion of the novel they address (no late papers accepted); they are required, but not graded. The purpose of these papers is to provide an incentive to attend class regularly, to keep up with the reading, and to initiate reflection on topics that will be taken up in class and thus improve the quality of discussion (at which, by the way, they are very successful). The longer paper provides an opportunity for the student to consider at greater length an issue of particular interest. The final, done at home over the period of a week, asks the student to explicate selected passages from the texts and through these brief essays to demonstrate an understanding of the novels and the themes of the course as a whole.

Obviously there are many novels I would like to include on this list if there were more weeks in the semester. I do distribute a list of suggestions for further reading. Other books that would fit well into this list and that I have taught successfully in this course or seriously considered using include: James Fenimore Cooper, *The Pioneers*; Nathaniel Hawthorne, *The Blithedale Romance* (instead of *The Scarlet Letter*); Harriet Beecher Stowe, *Uncle Tom's Cabin*; Edward Bellamy, *Looking Backward 2000–1887*; Kate Chopin, *The Awakening*; Edith Wharton, *The House of Mirth*; Theodore Dreiser, *Sister Carrie*; Willa Cather, *My Antonia*; Harriette Arnow, *The Dollmaker*; Ishmael Reed, *Yellow Back Radio Broke-Down*; Philip K. Dick, *Ubik*; Maxine Hong Kingston, *The Woman Warrior*.

Syllabus and Reading List

Week 1	Introduction
2	Nathaniel Hawthorne, *The Scarlet Letter* (1850)
3–4	Herman Melville, *Moby-Dick* (1851)
5	Mark Twain, *The Adventures of Huckleberry Finn* (1884)
6	Henry James, *The Portrait of a Lady* (1881)
7	Frank Norris, *The Octopus* (1901)
8	F. Scott Fitzgerald, *The Great Gatsby* (1925)
9	William Faulkner, *As I Lay Dying* (1930)
10	Toni Morrison, *The Bluest Eye* (1970)
11	Norman Mailer, *The Armies of the Night* (1968)
12	Margaret Atwood, *Surfacing* (1972)
13	Joanna Russ, *The Female Man* (1975); if unavailable, Marge Piercy, *Woman on the Edge of Time* (1976)

46
MALE AND FEMALE TRADITIONS IN AMERICAN FICTION
Carolyn L. Karcher
Proposal, 1982
Temple University
Philadelphia, PA 19122

Catalogue Description

Do men and women writers perceive social reality in the same ways? Do they use the same myths, archetypes, and literary conventions? Or do women writers sometimes have to modify the myths, archetypes, and literary conventions originated by their male precursors in order to adapt them to female experience? Might there be such a thing as a distinctively female imagination, with a symbolic language of its own? This course will attempt to answer such questions by comparing and contrasting pairs of tales and novels by men and women in the following literary modes: the supernatural tale, the realistic sketch, the historical romance, the novel of manners, the naturalist novel, the novel of black experience. Writers will be chosen from a pool that includes, among males, Washington Irving, Nathaniel Hawthorne, Herman Melville, Henry James, Upton Sinclair, David Bradley; among females, Lydia Maria Child, Harriet Beecher Stowe, Rebecca Harding Davis, Edith Wharton, Harriet Arnow, Toni Morrison.

Rationale

In the process of rediscovering forgotten women writers, feminist critics have come to recognize the need for a new body of literary theory that would apply to women as well as to men, or that would indicate wherein women's writings are distinctive. For example, when we include writers like Harriet Beecher Stowe, Sarah Orne Jewett, Mary Wilkins Freeman, Kate Chopin, Edith Wharton, Willa Cather, and Zora Neale Hurston in our definitions of American literature, it becomes apparent that we must revise those definitions; for we can no longer maintain, as did Richard Chase, R. W. B. Lewis, and Leslie Fiedler, that the American novel has a tendency to "ignore the spectacle of man in society," to concern itself with moral rather than social conflicts, to situate itself in the natural world rather than in the drawing room, and to substitute male camaraderie and man's struggle with nature for the novel's traditional themes: marriage and adultery. Clearly, women's fiction could not take this form, because most women simply could not escape society by going to sea or lighting out for the wilderness. Instead, the society to which they were confined became their chief subject.

The first decade or so of feminist criticism was oriented primarily toward reconstructing a separate female tradition—a chain of literary influences linking women writers of several continents to each other; exploring themes, images, and symbols that seemed typical of women's writings; and analyzing women's strategies for coping with the anxieties of authorship. Recently, however, feminist critics have begun to test their new theories by making systematic comparisons between male and female writers. I find this line of inquiry particularly promising, because it lays the groundwork for eventually reintegrating feminist criticism into the mainstream and evolving a richer and more inclusive theory of American literature.

The course I propose would contribute directly to this scholarly enterprise. Not only would it allow advanced students to re-examine their assumptions about American literature by making systematic comparisons between male and female writers; it would also encourage them to develop collectively a theory of American literature that could encompass a wider spectrum of writers, both male and female.

Methodology

In the first week of the course, I will familiarize students with the theories of American literature formulated by Richard Chase, Leslie Fiedler, R.W.B. Lewis, F.O. Matthiessen, and others, as well as with those put forward by feminist critics like Ellen Moers, Patricia Meyers Spacks, Annette Kolodny, Nina Baym, Jane Tomkins, Sandra Gilbert, and Susan Gubar. I will also introduce them to the concepts and tools they will need to read both male and female writers intelligently.

Thereafter the class will read pairs of short stories or novels by men and women, first taking on each work on its own terms and then analyzing it in relation to its counterpart and looking for similarities and differences. Frequent quizzes will help refine the students' analytical abilities by presenting them with passages from the works to identify and explicate. Class discussions will be supplemented by short lectures providing biographical and historical background on the assigned writers and the issues they fictionalize.

Reading List

The reading list is still tentative. The works are paired according to theme and literary mode. In order to make the comparison of male and female writers as broad as possible, I have chosen representatives of six different modes or genres.

Irving, "Rip Van Winkle"
Child, "Hilda Silfverling"
    —supernatural tales whose protagonists fall asleep in one time period
    and reawaken in another
Hawthorne, *The Scarlet Letter*
Stowe, *The Minister's Wooing*
    —historical romances set in the Puritan past and reassessing the
    Calvinist legacy from a nineteenth-century romantic perspective
Melville, "The Paradise of Bachelors and The Tartarus of Maids"
Davis, "Life in the Iron Mills"
    —sketches of factory life, in which each author focuses on workers of
    the opposite sex, entering imaginatively into their deprivations
James, *The Wings of the Dove*
Wharton, *The House of Mirth*
    —novels of manners, exploring the dilemma of a woman forced to
    marry for money, but from different points of view (I may choose a
    shorter James work)
Sinclair, *The Jungle*
Arnow, *The Dollmaker*
    —powerful naturalist novels depicting the disintegration of rural
    families migrating to the city, and exposing the corruption of the
    industrial system
Bradley, *The Chaneysville Incident*
Morrison, *Song of Solomon*
    —novels about the quest for identity and origins of a northern
    middle-class black protagonist OR
Richard Wright, *Native Son*
Zora Neale Hurston, *Their Eyes Were Watching God*
    —urban and rural black novels presenting diametrically opposite views
    of black culture (Wright reviewed Hurston's novel and attacked it for
    presenting too positive a view, thus implicitly denying black
    oppression)

47
THE CONTEMPORARY AMERICAN NOVEL
John M. Reilly
Fall, 1981
State University of New York
Albany, NY 12222

Course Objectives

This course is intended to consider important developments in contemporary American fiction. Among the obvious, most apparent developments are these: the appearance of writing that uses the experiences of sub-cultures generally ignored in early American writing (can you name an American Indian writer published in the 1920s? how many Jewish-American writers achieved wide readership before the late 1950s? name a black writer of fiction before Richard Wright); attacks on the premises of "realism" (why do we accept the idea that a story is about something outside the words on the page? is there a value perhaps in dropping the convention that a story begins at the chronological beginning, or that a reader should always know what is going on?); an attempt to employ new concepts of reality (if a writer accepts the validity of modern theoretical physics would that affect the way a story is written? do new social theories or philosophical practices issue in new ways to look at life? if so, what does one do about a literary form—the novel—that was formed back in the eighteenth century?).

Underlying my selection of texts for this course and directing my conduct of class discussions is an attempt to reconcile critical motives often thought to be in conflict. The first is the ethical desire to see literature work to enlighten an audience, perhaps to fight oppression. This is associated, of course, with the idea that art might change the world, and it ordinarily leads us to conceive of our teaching as at least partially political. The second motive is to engender appreciation of craft, which typically results in our concentrating on writers' ability to solve technical problems effectively. As academicians say, this is treating literature as literature. The political approach resulting from the ethical motive and the formalism following from the second often seem to be incompatible, especially if one or the other becomes the sole basis for teaching practice. As motives, however, we know they must relate, if only we can find the theory to link our belief in the political effects of literature with our fondness for the technical skill of craft.

This theory can be found, the motives reconciled, by attention to writers' reconstruction of genre. Genres are historical formations created to serve as templates for the way a group understands reality; thus, the realistic fiction with which our students are most familiar is informed by the empirical outlook of western culture (bourgeois and capitalist). Art, realism says, imitates familiar reality; what appears in conventional narrative exists, what is omitted does not exist. Suppose, however, that a Native American writer like Leslie Marmon Silko needs to assert the experience of fluid identity, or a Black American writer like Toni Morrison wishes to reanimate a folktale. The conventions of realistic fiction make no provision for those experiments. The writers must reconstruct the genre to accomodate their purposes. By repudiating old conventions and by advancing new technical solutions to the problems of narration, these writers provide a critique of the realistic model of consciousness. That is a political act we can present to satisfy the ethical motive for our teaching. At the same time it is an experiment in craft that we can explicate as a fully literary act.

Each time I teach "Contemporary American Novel" I replace some texts, but the choices I make are guided by the intention to help students understand the books they read as literary acts in the making of contemporary American history.

Booklist

Robert Coover, *The Universal Baseball Association*
John Gardner, *Grendel*
Ursula LeGuin, *The Left Hand of Darkness*
Clarence Major, *Reflex and Bone Structure*
Toni Morrison, *Song of Solomon*
Joyce Carol Oates, *Them*
Philip Roth, *The Ghost Writer*
Leslie Silko, *Ceremony*
Kurt Vonnegut, *Cat's Cradle*
Alice Walker, *Meridian*

48
TWENTIETH-CENTURY NOVELS
BY AMERICAN WOMEN
Patricia Sharpe
1981
University of Michigan Law School
Ann Arbor, MI 48109

Course Objectives

The course requirements and structure were, in large part, a response to smothering success. Typically, this course enrolled seventy-five to eighty students with a wide range of abilities and expertise. This precluded the ideal format (small class or seminar) for a course whose material often was disturbing and personally unsettling as well as thought-provoking to students. The use of frequent short writing assignments, required on a schedule to encourage students to keep up with the reading, was designed to assure an interaction even in a lecture course. These assignments were read by course assistants who were to commend students for use of detail and thoughtful exploration of issues, as well as to identify any who might have difficulty writing an acceptable term paper.

The discussion sections and frequent writing assignments were also intended to get the students involved actively in thinking about the material. The term papers were comparative because I wished to push them beyond consideration of any one novel into a more theoretical interpretation.

The reading list for the course was heavy, since my priority was to convince the students that women have written many wonderful books that one seldom hears about in the standard curriculum. The selections I offer here are somewhat arbitrary in that I can think of many other possibilities. I would like to use Gayle Jones's *Corregidora* but it has been out-of-print for several years. Gertrude Stein's *Ida* is another possibility; I would also consider a children's book that appeals particularly to girls, like Burnett's *The Secret Garden*.

Taken together, the novels should provide instances for discussing as many of the questions currently being debated by feminist scholars as possible. The list I propose would allow for discussion of the interaction of gender and genre, women's anxiety of authorship, women's psychological development and its effect on the plots women authors conceive, women's story-telling, creativity and procreativity as modes of defying prevailing ideology, the intersections of race, class and gender as well as the parallels women writers draw between patriarchy and American idealist imperialism. The course deals with women's internalization of cultural norms and the difficulty of resisting a masculinist ideology in a language and a literary

tradition that veil the masculine with an illusion of ungendered neutrality
and universality. By stressing recurring patterns and concerns in the novels,
I tried to draw the students' attention to the kinds of critical overviews one
might take, thus laying the groundwork for their selection of a term paper
topic.

Syllabus and Booklist

Week 1   Kate Chopin, *The Awakening*
   2   Ellen Glasgow, *Barren Ground*
   3   Edith Wharton, *The House of Mirth*
   4   Zora Neale Hurston, *Their Eyes Were Watching God*
   5   Willa Cather, *The Song of the Lark*
   6   Christina Stead, *The Man Who Loved Children*
   7   Carson McCullers, *The Member of the Wedding* and *Ballad
      of the Sad Cafe*
   8   Louise Meriwether, *Daddy Was a Numbers Runner*
   9   Sylvia Plath, *The Bell Jar*
  10   Ursula LeGuin, *The Left Hand of Darkness*
  11   Rosellen Brown, *Autobiography of My Mother*
  12   Annette W. Jaffee, *Adult Education, A Novel*
  13   Toni Morrison, *Song of Solomon*

49
THE AMERICAN POLITICAL NOVEL
Richard Yarborough
Spring, 1982
University of California
Los Angeles, CA 90024

Course Objectives

This course is a survey of the ways in which politics and specific
political issues have shaped American fiction from the mid-nineteenth
century to the present. As can be seen in any cursory glance at critical
attempts to determine just what a "political novel" is, the term is difficult to
define and useful more as a focusing aid than as a clearly demarcated

category. Accordingly, in this course I attempt to cover as many different types of political fiction as possible. I assign bestsellers as well as less popular novels, works of fantasy as well as thinly veiled renderings of contemporaneous historical events, "propagandistic" works as well as novels in which the writer is apparently not concerned with advocating a particular ideology. Political fiction also includes many different schools of writing: satires, utopias, historical romances, novels of sentiment, and postmodern, experimental works.

This course is useful to history and political science students because it examines one of the most powerful ways in which the average American is exposed to ideology. It is also valuable to English majors both because it covers works that are frequently considered to lie outside the mainstream of "classic" American fiction and also because it emphasizes that works of literature are grounded in specific sociohistorical contexts.

Books can be selected for this course according to a number of criteria. For instance, I have consistently begun my reading list with Harriet Beecher Stowe's *Uncle Tom's Cabin* not just because it is probably the singly most influential political novel ever published in this country but because it raises important racial and feminist issues, many of which have continued to concern American novelists. I teach Thomas Dixon's *The Clansman* and Charles Chesnutt's *The Marrow of Tradition* not only to present two radically opposed views of an important issue at the turn of the century but to suggest to the student that the connection between a novel's literary "quality" and its efficacy as a political weapon is extremely complex.

In the future, I will continue to diversify the texts of this course. One problem is that some of the more well-known political novels are simply too long for the ten-week quarter; Ayn Rand's *The Fountainhead*, Alan Drury's *Advise and Consent*, and Theodore Dreiser's *An American Tragedy* are three examples. Further, many works that deal explicity with political issues are rarely taught and, consequently, unavailable in paperback editions. There are, however, a number of books currently in print that I plan to teach in the near future: John Okada's *No-No Boy*, Norman Mailer's *Why Are We in Vietnam?*, Mark Twain's *A Connecticut Yankee in King Arthur's Court*, Mari Sandoz's *Capitol City*, William Lederer and Eugene Burdick's *The Ugly American*, Ayn Rand's *Anthem*, Richard Wright's *The Outsider*, and Henry Adam's *Democracy*, among others.

In other terms I have used Charlotte Perkins Gilman's *Herland* instead of Edward Bellamy, John Steinbeck's *In Dubious Battle*, Ann Petry's *The Street*, Ralph Ellison's *Invisible Man*, and Ernest J. Gaines's *The Autobiography of Miss Jane Pittman*.

Booklist

Class 1   Introduction
    2–8   Harriet Beecher Stowe, *Uncle Tom's Cabin*

9–11   Edward Bellamy, *Looking Backward*
12–15   Thomas Dixon, *The Clansman*
16–19   Charles W. Chesnutt, *The Marrow of Tradition*
20   Midterm
21–24   Sinclair Lewis, *It Can't Happen Here*
25–29   Richard Wright, *Native Son*
30–34   E. L. Doctorow, *The Book of Daniel*
35–39   Alice Walker, *Meridian*

Thematic Courses

Immigrant, Ethnic, and Minority Writing

50
THE IMMIGRANT EXPERIENCE
Edith Blicksilver (English)
Ronald Bayor (History)
Spring, 1981
Georgia Institute of Technology
Atlanta, GA 30332

Course Objectives

This course, offered jointly by the Social Sciences and the English Department, examines the history and the literature of the immigrant, stressing the following aspects: life in the Old World and reasons for emigrating, the passage to America, impressions of the Promised Land, and the problems of assimilation.

Various waves of immigrants are considered, beginning with the Colonial Period and including the twentieth century, in an effort to analyze the experience of being uprooted. The different concepts of the Melting Pot are studied through some personal testimonies of immigrant writers and historical literature. In addition, reactions to the immigrants with America's cycles of bigotry and restrictive immigration policy are interpreted.

Guests representing recently arrived Americans will visit the classroom, and a documentary film about immigrant problems will be viewed. Oral reports, a midterm and a final are required, in addition to a term paper reflecting individual interests. Prerequisite: consent of the departments.

Booklist

History
Ronald Bayor, *Neighbors in Conflict*

David Colburn and George Pozzetta, *America and the New Ethnicity*
Thomas Sowell, "Myths About Minorities," *Commentary*, August, 1979

English
Edith Blicksilver, ed., *The Ethnic American Woman: Problems, Protests,
    Lifestyles*
Lillian Faderman and Barbara Bradshaw, eds., *Speaking for Ourselves*
Edward Ifkovic, ed., *American Letter: Immigrant and Ethnic Writing*
Thomas C. Wheeler, ed., *The Immigrant Experience*

Syllabus: History

Week 1	Theories of Assimilation; Immigration During the Colonial Era. Sowell, "Myths About Minorities"
2	The Colonial Era: Voluntary and Involuntary Immigration. Colburn and Pozzetta, "Power, Racism, and Privilege"
3	The Irish: Adjustment and Nativism. Colburn and Pozzetta, "The Lasting Hurrah"
4	German Immigration: Assimilation and the World Wars. Bayor, chaps. 4, 6
5	The Asian Experience. Colburn and Pozzetta, "Japanese Americans on the Road to Dissent"
6	The Three Waves of Jewish Immigration. Bayor, all other chaps.
7	Southern and Eastern Europeans. Colburn and Pozzetta, "Risorgimento: The Red, White and Greening of New York," and "Polish America's Relations with the Rest of American Society"
8	The Hispanic Community. Colburn and Pozzetta, "Mexican Americans," "Right on With the Young Lords"
9	America Today and the Immigrant Experience. Colburn and Pozzetta, "The New Ethnicity," "Why Ethnicity," and all of section 4

Syllabus: English

Week 1–2	We will be discussing America's first immigrants, the English, Scotch-Irish, and Blacks—both the voluntary and involuntary immigrants. The topics for this unit and for the others will include life in the Old World, reasons for emigrating, adjustment to America, assimilation,

family life, love relationships, the generation gap, discrimination, and so forth. Doras Reed Benbow, "My Grandmother the Wasp" (English-American); Anne Webster, "My Father's War" (English-American); Avril Sutin, "No Problems, or Protests: I Like the Lifestyle" (English-American); select *five* works from those listed under "The Black Woman" in Appendix B (Blicksilver); "Introduction" to "Black American Writers" (Faderman and Bradshaw).

Additional readings (some will be discussed in class or assigned out-of-class, sometimes hand-out sheets will be used; some works will be used for oral/written reports): Dick Gregory, "America Was Momma's Momma" (Black-American); Langston Hughes, "Epilogue" (Black-American); Nathaniel Hawthorne, "Young Goodman Brown" (Puritan-American); William Bradford, "Of Plimouth Plantation" (English-American); Countee Cullen, "Incident" (Black-American); Charles W. Chesnutt, "The Sheriff's Children" (Black-American); Dudley Randall, "The Melting Pot" (Black-American); Alex Haley, "My Furthest-Back-Person 'The African' " (Black-American, Ifkovic); John A. Williams, "Roots of Black Awareness" (Black-American, Wheeler); Paul Laurence Dunbar, "We Wear the Mask" (Black-American, Faderman and Bradshaw

3   The Scandanavians: Theodore C. Blegen, "Room Here for All" (Norwegian-American, Ifkovic); Eugene Boe, 'Pioneers to Eternity" (Norwegian-American); H. Arnold Barton, "Two Letters from Swedish-American Women" (Swedish-American); Dorothy Burton Skardal, "The Norwegian-American Immigrant Girl and Morality" (Norwegian-American); May Swenson, "Things in Common" (Swedish-American); Thelma Jones, "My Norwegian-American Parents' Courtship" (Norwegian-American); Borghild Dahl, "Grandmother Skoglund's Advice to Lyng and the University Experience" (Norwegian-American, Wheeler)

4   The Irish, Germans: William Shannon, "The American Irish" (Irish-American); William Alfred, "Pride and Poverty" (Irish-American, Ifkovic); James T. Farrell, "The Oratory Contest" from *Studs Lonigan* (Irish-American, Faderman and Bradshaw); Peter Finley Dunne, "Mr. Dooley on the Anglo-Saxon" (Irish-American); Elizabeth Cullinan, "The Power of Prayer" (Irish-American); Betty Smith, "The Ethnic Child and the Classroom Experience" (Irish-American); Mary McCarthy, "To The Reader" (Irish-American); Lisel

Mueller, "The Cremona Violin," "More Light" (German-American); Heidi Rockwood, "The Best of Two Worlds" (German-American); Phyllis Scherle, "A Trace of Gold" (German-American); Sharon Renée Twombly, "Ethnicity to Humanity" (German-American, Ifkovic)

5   The Asian-Americans: Lin Yutang, "A Chinatown Family" (Chinese-American, Ifkovic or Faderman); Toshio Mori, "Slant-Eyed Americans" (Japanese-American); Ted Nakashima, "Concentration Camp: U.S. Style" (Japanese-American, Ifkovic); Jade Snow Wong, "Puritans from the Orient" (Chinese-American, Blicksilver and Wheeler); Robert Eng Dunne, "China of America" (Chinese-American, Ifkovic); Frank Chin, "Confessions of a Number One Son" (Chinese-American); Ferris Takahashi, "The Widower" (Japanese-American) Lee Yu-Hwa, "The Last Rite" (Chinese-American); Taruka Ogata Daniel, "Such, such were the Joys...George Orwell," "We Wise Children" (Japanese-American); Maxine Hong Kingston, "No Name Woman" (Chinese-American); Jeanne Wakatsuki Houstin, "Whatever He Did Had Flourish" (Japanese-American); Edith Maud Eaton [Sui Sin Far], "Mental Portfolio of an Eurasian"; Hisaye Yamamoto, "The Legend of Miss Sasagawara" (Japanese-American); Janet Mirikitani, "Lullabye," "Sing With Your Body" (Japanese-American); Rowena Wildin, "Children" (Japanese-American); Diana Chang, "An Appearance of Being Chinese" and two poems: "Saying Yes" and "Otherness" (Chinese-American); Ferris Takahashi, "Nisei, Nisei!" (Japanese-American, Faderman and Bradshaw)

6-7   Russian-American, Polish-American, Eastern European Jews and Others: Emma Lazarus, "The New Colossus" (Russian/Jewish-American); Philip Roth, "Eli the Fanatic" (Jewish-American); Konrad Berkovici, "Ghitza" (Roumanian-American); William I. Thomas and Florian Znaniecki, "Letters of the Polish Peasant"; Abraham Cahan, "I Lose My Mother" (Russian/Jewish-American); Henry Roth, "Prologue" to *Call It Sleep* (Russian/Jewish-American); Leslie A. Fiedler, "Negro and Jew: Encounter in America" (Ifkovic); Harry Roskolenko, "A Jewish Search for Freedom" (Russian/Jewish-American, Wheeler); Czeslaw Milosz, "A Polish Poet in California"; Isaac Bashevis Singer, "The Little Shoemakers" (Polish/Jewish-American); Karl Shapiro, "University" (Jewish-American); Richard Bankovsky, from *After Pentacost* (Polish-American);

Marya Zaturenska, "A Russian Easter" (Russian-American); Rhoda Schwartz, "Dark Moon," "Old Photographs" (Russian/Jewish-American, Faderman and Bradshaw)

7   Jewish-Americans: Jewish-American Woman, all items (Blicksilver). Polish-Americans: Monica Krawczyk, "For Dimes and Quarters"; Sister M. Florence Tumasz, "Growing up as a Polish-American" (Blicksilver). Slavic-Americans: listed under Russian-American Woman, all items (Blicksilver)

8–9   Mediterranean Immigrants—Italians, Greeks, Hispanic-Americans: Mario Puzo, "Amerigo Bonasera" from *The Godfather* (Italian-American, Ifkovic), "Italians in Hell's Kitchen" from *Choosing A Dream* (Wheeler); John Ciardi, "Letter to Mother," "Elegy" (Italian-American); Donald DeLillo, "Take the 'A' Train" (Italian-American, Ifkovic); Harry Petrakis, "The Wooing of Ariadne" (Greek-American); Pietro di Donato, from *Chirst in Concrete* (Italian-American); Gregory Corso, "Birth place Revisited," "Uccello" (Italian-American, Faderman and Bradshaw); Jack Agueros, "A Puerto Rican Pilgrimage" from *Halfway to Dick and Jane* (Wheeler); O.W. Firkins, "To a Greek Bootblack" (Hispanic-American); Carlos Bulosan, "America is in the Heart" (Hispanic-American); Oscar Lewis, "Simplicio: I'm Proud to be Poor" (Hispanic-American); Amado Muro, "Cecilia Rosas" (Hispanic-American); Victor Hernandez Cruz, "Going Uptown to Visit Miriam" (Hispanic-American, Ifkovic); Prudencio de Pereda, "Conquistador" (Hispanic-American); Emilio Diaz Valcárel, "Damián Sánchez, G.I." (Hispanic-American); Piri Thomas, "Alien Turf" from *Down These Mean Streets* (Hispanic-American), Omar Salinas from "Aztec Angel" (Hispanic-American, Faderman and Bradshaw); Filipina-American, Chicano, Puerto Rican-American, Greek-American, Italian-American—all sections (Blicksilver)

51
THIRD WORLD WOMEN WRITERS IN THE UNITED STATES
Roberta Fernández
Spring, 1983
Smith College
Northampton, MA 01063

Course Objectives

This course was originally offered as "Bay Area Ethnic Women Writers" at Mills College through the Department of Ethnic Studies in the Fall of 1980. The course was a positive reaction to an initial anger I experienced when attending a festival of literature written by women in Northern California. At that particular three-day event, at which dozens of women read, only a handful of ethnic minority women had been invited to partipate. I decided to create a course dealing with the literature of contemporary ethnic women writers in the Bay Area in which their literature would be approached comparatively based on the particular group experiences that had shaped the present state of creativity in the Third World community. For this reason, texts selected were mainly published by small presses in the San Francisco Bay Area. When I came East I enlarged the scope of the course and discovered that "Ethnic Women Writers" had a different connotation on the East Coast than it had on the West Coast, where Ethnic Studies Departments deal with the history and culture of Asian-American, Black, Chicano/Latino, and Native American peoples. The course was retitled but I am quite aware of an ambiguity in terminology which I feel reflects the present state of reaction by mainstream society to people of color in the United States as well as our own present process as we begin to truly interact with one another in a comparison of commonalities and an understanding of our differences.

In presenting the literature of relatively new writers I also discovered a lack of literary criticism dealing with individual writers, particularly from a comparative approach. For this reason I have been interviewing the writers for a book-length study that will focus on the search for a correspondence of content and form, based on a cultural context. I believe that this search for new forms is greatly enchancing the corpus of American literature.

The course itself is an exploration of contemporary works by women of color living in the United States. Themes that are covered are the following: cultural indentifications, celebrations and rituals, the role of the oral tradition and its transmission and transformation in written works, stylistic innovations, the use of language, women as individuals and as members of a community, Third World feminism.

Booklist

Dexter Fisher, ed., *The Third Woman: Minority Women Writers in the United States* (Boston: Houghton Mifflin, 1980)
Gloria Anzaldúa and Cherríe Moraga, eds., *This Bridge Called My Back: Writings by Radical Women of Color* (Watertown, MA: Persephone Press, 1981)

Individual Authors (in order of presentation):
Maya Angelou, *I Know Why the Caged Bird Sings* (New York: Bantam, 1980)
Ntozake Shange, *For Colored Girls Who Have Considered Suicide/When the Rainbow is Enuf* (New York: Bantam, 1980)
———, *Nappy Edges* (New York: St. Martin's Press, 1978)
Leslie Silko, *Ceremony* (New York: Viking/Penguin, 1977)
Wendy Rose, *Lost Copper* (Banning, CA: Malki Museum Press, Morongo Indian Reservation, 1980)
Lucha Corpi, *Palabras de mediodía/Noon Words* (Berkeley: Fuego de Aztlan Publications, 1980)
Barbara Brinson Pineda, *Nocturno* (Berkeley: Fuego de Aztlan Publications, 1979)
Lorna Dee Cervantes, *Emplumada* (Pittsburg: University of Pittsburg Press, 1981)
Jessica Tarahata Hagedorn, *Dangerous Music* (San Fransisco: Momo's Press, P.O. Box 14061, 1978)
Nina Serrano, *Heart Songs* (San Fransisco: Pocho Che Publications, 1980)
Nicholasa Mohr, *In Nueva York* (New York: Dial Press, 1977)
Maxine Hong Kingston, *The Woman Warrior* (New York: Vintage, 1977)

Secondary Sources
Barbara Christian, *Black Woman Novelists* (Westport, CT: Greenwood, 1980)
Elaine Kim, *Asian American Literature* (Philadelphia: Temple, 1982)
Beth Miller, ed., *Women in Hispanic Literature* (Berkeley: University of California, 1983)

Syllabus

Black Women Writers:
1. Presentation on Black women writers, the literature of Black nationalism, the development of a Black aesthetic: themes, style, language. Introduction to Maya Angelou and the autobiography of the Black woman: *I Know Why the Caged Bird Sings.* Topics to be covered: the rural community as a character, the education of a young girl, the role of literature in the formation of Maya Angelou's girlhood, the role of race relations in the book

with a particular focus on the presentation of white women's racism. Who is the writer's audience? How does this affect her style? What are the particular resources in her rural community that shape Maya Angelou's perspective?

2. Video-tape of Maya Angelou at the University of Massachusetts. Discussion of her comments, particularly on the role of Black popular music and the "troubadours" as these shaped her relationship to language.

3. Poetry by Black women in *The Third Woman*. What are their themes? What style(s) are used? How are Black aesthetics shaping some of the poems? Focus on three themes: Writers writing about writing; The transmission of women's culture; The Black woman as individual and as member of a community. Comparison of the thematics and style of the poetry with Maya Angelou's autobiography. (Handout of Andrea Rushing article on Ntozake Shange's *For Colored Girls...*)

4. Record of *For Colored Girls Who Have Considered Suicide/When the Rainbow Is Enuf*. Follow text in class.

5. Class discussion of Ntozake Shange's *For Colored Girls* in the context of her own comments as expressed in the essays of *Nappy Edges*. Presentation of the San Francisco Bay Area Third World aesthetics from which *For Colored Girls* developed. Contrast of the urban experience with the rural experience: the role of place in the shaping of a writer's development. What are the historical differences that shaped Angelou and Shange? Critique of the Rushing article. Reports due on *Nappy Edges*.

6. Continuation of reports by a group of four students. Each student is taking a section of *Nappy Edges* and selecting one or several poems that are representative of the section. Short paper on Shange due.

7. A close reading of selected poems in *Nappy Edges* which indicate the attention that the author has given to structure both in individual works and in the presentation of the book. Particular attention is paid to the feminist poems. Introduction of the concept of Third World feminism.

Native American Women Writers:
1. Introduction to Native American writers: the historical milestones. Native American cosmology: the circular view of the world, the rhythms in the universe, cycles, inherent positive views of the universe, the myths of creation, regeneration, duality. The role of the oral tradition. *Visuals:* the landscape and Indian peoples.

2. Thematics and style in the poetry of Native American women in *The Third Woman*. Reports: students select representative poems. (Most classes tend to choose the same poems: "Thomas Ironeyes" by Marnie Walsh, "Grandmother" by Paula Gunn Allen, "Iridescent Child" by Nia Francisco and "Where Mountain Lion Lay Down with Deer" by Leslie Silko—very good choices.)

3. Introduction to Leslie Silko's *Ceremony*: a close reading of the opening passages. The role of the myth of regeneration. The cyclical structure. The non-Western interpretation of literature that does not make a distinction between prose and poetry—how this affects the style and corresponds to the content of the novel.

4. Continuation of *Ceremony:* themes of sickness and the loss of balance; the role of evil and the forces of evil; the necessity of adaptation to a new reality; the blending of races as a thematic unity: the "half-breeds" and the new race of cattle; survival. A close reading of passages that deal with that ceremony Tayo must undergo in order to cleanse himself. Connection of the myth of regeneration with Tayo's regeneration. Correspondence of style and content, the cycles, the completion of the ceremony.

5. The forces of evil and the introduction of the atomic bomb, which makes all people one again. Silko's political themes. Comparision of "Storyteller," from *The Third Woman*, to *Ceremony:* What thematics and stylistic devices does Silko use in both stories? How do the correspondences between theme and style stem from a particuarly Native American perspective? How do the flashbacks within flashbacks and flashforwards within flashbacks stem from the Native American perspective rather than from the Western concept of fragmentation of time?

6. Summary of Silko's work. Selected poetry of Wendy Rose. (Students have been given a list of the specific poems to be discussed.) Comparison of a Leslie Silko with a Maya Angelou (writers with a strong sense of their own culture as developed in a particular geographic area) and a contrast/comparison of a Ntozake Shange with a Wendy Rose (writers who have experienced the urban diffusion of culture). Particular attention paid to the different expressions used to present the theme of cultural diffusion. Rose's attention to the craft of poetry: imagery and inner rime.

7. Wendy Rose: Last section of *Lost Copper:* the journey and resolution through poetry. Particular attention paid to the role of creativity as a resolution for the conflicts the writers experience. Summary and comparison/contrast between Black and Native American women writers. Midterm due.

Chicana/Latina Women Writers:
1. Introduction to the Chicana/Latina writers. *Definition of terms:* Mexican American, Chicana, Mexicana, Hispana, Hispanic, Latina, Puerto Rican, Boricua. *Historical presentation:* a) The Mexicans living in Aztlán prior to 1848; b) The Great Migratory Wave of 1910-1917; c) The more recent immigrants: Mexican, Cuban, Puerto Rican, Salvadoran, other Central Americans. Development of a literature in Spanish that parallels the development of a literature in English on the Eastern seaboard. "The Burning," story by Estela Portillo in *The Third Woman*. A story situated in the Southwest. Make connections with Native American culture.

2. Thematics and style in the poetry of Chicanas as presented in *The Third Woman*. Reports due (student selections: Ana Castillo, Sylvia Gonzalez, Estela Portillo; the use of bilingual style; dealing with basics; the sense of history and double conquest; anger in the works of these writers.)

3. The California poets: Lucha Corpi and Barbara Brinson Pineda. Corpi (Mexican born, the writer in self exile): *Palabras de Mediodía/Noon Words*.
The Marina poems: Giving voice to the mother of the race—

"Solario nocturno"/"Nocturnal Sunscape," "Emily Dickinson,"
"Como la semilla en espera"/"Like the Seed that Waits,"
"Quedarse quieto"/"Keeping Still" (on writing)

Barbara Brinson Pineda (third generation Californian): *Nocturno*.
"María la O,"· "Fire," "Tú eres como yo—A Celia Kruse"

4. The California poets: colonialism and the question of identity; the poetry about the process of writing—wanting to write one way/having to deal with reality.

Lorna Dee Cervantes (fifth generation California Chicana): *Emplumada*.

"The Woman in My Notebook," "Beneath the Shadow of the Freeway," "Poem for the Young White Man Who Asked Me How I, An Intelligent, Well-Read Person, Could Believe in the War between Races," "Visions of Mexico While at a Writing Symposium...," "Uncle's First Rabbit," "For Virginia Chavez," "Refugee Ship," "Oaxaca," "Emplumada"

Jessica Hagedorn (Filipina of Filipino, Spanish, Scottish ancestry): *Dangerous Music*.

"Sorcery," "Something about You," "Souvenirs," "Song for My Father," "Solea," "The Blossoming of Bongbong" (short story)

Nina Serrano (New Yorker, Colombian/Anglo ancestry): *Heart Songs*.

5. Continuation of Cervantes, Hagedorn, Serrano: the question of identity seen by someone who has been colonized—contrasts and contradictions, learning to make adjustments. The *Ars Poetica:* Discussion of the stylistic characteristics in the poetry studied up to this point. What makes this political poetry "poetry"? Expanding and projecting: Characteristics of Third World poetry in the Third World. (Handout of examples to be commented on at a social event). The poetry of the twenty-first century.

6. Two short stories by Nicholasa Mohr (Neuyorican). The immigrant experience. What stylistic similarities does she have with the Chicana writers? Compare her presentation of the immigrant experience with Hagedorn's in "The Blossoming of Bongbong."

7. Film: "Mitsuye and Nellie." (Read their section in *This Bridge Called My Back.*) Discussion of the Asian American experience as portrayed in the film.

8. *The Bridge Called My Back.* A personalized approach to the book. Open up the discussion with a quote from Mitsuye Yamada, p. 35: "*Their* anger made *me* angry." Relate this statement to reactions which students have had to previous writers read in class. How does society hope that people who have been forced to experience racism will react? Give examples from your own life that point out this unsaid expectation. The entire approach to the book will focus on the fact that indeed there is a theory being presented throughout the texts. Topics to cover: The politics of identity. Specificity. "The danger lies in attempting to deal with oppression purely from a theoretical base." Relate this idea to Lorna Dee Cernvates's "Racism is not intellectual. I cannot reason these scars away." Read the following poems: "The Bridge Poem," "When I Was Growing Up," "He Saw," "I Walk in

the History of My People," and "The Welder." Students' reactions to the poems and to each other. An open discussion dealing with anger, and racism. How to make connections with each other. Specify!

9. Continuation: *The Bridge*. (At least three hours are needed to deal with the issues and feelings.) Topics to cover: Individual responsibility to transform the system (p. 79). Learning to take our differences and make them strengths (p. 99). Third World feminism (p. 142). Writing directly and immediately—be specific (p. 170). Identity politics (p. 212). Conclusion: the specific theory stemming from this book.

10. Extra class/social/dinner. Very important that this gathering takes place in a warm atmosphere, with good food. Class listens to tapes of writers reading from their own works: Cervantes, Corpi, Hagedorn. Comments on handouts of Third World poetry from the Caribbean, Latin America, and Africa. Resolutions.

Asian American Women Writers:

1. Historical introduction. "Asian American" as an umbrella term. Historical differences for each group. Make connections with Asian American writers we have already read: Jessica Hagedorn, Nellie Wong, Merle Woo, Mitsuye Yamada. Thematics and style in the poetry of Asian American women as presented in *The Third Woman*: Diana Chang, Janice Mirikitani, Geraldine Kudaka, and Fay Chiang. Reports due. (Handout of questions/study guide for each one of the stories in *The Woman Warrior*.)

2. *The Woman Warrior*: "No Name Woman" and "White Tigers." Generally, focus discussion on the set of questions students have thought about as they read the work.

3. *The Woman Warrior*: "Shaman" and "At the Western Palace."

4. *The Woman Warrior*: "At the Western Palace" and "Song for a Barbarian Reed Pipe." Present the closing passage of the book as a metaphor for writing by Third World women writers in the United States. Summary of class. Pass out final take-home exams.

52
BLACK AND ETHNIC LITERATURE
Jean Allen Hanawalt
Fall, 1981
Seattle Pacific University
Seattle, WA 98119

Course Objectives

"Black and Ethnic Literature" explores the literature of the minority experience in the United States, whether the minority be racial, religious, or "ethnic." The student should gain a familiarity with the group of writers and representative works, develop critical understandings of the literature and its relation to a particularized American experience, and increase his/her skill in reading literature and writing about it.

One emphasis of the course that the syllabus does not make clear is the distinction between the visible and invisible minority, the permanent and the temporary, the involuntary and the voluntary. The visible, permanent, and involuntary minorities are, of course, those with a racial identity different from that of the majority group. The invisible and temporary include first generation European immigrants while the voluntary minorities number such groups as the Hasidic Jews and the Mennonites. Not all lines are clear cut; for example, some European immigrants may feel themselves visibly identifiable for several generations.

The distinctions provide one more valuable way of approaching the literature as they encourage students to analyze both the works and their own responses more thoughtfully; for this reason students are required to use a visible minority (work or author) as the topic for at least one paper.

Gordon Allport's *The Nature of Prejudice* (Addison Wesley, 1954) has helpful material on language and prejudice.

Booklist

Lillian Faderman and Barbara Bradshaw, eds., *Speaking for Ourselves* (abbreviated F&B)
Rudolfo Anaya, *Bless Me, Ultima*
Willa Cather, *My Antonia*
Ralph Ellison, *Invisible Man*
Chaim Potok, *My Name is Asher Lev*
Kenneth Rosen, ed., *The Man to Send Rain Clouds*
Richard Wright, *Black Boy*

Syllabus

Class 1   Introduction: Who Are We?

2   History of Black Literature. James Baldwin, from *Go Tell It On the Mountain*; Langston Hughes, "Let America Be America Again"; Paul Laurence Dunbar, "We Wear the Mask," "At Candle-Lightin' Time"; Claude McKay, "If We Must Die," "The White House" (F&B)

3   Wright, *Black Boy*

4   Immigrant literature. Cather, *My Antonia*; Michael Novak, "White Ethnic"; Harry Mark Petrakis, "The Wooing of Ariadne"; James T. Farrell, "The Oratory Contest"; Robert Laxalt, from *Sweet Promised Land*; Joe Papeleo, "Italian to the Moon Over New York"; Sharon Hucklenbroich, "Genealogy" (F&B)

5   The Mexican-American in U.S. Literature. Rudolfo Anaya, *Bless Me, Ultima*

6   Manuel J. Martinez, "The Art of the Chicano Movement and the Movement of Chicano Art"; Prudencio de Pereda, "Conquistador"; Oscar Zeta Acosta, "Perta Is a Pig"; Luis Valdez, "Los Dos Caras del Patroncito" (F&B)

7   Native American Experience in American Literature. Kenneth Rosen, *The Man to Send Rain Clouds*; Vine Deloria, "The Cheyenne Experience"; N. Scott Momaday, "A Vision Beyond Time and Place"; Juanita Platero and Siyowin Miller, "Chee's Daughter"; Hyemeyohsts Storm, "Jumping Mouse"; Traditional songs: "Child's Night Song," "Song of Failure," "Spring Song," "Glyph," "May I Walk"; Wendy Rose, "Grebes at Sunset," "Hopi Roadrunner, Dancing, Dancing" (F&B)

8   The religious "minorities" in United States literature. Chaim Potok, *My Name is Asher Lev*

9   Donato, from *Christ in Concrete*; Richard Bankowsky, from *After Pentecost*; Isaac Bashevis Singer, "The Little Shoemakers"; Bernard Malamud, "The First Seven Years"; Saul Bellow, from *The Adventures of Augie March*; Muriel Rukeyser, from *Letter to the Front* (F&B)

10   Frank Chin, "Confessions of a Number One Son"; Ferris Takahashi, "The Widower," "Nisei, Nisei"; Hisaye Yamamoto, "The Legend of Miss Sasagawara"; Toshio Mori, "The Eggs of the World," "The Seventh Street Philosopher"; Lin Yutang, from *Chinatown Family*; Bienvenido Santos, "The Day the Dancers Came"; Chiang Yee, "Arrival at Boston"; Kuangchi C. Chang, "Garden of My Childhood"; Diana Chang, "On Seeing

My Great-Aunt in a Funeral Parlor," "Four Views in
Praise of Reality"; José Garcia Villa, "Inviting a Tiger,"
"Be Beautiful, Noble, Like the Antique Ant" (F&B)

11   The Asian-American in Literature
12-13   Contemporary Black literature. Ellison, *Invisible Man*
14   Term paper due
15   Again, Who Are We? Review and Synthesis

Oral Report

Oral reports consist of a prepared presentation to the class by each
student, either singly or in a group, of material

1. Exploring another literary work related to one of the books assigned.
2. Examining another work in this area by an assigned author.
3. Describing the historical and/or social/economic background of the
   situation dealt with in one or more of the assigned books.

Oral reports by individuals generally focus on a work or an author not
discussed or read by the class. Examples of such topics include Wright,
Native Son, Frederick Douglass, O.E. Rolvaag, or Cather, *Song of the Lark*.
Group presentations have varied from straight-forward panel discussions,
usually exploring a theme in a group of works, to a production of "Los Dos
Caras Del Patroncito" by Luis Valdez, which is in Faderman and Bradshaw.
(This was done by a group of mature women students with great success.)
Since many of the students in the class are preparing to be secondary
teachers, panels may demonstrate ways to introduce a segment of the
literature to a high school class. For example, one on Japanese American
literature included tea and seaweed cookies as well as some stories and poems
and a discussion of how best to present such materials.

53
AMERICAN LITERATURE
OF SOCIAL JUSTICE
John Lowe
Autumn, 1982
Saint Mary's College
Notre Dame, IN 46556

Course Objectives

When I first arrived at Saint Mary's College to teach most of the American Literature courses, I discovered there were no courses dealing specifically and exclusively with Afro-American, immigrant, or women's literatures, although a few texts by these various types of writers had found their way into survey and genre courses. Seeking to find a way of addressing this vacuum at once, I devised a course that integrated all three "minority canons" together, using the common theme of oppression. I found this useful, since Saint Mary's quite rightly seeks to expose students to the issues of social justice that the Church is now addressing so effectively all over the world. A fortunate result was an increased sensitivity on the part of my students, all of whom are female and Catholic; most have immigrant backgrounds as well. They therefore were able to transfer their understanding of elements in the novels written by women and immigrants to novels written by blacks. This was imperative, since very few of our students are black.

I have since incorporated many other texts by women and minorities into the "standard" American Literature survey and genre courses as well. This year I changed the title "American Literature of the Oppressed" to "Literature of Social Justice" for a number of reasons. First, Professor Chester Fontenot convinced me, at the Yale Summer Institute on Reconstructing American Literature, that labelling the literatures of women, blacks, and immigrants as that of the "oppressed" tended to perpetuate the unconscious presumption that all such people were always in this category, and worse, that their literature was oppressive. Second I didn't want the prospective students to be scared away by the thought that this literature would oppress *them* in the classroom. Finally, issues of social justice are so widely discussed on our campus that the title "Literature of Social Justice" immediately attracts the attention of concerned students.

The following is the course description in our departmental pre-registration booklet:

> Some of the most stimulating and moving literature of our time has been produced by men and women who have tried to right the wrongs inflicted upon them by society. This has been especially true in Afro-

American novels, in Immigrant literature of the cities, and in books written by angry and determined women. This course will examine the joys and sorrows of their fight for dignity and justice. Thematic issues will include ethnicity, urbanization, economic inequities, racial and sexual oppression, and that delightful weapon, ethnic humor. Some of the writers to be covered: Kate Chopin, James Weldon Johnson, Abraham Cahan, Henry Roth, Richard Wright, Zora Neale Huston, Saul Bellow, and Toni Morrison.

Booklist

Saul Bellow, *The Victim* (Signet)
Abraham Cahan, *Yekl and The Imported Bridegroom* (Dover)
Kate Chopin, *The Awakening* (Signet)
Pietro Di Donato, *Christ in Concrete* (Bobbs-Merrill)
Frederick Douglass, *Narrative of the Life of Frederick Douglass* (Signet)
Zora Neale Hurston, *Their Eyes Were Watching God* (Illinois)
Toni Morrison, *Song of Solomon* (Signet)
Tillie Olsen, *Yonnondio* (Delta)
Henry Roth, *Call It Sleep* (Avon)
Three Negro Classes (Avon); contains *The Autobiography of an Ex-Colored Man*, *Up From Slavery*, and *The Souls of Black Folk*
Richard Wright, *Native Son* (Harper)

Syllabus

Class 1	Introduction: close reading of Ursula K. LeGuin, "The Ones Who Walk Away from Omelas"
2–3	Douglass, *Narrative*
4–5	Chopin, *The Awakening*
6	Cahan, *Yekl*
7	Cahan, *The Imported Bridegroom*
8	Johnson, *The Autobiography of an Ex-Colored Man*
9–11	Hurston, *Their Eyes Were Watching God*
12–14	Roth, *Call It Sleep*
15	Midterm exam
16–17	Di Donato, *Christ in Concrete*
18–19	Olsen, *Yonnondio*
20–22	Wright, *Native Son*
23–24	Bellow, *The Victim*
25–27	Morrison, *Song of Solomon*
28	Review/Concluding discussion

Midterm Examination

Part I.
Short Answer Questions—15 minutes/20 points/Choose five
1. Who is Mrs. Kavarsky? What role does she play?
2. What happens during Douglass's confrontation with Covey? Why is it important?
3. Tell why the scene with Shiny towards the end of the novel is important in *Autobiography of an Ex-Colored Man*.
4. How is food used symbolically in *The Awakening*? List at least three examples.
5. How is Asriel's attitude towards Shaya similar to that of Albert towards David?
6. Discuss the symbolism of the Cabin in *Their Eyes Were Watching God*.
7. List at least three ways in which religion plays an important role in *Call It Sleep*.

Part II.
Essay Questions—60 minutes/80 points/Choose two
1. David Scherl and members of his family go through a process of awakening; so does Edna Pontellier. How are their quests/ordeals alike? How are they different?
2. Yekl, Shaya, and the narrator of *Autobiography of an Ex-Colored Man* all leave their former lives behind them , but not without cost. What has each gained and lost?
3. Frederick Douglass and Janie Mae Crawford Killicks Starks tell male and female versions of a liberation story. Which story moved you most? Why? Note: you must discuss elements in *both* narratives.

Final Examination

Part I.
Short answer questions—25 points/30 minutes/Choose five
1. Describe "The Cripple's" role in *Christ in Concrete*. Why does she relate so well to the central figures of the novel?
2. How are Bigger's dreams for the future visualized by Wright in *Native Son*?
3. Why did Tillie Olsen choose the title *Yonnondio*? Why is it appropriate for her subject matter?
4. Bellow uses the public transportation system in New York City quite frequently in *The Victim*; his characters are constantly in motion. List some examples and show how this translates into effective imagery.

   5. How does Guitar function as Milkman's "double" in *Song of Solomon*?
   6. What is the purpose of Hagar's wild "shopping spree"? What does she buy, and what does it lead to?
   7. How is the image of the dying garden used in *Yonnondio*?

Part II.

   Essay questions—75 points/90 minutes/Choose one question from each set.
   1.A. Bigger Thomas and Milkman Dead both desperately try to fashion new identities for themselves in a hostile world. Their quests are similar, but the people they turn out to be are very different. Discuss, citing key passages in the novels.
     B. Racial and religious persecution are examined in detail in *The Victim* and *Native Son*. Show how this is dramatized in each novel. Do you see a pattern common to both? How does this fit in with the concepts of injustice we have been discussing this term?
   2.A. Anna Holbrook, Pilate Dead, and Annunziata are all mothers who must do the best they can for their children in the face of oppressive circumstances. Describe each in turn, detailing the burdens she must bear; then state which mother you admire most, and why.
     B. Asa, Kirby, Jim Holbrook, and Paul all must find work. In the novels they populate, each author takes a critical attitude toward the labor situation in a capitalist society. Who among them does the best job of delineating the unfair practices of the world of work?

54
STUDIES IN ETHNIC AMERICAN LITERATURE
James R. Payne
Spring, 1981
New Mexico State University
Las Cruces, NM 88003

Course Objectives

The course offers students an opportunity to read and discuss important works of Black, Chicano, Jewish-American, Asian-American, and Native American fiction, poetry, and autobiography. In the course of our studies we may consider ethnic American literary texts from three points of view: from the point of view of the particular ethnic groups from which they derive, from a universal point of view, and from the point of view of the individual reader—each one of us.

Booklist

Rudolfo Anaya, *Bless Me, Ultima*
Maya Angelou, *I Know Why the Caged Bird Sings*
Abraham Cahan, *Yekl and The Imported Bridegroom*
Ralph Ellison, *Invisible Man*
Maxine Hong Kingston, *The Woman Warrior*
Philip Roth, *Goodbye Columbus and Five Short Stories*
Leslie M. Silko, *Ceremony*
Poetry handouts for the first group of classes

Syllabus

Class 1   Introduction. In-class reading and discussion of the following poems takes place during the first four sessions: Paul Laurence Dunbar, "We Wear the Mask," "Sympathy"; Anne Spencer, "Letter to My Sister"; Langston Hughes, "Cross," "Mother to Son," "Lenox Avenue Mural"; James A. Emanuel, "Get Up, Blues"; Fenton Johnson, "The New Day," "Tired"; Claude McKay, "The Lynching," "If We Must Die," "To The White Fiends"

2–6   Ellison, *Invisible Man*
6–8   Angelou, *I Know Why the Caged Bird Sings*
9   Overview on Black American literature
10–13   Kingston, *Woman Warrior*
14   In-class essay
15–17   Silko, *Ceremony*
18–20   Anaya, *Bless Me, Ultima*
21–24   Roth, stories
25–28   Cahan, *Yekl, The Imported Bridegroom*, and other stories
29   Review
30   Papers due
31   In-class essay

Women's Experience

55
THE NEW WOMAN—SEX AND
SOCIAL CHANGE
IN AMERICAN FICTION, 1870-1940
Elaine Hedges
Spring, 1982
Towson State University
Towson, MD 21204

Course Objectives

Toward the end of the nineteenth century, changing economic and educational conditions led to the emergence of what was called the "new woman"—women who questioned and departed from their traditional domestic roles. The course will examine the treatment in fiction of this new woman, who was the subject of extensive and heated debate during a half century of important and continuing social change in the United States. We shall look at stories and novels by male and female authors as they reflect and interpret society's and their authors' attitudes toward the new woman: Were old images of women revised? Were the new images based on fantasy or fact? Does our literature reflect the realities of women's lives? What does it reveal about the hopes and fears of American society during the period?

Booklist

Kate Chopin, *The Awakening*
Charlotte Perkins Gilman, *Herland*
Ernest Hemingway, *The Sun Also Rises*
Zora Neale Hurston, *Their Eyes Were Watching God*

Meridel LeSueur, *The Girl*
Katherine Anne Porter, *The Old Order*
Elizabeth Robins, *The Convert*
Agnes Smedley, *Daughter of Earth*
Anzia Yezierska, *Bread Givers*

Syllabus

Class 1   Introduction to course
I. The Image and Status of Woman in the Nineteenth Century
    2   Edward Ross, "The Cause of It All"; Barbara Welter, "The
                Cult of True Womanhood"; Edith Wharton, from *The
                Age of Innocence* (handouts)
    3–4   Chopin, *The Awakening*
II. The Feminist Movement in the United States and England
    5   Seneca Falls "Declaration of Sentiments"; Henry James,
                from *The Bostonians* (handouts)
    6–7   Robins, *The Convert*
    8–9   Gilman, *Herland*
III. The Older Woman as Heroine
    10–13   Porter, "Grandmother," "The Last Leaf," "Old Mortality,"
                from *The Old Order*
                William Faulkner, "A Rose for Emily"; Mary Wilkins
                Freeman, "The Revolt of 'Mother,'" "Old Woman
                Magoun" (handouts)
    14   Catch-up and review
    15   Mid-term exam
IV. The "New Woman" in the Twentieth Century
    16–22   James R. McGovern, "The American Woman's Pre-World
                War I Freedom in Manners and Morals"; Florence Sea-
                bury, "Stereotypes" (handouts); Hemingway, *The Sun
                Also Rises*, "The Short Happy Life of Francis Ma-
                comber" (handout)
V. Working-Class, Immigrant, and Black Women
    23–24   Smedley, *Daughter of Earth*
    25–26   Yezierska, *Bread Givers*
    27–28   Hurston, *Their Eyes Were Watching God*
VI. The Depression Decade of the 1930s
    29–30   LeSueur, *The Girl*
    31–32   Student Reports

Suggested Works for Written Papers

The following is a list of suggested works (mostly novels) from which you can draw for your paper. The list is far from exhaustive, and I'll be glad to suggest other possibilities. Your paper may be a study of a single work, or a comparison of two works, focusing on an analysis of one or more of the female characters. (More specific directions will be given later, and in individual conferences.) In some cases, reading an autobiography or biography will be encouraged.

Henry Adams, *Esther* (1884)

Adams, a leading intellectual at the end of the nineteenth century and alert to contemporary scientific, political, and social developments, found the American woman, he said, more interesting and impressive than the American man. In *Esther* he depicts a woman's conflict between her own beliefs and her traditional womanly role of acquiescence.

A major statement by Adams about "Woman" is to be found in chapter 25 of his autobiography, *The Education of Henry Adams*, "The Dynamo and the Virgin."

Louisa May Alcott, *Work* (1873)

A bit earlier than our period, but an interesting work. Based on Alcott's life, the novel describes the life of a working girl as maid, governess, seamstress, and actress, and her eventual organization of a community of women who will live and work together.

Mary Austin, *A Woman of Genius* (1912)

An autobiographical novel describing its heroine's struggle for autonomy first within and then outside marriage, and her relation to the birth control and suffrage movements. You may or may not like its somewhat florid style.

Edward Bellamy, *Looking Backward* (1888)

Described in 1935 as "the most influential work of the previous 50 years," this utopian novel did have enormous impact on American writers and thinkers, including Charlotte Perkins Gilman. But do women achieve real equality in a male utopia?

Fielding Burke (pseudonym for Olive Dargan), *Call Home the Heart* (1932)

A novel, recently republished, that needs to be rediscovered and more widely read, describing the economic struggles and growing political awareness of a Southern rural woman who fights against the exploitation of textile workers in the 1920s.

Kate Chopin

Chopin wrote large numbers of short stories, many with portraits of women unusual for their time. You might wish to analyze a selected group.

John Dos Passos, *The Big Money* (1936)
    One volume of a trilogy of novels called *USA* which provide a vast, panoramic view of social, intellectual, economic, and political currents in American life from the decades before World War I until 1936. *The Big Money* explores the interlocking fates of a variety of characters who represent the new tendencies at work in American society in the years after World War I. The social worker and political activist, Mary French, is a sympathetically drawn character. Other female characters provide other portraits of "the new woman."

Theodore Dreiser, *Sister Carrie* (1900)
    From an impoverished background, Carrie "rises" to success as an actress, but through means considered immoral in 1900. (The novel's publisher was reluctant to publicize or distribute it.) How sympathetic to Carrie is Dreiser?

William Faulkner, *The Sound and the Fury* (1929)
    Caddie is one version of the liberated woman, or the woman trying to liberate herself, seen by her author as the "bitch." How do her father and her brothers react to her, in this rich and complex novel, one of Faulkner's most famous, of the declining fortunes of a Southern family?

F. Scott Fitzgerald, *The Great Gatsby* (1925)
    Like *The Sound and the Fury*, another "classic" of male literature of the 1920s. The impact of this novel on the male literary imagination and on American literary history has been profound. Its three female characters, Daisy Buchanan, Jordan Baker, and Myrtle Wilson have been described as a bitch, a liar, and a whore.

Dorothy Canfield Fisher, *The Homemaker* (1924)
    Fisher is a neglected writer who deserves to be better known. In this novel she describes a marriage in which, because of the husband's illness, he becomes the homemaker and the wife becomes a businesswoman. A sympathetic portrayal of men and women trying to adopt new roles, and their struggle to retain them against public opinion.

Mary Wilkins Freeman, *A New England Nun and Other Stories* (1891)
    Short stories, most focusing on women (and usually older women) whose lives are confined within the limits of a declining New England village way of life, but who survive, often with special strengths.

Harold Frederic, *The Damnation of Theron Ware* (1896)
    Thereon is a naive, provincial minister, fascinated by the sophisticated Celia, who introduces him, for better or worse (does the novel decide?), to a larger intellectual and sexual/emotional world. The novel is an example of the interest in and ambivalence about the new woman at the end of the nineteenth century.

Hamlin Garland
    A midwestern author who sympathized with and wrote of the hardships of the life of rural women (using his own mother's life as his model), Garland

also became interested in the new woman. In *A Spoil of Office* (1892) and *The Rose of Butcher's Cooly* (1895) he celebrates the new educational opportunities available to women but in the end reveals that he cannot free himself of certain traditional conceptions and expectations.

Ellen Glasgow, *Vein of Iron* (1935)

Glasgow writes of social classes in Virginia, both the Tidewater aristocracy and the middle and rural classes. *Vein of Iron* traces its heroine's struggle to survive war and economic depression and to take control of her life. Glasgow's autobiography, *The Woman Within*, is also worth reading.

Zora Neale Hurston

If you are interested in reading more by Hurston, who was important in the Harlem Renaissance of the 1920s, you can consider her works, *Mules and Men* or *Dust Tracks on the Road*, or the selections from her writings provided in the new collection, *I Love Myself When I am Laughing* ... (ed. Alice Walker, 1979). There is also an excellent biography by Robert Hemenway.

Henry James, *The Portrait of a Lady* (1881)

One of our literature's most engaging heroines, Isabel Archer is launched on a search for her personal freedom with all of Europe as her territory to explore. To what extent does she achieve autonomy, and what is James's attitude toward her? Several other female characters are worth noting, including an example of the new career woman.

Or there is *The Bostonians* (1886), James's complex, often perceptive but often infuriating treatment of women in reform movements in the nineteenth century.

Sarah Orne Jewett, *The Country of the Pointed Firs* (1896)

A loosely related collection of short stories describing life in a backwater Maine village in the late nineteenth century. It is largely a community of women, focused on Mrs. Todd, an engaging character who practices herbal medicine. Not an "eventful" story, but beautifully told, with a subdued lyricism and love for its characters, who are not "new women" but members of an older generation that Jewett wishes to commemorate.

Jewett, *A Country Doctor* (1884)

Nan Prince must overcome the skepticism of relatives and make the choice between marriage and her desired medical career. The novel draws on Jewett's own life, her relation to her doctor father, and her choice of career over marriage.

Edith Summers Kelley, *Weeds* (1923)

A lost and recently discovered novel, which has been described as the "story of one of the fullest heroines in modern fiction, Judith Blackford, who must battle the institutions of marriage and the social forces that threaten to cripple and ultimately destroy her potential." Despite the excesses of that publicity blurb, it is a powerful novel, in the tradition of naturalism.

Kelley, *The Devil's Hand* (1920s)

This novel was never published in Kelley's lifetime and was discovered after her death in 1956. The story of two young women who determine to break free of traditional female roles and become economically independent by farming in the Imperial Valley in California.

Meridel LeSueur

If you are interested in reading more by LeSueur, whose career extended from the 1920s through the depression decade of the thirties up to the present, I can supply you with further works by her, including a new collection, *Ripening: The Selected Writings of Meridel LeSueur*. She is another of our "rediscovered" women writers, whose career of writing and radical political activism spans over half a century.

Sinclair Lewis, *Main Street* (1920)

Lewis was a Nobel Prize winner and the major literary analyst of small town, midwestern life; he put "Main Street" and its complacent, commercially-oriented exemplar, Babbitt, on the literary map. In this novel, Carol Kennicott is an example of the new woman, restless with her conventional life, but experiencing only limited success in breaking away from it.

Elizabeth Stuart Phelps, *The Story of Avis* (1877)

Like Alcott, Phelps wrote in a period slightly earlier than we study, but this novel was unusual for its time, graphically and convincingly detailing a woman's conflict between marriage and her career as an artist.

Phelps, *The Story of Dr. Zay* (1882)

An interesting experiment in role reversal. The woman is the doctor, the man is the sickly, dependent patient. What happens when he falls in love with her but finds that because she has risen above the "feminine" role in courtship he can't act the "masculine" one?

Tess Slesinger, *The Unpossessed* (1934)

Skeptical treatment of men and women of the Left in the thirties. In Margaret Flinders, Slesinger explores the conflicts a woman experiences between personal and political life, between her husband's political radicalism and his traditional male treatment of her. In Elizabeth Leonard she presents a woman unsatisfactorily living the gospel of personal freedom.

Gertrude Stein, *The Autobiography of Alice B. Toklas* (1933)

The life story of this highly idiosyncratic, independent, and important writer, whose way of life in Paris from the 1900s until her death in 1946 contrasts strongly to her friend, Hemingway's, portrayal of expatriate life in *The Sun Also Rises*.

Dorothy West, *The Living is Easy* (1948)

Recently rediscovered and republished novel describing a black family living on the outskirts of Boston in the first half of the twentieth century. The main character is a fascinating woman whose independence and self-determination have been seen as destructive by some readers, admirable by others.

Edith Wharton, *The House of Mirth* (1905)

Poignant story of a well-bred but suddenly penniless New York society woman confronted with the need to find security by selling herself in marriage. Shrewd analysis of the "marriage game" in upper-class, turn-of-the-century life.

Wharton, *The Age of Innocence* (1920)
    Wharton's treatment of those perennials of American fiction, the Fair Lady and the Dark Lady. Another shrewd analysis of women and men locked into stifling roles and their efforts to break free.

Background Reading

Literature

Mary Allen, *The Necessary Blankness: Women in Major American Fiction of the Sixties* (1976)
    A critique of major male writers (Philip Roth, John Updike, John Barth, Thomas Pynchon) as well as studies of Joyce Carol Oates and Sylvia Plath. Argues that even in a time of social and sexual expansiveness male writers continue to portray women in stereotypical and derogatory ways, and show "an astonishing bias against the professional woman."

Nina Baym, *Woman's Fiction: A Guide to Novels by and about Women in America, 1820-1870* (1978)

Roseann P. Bell, ed., *Sturdy Black Bridges: Visions of Black Women in Literature* (1979)

Warner Berthoff, *The Ferment of Realism: American Literature 1884-1919* (1965)
    A general history of authors and trends in the period covered.

Cheryl Brown and Karen Olson, eds., *Feminist Criticism: Essays in Theory, Poetry, and Prose* (1978)

Arlyn Diamond and Lee Edwards, eds., *The Authority of Experience: Essays in Feminist Criticism* (1977)
    This and the preceding collection demonstrate feminist approaches to traditional literary works. They might contain discussions of your particular author; they can provide examples of how a novel might be analyzed.

Judith Fetterley, *The Resisting Reader: A Feminist Approach to American Fiction* (1978)
    A provocative study which argues that the woman reader must learn to resist the sexist designs a text may make on her when it asks her to identify with male heroes and belittles or distorts its female characters. Authors studied include Nathaniel Hawthorne, Henry James, William Faulkner, F. Scott Fitzgerald, and Norman Mailer.

Leslie Fiedler, *Love and Death in the American Novel* (1960)
    A wide-ranging and challenging survey of major male American writers which argues that they stereotype women, especially into Virgins and Dark Ladies (or Bitches), and that such stereotyping indicates both a

fear of women and immaturity on the part of the authors. A landmark study for its time.

Judith Fryer, *The Faces of Eve: Women in the Nineteenth-Century American Novel* (1976)

The American Adam, freely and self-reliantly ranging through the Garden of the New World, has been a major American literary type. Fryer analyzes the American "Eve," and finds that female characters in fiction from Nathaniel Hawthorne to Henry James are locked into roles based on a patriarchal culture.

Jay Martin, *Harvests of Change: American Literature 1865-1914* (1967)

A general history of major writers and literary, social, and political developments during the period covered. Primarily male writers, but with some coverage of women writers.

History

Lois Banner, *Women in Modern America: A Brief History* (1974)

Discussions of women's status, and of social and political changes, in the 1890s, the period from 1900 to World War I, and the 1920s-30s.

Mary Beard, *America Through Women's Eyes* (1933)

A history based on the words and records of women themselves, by the wife of the well-known historian, Charles Beard, written in a period when there was little recognition of the history of women.

William Chafe, *The American Woman: Her Changing Social, Economic, and Political Roles, 1920-1970* (1972)

A thoughtful study by an historian sympathetic to feminism.

Nancy Cott and Elizabeth Pleck, eds., *A Heritage of her Own: Toward a New Social History of American Women* (1979)

Articles by a variety of scholars, including Carroll Smith-Rosenberg's "The Female World of Love and Ritual: Relations between Women in Nineteenth-Century America" and others on the role and status of nineteenth-century white, black, and ethnic women.

Esther Katz and Anita Rapone, eds., *Women's Experience in America: An Historical Anthology* (1980)

Essays and articles on women in colonial, nineteenth-, and twentieth-century society, including several on the "new woman" of the early twentieth century.

Freda Kirchwey, ed., *Our Changing Morality* (1924)

A collection of articles written by men and women in the early 1920s who were struggling to define "the new woman," and the new sexual and moral standards in American society after World War I. The analyses in the articles are extremely interesting, providing a spectrum of opinion on whether women had been in fact genuinely "liberated," or not.

Gerda Lerner, ed., *Black Women in White America: A Documentary History* (1972)

Primary source materials describing the experience of black women from slavery through the twentieth century.

Lerner, ed., *The Female Experience: An American Documentary* (1977)
Primary source materials (as with the above, many rare and inaccessible) covering women's experience over several centuries. Book is organized in terms of the female life cycle, with sections also on paid work, participation in politics, and efforts for autonomy.

Mary Ryan, *Womanhood in America: From Colonial Times to the Present* (1975)
A compact and useful survey.

June Sochen, *Movers and Shakers: American Women Thinkers and Activists 1900–1970* (1973)

Sochen, *The New Feminism in 20th Century America* (1971)
Includes sections on the suffrage movement and feminism in the 1910s.

Sochen, *The New Woman: Feminism in Greenwich Village 1910–1920* (1972)
Chapters on selected women who were political activists, social workers, and writers, including Susan Glaspell, Ida Rauch, Crystal Eastman, Harriet Rodman.

Anne F. Scott, ed., *The American Woman—Who Was She?* (1971)
Primary source materials detailing the history of the struggle for equality of American women since the Civil War in the areas of work, education, marriage, family, and sex.

Elaine Showalter, ed., *These Modern Women: Autobiographical Essays from the Twenties* (1978)
Essays originally published in *The Nation* magazine by professional women who discussed their lives, ambitions, marriage and career conflicts.

Biographical and Bibliographical Reference works

Edward T. James, ed., *Notable American Women*, 3 volumes (1971)
Excellent biographies of writers and discussions of their work. Consult for overview of the life and career of your author, and for bibliography. Note: covers only women who died by 1950. Consult the new suplementary volume for later entries.

Lina Mainiero, ed., *American Women Writers* (1981)
Multivolume set of biographical-critical articles on women writers, with bibliography, in process of being published. Library should have first part of alphabet.

56
HER-LAND: AMERICAN LITERATURE
OF WOMAN AND THE LAND
Joann Peck Krieg
Spring, 1981
Hofstra University
Hempstead, NY 11550

Course Objectives

America as a state of mind and a dream of fulfillment was associated in its earliest literary and pictorial representations with the idea of a voluptuous, yielding, and bountiful woman. This female topography is reflected in a literature rife with characterizations that tie the idea of the land to that of a woman. Conquest of the land/woman, however, involved a lost virtue, and the literary image of the Virgin Land is soon countered by an anti-image of sordid industrialization and materialism. Attempts to reclaim the lost land/woman have produced asexual female images such as the mother or the girl child, and even these are confined to a literature of fantasy.

Texts

Required
L. Frank Baum, *The Wonderful Wizard of Oz*
Willa Cather, *A Lost Lady; O Pioneers!*
Stephen Crane, *Maggie, A Girl of the Streets*
Rebecca Harding Davis, *Life in the Iron Mills*
John Donne, "Elegy XIX"
William Faulkner, *As I Lay Dying*
F. Scott Fitzgerald, *The Great Gatsby*
Charlotte Perkins Gilman, *Herland*
Nathaniel Hawthorne, *The Scarlet Letter*
Washington Irving, "The Legend of Sleepy Hollow"
Herman Melville, "The Paradise of Bachelors and the Tartarus of Maids"
John Milton, *Paradise Lost*, Book IX; *Comus*

Recommended
Willa Cather, *My Antonia*
Ellen Glasgow, *Barren Ground*
Annette Kolodny, *The Lay of the Land*

Page Smith, *Daughters of the Promised Land*
Harriet Beecher Stowe, *Uncle Tom's Cabin*

Syllabus

Week 1	The Discovered Land: Discussion of early discovery narratives that speak of the New World in terms of the female body. The female body as the ideal place; erotic poetry of the sixteenth and seventeenth centuries. Donne, "Elegy XIX"
2	Slide series on allegorical representations of America from sixteenth and seventeenth centuries. The Pochahantas legend.
3	The Moral Landscape: Spenser and Milton. Milton, *Paradise Lost*, Book IX; *Comus*
4	The American Puritans: Witches and Wives. Smith, *Daughters of the Promised Land*, Chapters 1, 2
5-6	Hawthorne, *The Scarlet Letter*
7	The Fruitful Land: Image. Irving, "The Legend of Sleepy Hollow"; Cather, *O Pioneers!*, *My Antonia*
8	The Fruitful Land: Anti-Image. Melville, "Paradise of Bachelors and Tartarus of Maids"; Davis, *Life in the Iron Mills*; Crane, *Maggie*
9	Lost Land/Lost Lady. Cather, *A Lost Lady*
10-11	Fitzgerald, *The Great Gatsby*
12-13	Faulkner, *As I Lay Dying*
14	Reclaiming the Land. Gilman, *Herland*; Baum, *The Wonderful Wizard of Oz*

Suggested Topics for Research Papers

Images of the Southland and the woman
Cityscapes and the woman (Dreiser is a good source)
The Indian woman in American and/or Native American literature
As I Lay Dying, *The Scarlet Letter*, and female viture
Cather's earth mother figure
A comparison of Melville's short stories with *The Lowell Offering* and a
    history of Lowell, Massachusetts
The Scarlet Letter with reference to Anne Hutchinson
Herland, erotic poetry conventions, and the female landscape
Female beauty and national consciousness

57
REGIONAL LITERATURE
AND WOMEN'S CULTURE
Candace Waid
1980
University of Alabama
Currently at Yale University
New Haven, CT 06520

Booklist and Syllabus

Week 1	Emily Dickinson, "I tie my hat," "A light exists in spring," other selected poems; Henry David Thoreau, *Walden* (selections)
2	Rose Terry Cooke, "Rootbound," Polly Mariner, Tailoress," "Poll Jenning's Hair"; Mary Wilkins Freeman, "A New England Nun," "The Revolt of 'Mother'" Sarah Orne Jewett, "The White Heron"; Edgar Allan Poe, "The Fall of the House of Usher"; Susan Smulyan, "The Female Local Colorist and Hawthorne"
3	Sarah Orne Jewett, *The Country of the Pointed Firs*, "The Foreigner"; Willa Cather, *Not Under Forty* (selections); A.D. Wood, "The Literature of Impoverishment"
4	Edith Wharton, *Summer, Ethan Frome, A Backward Glance* (selections)
5	Mary Austin, *Land of Little Rain*, "One Hundred Miles on Horseback," *Earth Horizon* (selections), "Regionalism in American Fiction"; Thoreau, *Walden* (selections)
6	Cather, *My Antonia*; Eudora Welty, "The House of Willa Cather"; Tremaine McDowell, "Regionalism in American Literature"
7	Kate Chopin, *The Awakening*; Jules Chametzky, "Our Decentralized Literature: A Consideration of Regional, Ethnic, Radical, and Sexual Factors"
8	William Faulkner, *Absalom, Absalom!*
9	Zora Neale Hurston, *Their Eyes Were Watching God, Dust Tracks on a Road* (selections); Kathryn Morgan, "Caddy Buffer Stories"; Flannery O'Connor, "The Regional Writer"
10	Welty, "The Wide Net," "First Love," "Some Notes on River Country," "Place in Fiction"
11	Welty, *Losing Battles*
12	Rudolfo Anaya, *Bless Me, Ultima*

Place and Region in American Literature

58
THE SENSE OF PLACE: REGIONALISM
Ellen O'Brien
Spring, 1978
Guilford College
Greensboro, NC 27410

Course Objectives

An exploration of regionalism in American Literature, the course will be concerned both with the best of the "local color" literature which flourished in the late nineteenth century and with literature that defies such categorization but which nonetheless has deep regional roots. Major issues will include the vanishing frontier, the importance of place and history in the American identity, and embodiments and distortions of American values. Questions of literary form and its relation to regionalism will also be raised in the study of poetry, short fiction, and novels.

Booklist

George Washington Cable, *The Grandissimes*
Willa Cather, *O Pioneers!*
Charles W. Chesnutt, *The Conjure Woman*
Philip Durham and Everett L. Jones, *The Western Story*
William Faulkner, *Go Down, Moses; Absalom, Absalom!*
Arthur Kopit, *Indians*
Jean Toomer, *Cane*

Recommended Readings (on reserve)

Background reading
Jay B. Hubbell, *The South in American Literature*
Frederick Jackson Turner, "The Significance of the Frontier in American History"
Henry Nash Smith, *Virgin Land*
Leslie Fiedler, *The Return of the Vanishing American*

Southern Literature
William Faulkner, *Light in August; The Sound and the Fury*
George Washington Cable, *Old Creole Days*
Robert Penn Warren, *All The King's Men*

Western Literature
Mark Twain, *Roughing It; The Adventures of Huckleberry Finn*
James Fenimore Cooper, *The Deerslayer*
Wright Morris, *Ceremony in Lone Tree*
Ishmael Reed,*Yellow Back Radio Broke Down*

Syllabus

Class 1   Introduction
     2   Chesnutt, *The Conjure Woman*
     3   Readings in Southwest humor (handout)
     4–6   Cable, *The Grandissimes*
     7–9   Faulkner, *Go Down, Moses*
     10–13 Faulkner, *Absalom, Abasalom!*
     14–15 Toomer, *Cane*
     16   Jack London, "All Gold Canyon"; Bret Harte, "Tennessee's Partner"; Owen Wister, "Balaam and Pedro" (*The Western Story*)
     17   Clarence Mumford, "Hopalong Sits In"; Zane Grey, "Canyon Walls"; Vardis Fisher, "The Scare Crow" (*The Western Story*)
     18   Clay Fisher, "The Trap"; Luke Short, "Top Hand"; Walter Van Tilberg Clark, "The Indian Well" (*The Western Story*)
     19   Stephen Crane, "The Bride Comes to Yellow Sky," "The Blue Hotel" (*The Western Story*)
     20–21 Cather, *O Pioneers!*
     22–23 Kopit, *Indians*
     23   Native American Chants and Songs (handout)
     24–25 Final Seminars (see below)

Final Seminars

The last two class meetings will be devoted to seminars intended to draw together the readings and discussions for the semester. In preparation for these seminars, you should review your notes and texts, read the assigned readings and submit a set of informal notes (*not* eassys) in response to the questions below. Evaluation will be based on the notes and on your oral contributions to the seminar.

Seminar 1: The Fate of Western Literature

Readings: Frank Norris, "A Neglected Epic"; T.K. Whipple, "American Sagas" (*The Western Story*); John Williams, "The 'Westerner': A Definition of the Myth," *The Nation* (Nov. 18, 1961), pp. 401-06 (on reserve); Leslie Fielder, "Boxing the Compass," *The Return of the Vanishing American*, pp. 16-28 (on reserve).

It is generally conceded that while the South has produced a number of literary masterworks that are distinctly regional, the West has yet to produce such a work. At the same time, the importance of the West as an influence on American thought and literature has become a commonplace of critical thinking, at least since the publication of Turner's frontier thesis. In this context, we will consider the following issues:

1. Several of the critics we have read suggest reasons for the failure of Western literature. How persuasive do you find each of these suggestions? Why?

2. A genre for Western literature: epic, comedy, tragedy, myth, or pastoral? Arthure K. Moore, in *The Frontier Mind*, asserts that Western literature has failed to fulfill its potential through failure to recognize the epic as its proper mode; John Williams insists that "the Western adventure ... is not really epical" and that the attempt to write epic has been the downfall of much Western literature. What do you see as the most appropriate mode or modes for Western literature?

3. If we assume *Indians* to be representative of recent serious treatments of the West in literature, what conclusions might we draw on the future of Western literature? Is this a step toward or away from a more complex and satisfying literature of the West?

4. Open forum: What do you see as important or interesting questions on this subject?

Seminar 2: The Sense of Place in Southern and Western Literature

Readings: Review notes and readings in Southern literature.

1. Review the mid-term questions you submitted on Southern literature. Can any of these be profitably expanded to reflect on Western Literature?

2. How would you define the nature and character of Southern literature? The question can be addressed in terms of theme, style, recurrent structures, essential question, genre, etc.

3. How would you define the nature and charracter of Western literature?

4. How is the sense of place defined in each of these literatures? What is its significance?

5. Open forum: What other issues are important to an understanding of Western and/or Southern literature?

59
THE URBAN FRONTIER
Joan Hedrick
1982
Trinity College
Hartford, CT 06106

Course Objectives

Frederick Douglass wrote, "A man is worked on by what he works on; he may carve out his circumstances, but his circumstances will carve him out, as well." Studs Terkel's interviews with workers confirm Douglass's perception that, to some degree, we are what we do. This course recognizes the centrality of the institution of work, attempts to understand the effects of scientific management, and takes into account the ways in which the work experience is shaped by what we bring to it, whether these cultural assumptions come from Horatio Alger books or from a particular subculture. The city is the setting rather than the subject of this exploration. The goal of the course is to understand the interrelationships between work, ideology, ethnicity, gender, and communtiy in twentieth-century America.

Booklist

Horatio Alger, *Ragged Dick and Mark the Match Boy*
Rosalyn Baxendall, et al., *America's Working Women*
Harry Braverman, *Labor and Monopoly Capital*
Theodore Dreiser, *Sister Carrie* (new, restored edition)
Charlotte Perkins Gilman, *Women and Economics*
Jack London, *Martin Eden*

Ruth Rosen and Sue Davidson, eds., *The Maimie Papers*
Lillian Rubin, *Worlds of Pain: Life in the Working-Class Family*
Studs Terkel, *Working*

Syllabus

Class 1   Introduction
2   Terkel, *Working*. Read entire; be prepared to discuss in detail
            one of the interviews that especially struck you.
3   Braverman, *Labor and Monopoly Capital*. Short paper:
            Choose a point you take to be important to Braverman's
            argument; then use material from Terkel either to prove
            or disprove it.
4   Herbert Gutman, "Work, Culture and Society in Indus-
            trializing America" (on reserve); John Ibson, "Virgin
            Land or Virgin Mary? Studying the Ethnicity of White
            Americans," *American Quarterly*, 33 (Bibliography,
            1981), 284–308 (on reserve); Baxandall, *America's
            Working Women*, pp. 128–41.
5   Alger, *Ragged Dick and Mark the Match Boy*. Short paper on
            Alger
6   London, *Martin Eden*. Short paper on *Martin Eden* (or, later,
            you can write on *Sister Carrie* or *The Maimie Papers*)
7   Drieser, *Sister Carrie*. Suggested topic for paper: compare
            and contrast *Carrie* and *Martin Eden*
8   Gunther Barth, *City People*, chapters 4 and 6 (on reserve);
            Sophie Tucker, *Some of These Days*, pp. 1–78 (on
            reserve); Eric E. Lampard, "American Historians and
            the Study of Urbanization," *American Historical Review*,
            67 (Oct., 1961), 49–61 (on reserve); Vladimir C.
            Nahirny and Joshua A. Fishman, "American Immigrant
            Groups: Ethnic Identification and the Problem of
            Generations," *Sociological Review*, 13 (1965), 311–26 (on
            reserve)
9   Gilman, *Women and Economics*
10   *The Maimie Papers*. Suggested topic for papers: In what way
            is Gilman's analysis applicable to Maimie's story? Or,
            compare and contrast the interview with Roberta Victor
            (*Working*) with Maimie's story.
11   Baxandall, *America's Working Women* (rest). Film: "Union
            Maids"
12   Rubin, *Worlds of Pain*
13   Rubin Pawlowski, *How the Other Half Lived* (on reserve).
            Class reports on final projects.
14   Class reports on final projects

60
THE CITY IN AMERICAN LITERATURE
Amy Kaplan
Fall, 1982
Yale University
New Haven, CT 06520

Course Objectives

A course on the city in literature provides an excellent opportunity to discuss literature in its social context. In this course, I explore the ways in which literary forms respond to and are shaped by the urban experience. My major premise is two-fold: 1) that there is a body of American literature with common themes and concerns that constitutes an urban literary tradition; 2) within this continuity, urban literature in America changes over time and varies according to the particular social perspective of the writer. I have organized the course into units that reflect this variety of literary and social perspectives, and I have placed these units within a historical chronology. In units one and three I discuss realism and modernism as literary forms for confronting new urban experiences. (I do this from the point of view of what is seen as the dominant literary tradition.) In units two and four, I explore the ways in which white women writers and Afro-American writers use these forms and create new forms to express their own experiences of the American city.

In selecting texts, I have tried to combine well known and relatively unknown authors (Richard Wright and Ann Petry, for example). In each unit, I have also added very short readings from historical sources to create a sense of social context for the literature. (Many other texts would suit this scheme: Richard Wright, *Native Son*; Henry Roth, *Call It Sleep*; T.S. Eliot, *The Wasteland*; detective novels by Dashiell Hammett or Raymond Chandler; Hart Crane, *The Bridge*; Upton Sinclair, *The Jungle*.)

Booklist

Abraham Chapman, ed., *Black Voices*
Kate Chopin, *The Awakening*
John Dos Passos, *Manhattan Transfer*
Theodore Dreiser, *Sister Carrie*
Ralph Ellison, *Invisible Man*
William Dean Howells, *A Hazard of New Fortunes*

Alan Trachtenberg, *The Incorporation of America*
Edith Wharton, *The House of Mirth*
William Carlos Williams, *Paterson*
Anzia Yezierska, *Bread Givers*

Syllabus

Week 1   Introduction: Nineteenth-Century Precedents. Walt
                   Whitman, "Crossing Brooklyn Ferry" (handout)
   I. Realism: Confronting the New Urban Order (and Disorder)
           2   Howells, *A Hazard of New Fortunes* (1890); Trachtenburg,
                   Incorporation of America, Chap. 3
           3   Henry James, *The American Scene* (1907), pp. 72–146,
                   158–65, 174–78, 182–85 (on reserve); Stephen Crane,
                   "The Men of the Storm," 'Experiment in Misery,"
                   "Experiment in Luxury" (1894) (on reserve); Jacob Riis,
                   How the Other Half Lives (1890), Introduction, chaps. 3,
                   10, 11 (on reserve); Trachtenberg, *Incorporation*, chap. 4
           4   Dreiser, *Sister Carrie* (1900); Trachtenberg, *Incorporation*,
                   chap. 7
  II. Women Writers and Urbanization: Private and Public Spaces
           5   Chopin, *The Awakening* (1899); Charlotte Perkins Gilman,
                   The Home (1902), selections (on reserve)
           6   Wharton, *House of Mirth* (1905): Thorstein Veblen, *Theory of
                   the Leisure Class* (1899), chap. 7 (on reserve)
           7   Yezierska, *Bread Givers* (1925); Elizabeth Ewen, "City
                   Lights: Immigrant Women and the Rise of the Movies,"
                   Women and the American City, Catherine Stimpson, et
                   al., eds. (on reserve)
 III. Modernism: The Fragmentation of Urban Life
           8   Dos Passos, *Manhattan Transfer* (1925); George Simmel,
                   "The Metropolis and Mental Life," *Classic Essays in the
                   Culture of Cities*, ed. Richard Sennet (on reserve)
           9   Nathaniel West, *The Day of the Locust* (1939) (on reserve);
                   Williams, *Paterson*, Books III–VI (1946–1958)
 IV. Black Writers and Urbanization: Invisible Cities Made Visible
          10   Richard Wright, "The Man Who Lived Underground"
                   (1942), *Black Voices*; Ann Petry, "Darkness and Con-
                   fusion," *Black Voices*, "Mother Africa," *Miss Muriel and
                   Other Stories* (on reserve); Allan Schoener, ed., *Harlem
                   on My Mind*, pp. 171–202 (on reserve)
          11   Ellison, *Invisible Man* (1952)
          12   Ellison, *Invisible Man*; Gwendolyn Brooks, *Maud Martha*
                   (1953) (on reserve)

61
SOUTHERN LITERATURE
Kathryn L. Seidel
Spring, 1981
University of Maryland
College Park, MD 20742

Course Objectives

The Southern Literature course is ideal for consideration of works by Whites, Blacks, and Indians because Southern history has been so shaped by these groups. That said, the course continues to be hampered by what works are and are not in print. Nonetheless, the colonial and revolutionary periods are handled well in material from William Byrd and Thomas Jefferson, especially his *Notes on the State of Virginia* but also in his letters to his daughter. Antebellum materials can include Edgar Allan Poe and William Gilmore Simms, but must include a plantation novel. Few are in print; one recently out-of-print but semi-available is John Pendleton Kennedy's *Swallow Barn*. For most courses, Harriet Beecher Stowe's *Uncle Tom's Cabin* suffices as an example of the plantation novel and as itself, one of the most essential novels in American literature. The antebellum works can be supplemented with handouts from Mary Chesnut's *Diary from Dixie*, and by using Frederick Douglass's *Narrative*.

The post-bellum period, with its rapid mythologizing, can be observed in Thomas Nelson Page's and Joel Chandler Harris's stories. *The Clansman* by Thomas Dixon, Jr. is in print and certainly encapsulates the worst of the prejudices of this period.

The specialized literature from New Orleans can be handled with Kate Chopin or George Washington Cable's *The Grandissimes*, or with stories from both.

The Southern Renaissance can include Ellen Glasgow's *Barren Ground*, although fortunately the superior novel, *The Sheltered Life*, remains in print. Frances Newman's eccentric and brilliant novel, *The Hard-Boiled Virgin* and William Faulkner's *Light in August* can also be used. The agrarian impluse is found as much in Faulkner's *Absalom, Absalom!* as it is in Margaret Mitchell's *Gone With the Wind*, both historical novels typical of fiction in the 1930s. Short stories from the thirties through the fifties work well to cover Katherine Anne Porter, Carson McCullers, Flannery O'Connor, and Eudora Welty.

Later fiction can include works by Ralph Ellison or Richard Wright and several contemporary Black writers; a unit on Black poetry is an alternative. One can also look at existentialism in modern Southern literature with

William Styron's *Lie Down in Darkness*, *Invisible Man*, and Walker Percy's *The Moviegoer*. An undiscovered classic, Harriet Arnow's *The Dollmaker*, makes a nice alternative to Welty's works.

Southern drama is well represented by Tennessee William's works, but Beth Henley's recent *Crimes of The Heart* is in print and is very fine.

Booklist

Harriette Arnow, *The Dollmaker*
Kate Chopin, *The Awakening*
Ralph Ellison, *Invisible Man*
William Faulkner, *The Sound and the Fury*
Ellen Glasgow, *The Sheltered Life*
Margaret Mitchell, *Gone With the Wind*
Harriet Beecher Stowe, *Uncle Tom's Cabin*
William Styron, *Lie Down in Darkness*
Robert Penn Warren, *All the King's Men*
Tennessee Williams, *A Streetcar Named Desire*

Syllabus

Class 1	Introduction
2	Colonial Beginnings. William Byrd, Thomas Jefferson, and others (handouts)
3	The Antebellum Period; Plantation novels. Stowe, *Uncle Tom's Cabin*
4	Edgar Allan Poe and William Gilmore Simms
5	The War and Post-Bellum Period—Mythmaking. Thomas Nelson Page (handout)
6	Local color. J. C. Harris (handout)
7	New Orleans. Chopin, *The Awakening*
8	George Washington Cable (handout)
9-10	The Southern Renaissance. Glasgow, *The Sheltered Life*
11	Faulkner, *The Sound and the Fury*
12-13	The 1930s—The Agrarians. Mitchell, *Gone With the Wind*
14-15	Warren, *All The King's Men*
16	Midterm exam
17	Williams, *A Streetcar Named Desire*
18	Southern Drama
19	Ellison, *Invisible Man*
20	Black and Ethnic Literature
21	Arnow, *The Dollmaker*
22	Existential Influences
23-24	Styron, *Sophie's Choice*
25	Some Poets

62
THE SOUTHERN RENAISSANCE
Anne Bradford Warner
1981
Spelman College
Atlanta, GA 30314

Course Objectives

This course examines the twentieth-century flowering of Southern writing, the Southern Renaissance, in the light of literary and historical trends. Close attention will be given to the powerful way in which selected authors use class, place, racial conflict, regional religion, and oral tradition to shape their fiction.

Booklist

Kate Chopin, *The Awakening and Selected Short Stories*
William Faulkner, *As I Lay Dying*
Zora Neale Hurston, *Their Eyes Were Watching God*
Flannery O'Connor, *Three by Flannery O'Connor*
Allen F. Stein and Thomas N. Walters, eds., *The Southern Experience in Short Fiction*
Eudora Welty, *The Optimist's Daughter*

Syllabus

Class 1-2   Introduction to the course. "Introduction" to Stein, *The Southern Experience*
3-5   Chopin, *The Awakening*
6-8   Card report on *The Awakening*. Chopin, "La Belle Zoraide"; optional: Chopin, "Desiree's Baby" (if possible to get a copy)
9-11   Faulkner, *As I Lay Dying*
12-14   Faulkner, *As I Lay Dying*; "Barn Burning" (Stein); card report on "Barn Burning"
15-17   Richard Wright, "Long Black Song," "The Man Who Was Almost a Man" (Stein)

18-22   Hurston, *Their Eyes Were Watching God*; read contemporary
        reviews (library)
23   Midterm exam
24-26   Ralph Ellison, "Flying Home," "Battle Royal" (Stein);
        optional "Kings of the Bingo Game" (if possible to get a
        copy)
27-29   O'Connor, "Wise Blood" (*Three by O'Connor*); read reviews
        of book and movie (library)
30-32   O'Connor, "The River," "A Late Encounter With the
        Enemy" (Stein); "A Good Man is Hard to Find" (*Three
        by O'Connor*)
33-35   Peter Taylor, "Venus, Cupid, Folly, and Time"; Jesse Hill
        Ford, "To the Open Water"; George Garrett,
        "Texarkana Was a Crazy Town" (Stein)
36-38   Ernest Gaines, "The Sky is Gray"; Edward J. Cabbell,
        "Soul's Sting"; Welty, "Where is the Voice Coming
        From" (Stein)
39-41   Welty, *The Optimist's Daughter*
42-43   Review of material and summary

Card Report

The card report should help students analyze works of fiction. Summarize information about the story or novel assigned by describing appropriate material for the following categories:

1. The title of the story and the date of its original publication.
2. The author's name and dates.
3. A terse summary of the main events of the story, given in chronological order.
4. The name (if any) of the central character, together with a description of that character's main traits or features.
5. Other characters in the story, dealt with in the same fashion.
6. A short description of setting.
7. The narrator of the story. (In other words, clarify the fine distinctions about point of view, central consciousness, stream-of-consciousness.)
8. A descriptiion of the general tone of the story, as well as it can be sensed: the author's apparent feelings toward the central character or the main events.
9. Some comments on the style in which the story is written. (Brief illustrative quotations are helpful, insofar as space permits.)
10. Whatever kinds of irony the story contains, and what they contribute to the story.
11. In a sentence, the story's main theme.

12. Leading symbols (if the story has any), with an educated guess at whatever each symbol suggests.

13. Finally, an evaluation of the story as a whole, concisely setting forth the student's opinion of it.

(Note: These categories, with a slight change in #7, are excerpted from X. J. Kennedy, *Literature, An Introduction to Fiction, Poetry, and Drama,* 2nd ed. (Boston: Little, Brown, 1979), pp. 224–25.)

When you have completed these short sections, choose one topic (from #s 7, 9, 10, or 12) for a brief essay of 500–700 words.

Use the attached sheet of definitions, adapted from the handbook by Thrall, Hibbard, and Holman, as a guide for these categories.

Varying Themes

63
THE AMERICAN DREAM
Bette S. Weidman
Fall, 1981
Queens College/City University of New York
Flushing, NY 11367

Course Objectives

The Queens College catalog description for English 83, "The American Dream," describes it broadly as a course considering "political, social and economic visions of America based on a selection of literature from the Puritans to the present." The course is an elective acceptable toward the English major and open to other interested students, primarily juniors and seniors. In our numbering system, it follows and is more specialized than our two-semester survey of American literature or our American Novel course; the readings and course shape vary with the instructor each semester.

Although chronological arrangement of readings is not required in English 83, I wanted to treat "the American dream" as an expression of an historical reality: the widespread yearning for a better future based on association with the mythic past—Eden, Atlantis. My goal was to respect, not reduce, the mythic element in the Dream, not to disregard the social and economic realities it represented in various periods, but to recognize the complexity of human motives that generated vast movements of people.

My own impulse, which is to be inclusive and historical and to insist on the representation of women, blacks, and Indians, confronted my practical position: to avoid an expensive booklist of "mainstream" materials that would make it difficult to justify the purchase of books I regarded as major for the course. I decided on four central novels by women—*O Pioneers, Life in the Iron Mills, Chinamen, and Yonnondio*—placed in the stream of the course at the correct historical moment, and I arranged, to flow around these, crucial texts from which I photocopied short passages. I also included as key texts three works of non-fiction, each for a different purpose: *Heavens on Earth*, an (inexpensive) excellent discussion of Utopias, allowed me to explore the radical solutions of one period and to introduce folk art and music of the Shakers; *The Souls of Black Folk* allowed me to explore the situation of one people through the work of an eloquent spokesman and to include the music of the sorrow songs; *Wilderness and the American Mind* permitted discussion of the history of a central idea associated with landscape and natural history.

I started with the Eskimo myth of "Sedna, Mistress of the Underworld," an immigrant who expected paradise, but found disaster; out of her body are made the creatures that now support life. In a series of other short myths (see Stith Thompson, *Tales of the North American Indians*, Indiana University Press, 1966), including "The Woman Who Fell From the Sky" (Seneca), "The Beginning of Newness"(Zuni), and "Raven's Adventures— The Theft of Light" (Northwest Coast), we established some new-world sources for images of the land of milk and honey, the generative force of women—mystical but powerless to choose, the hope for children, and the trickster (Prometheus) theme. Each time I brought photocopied materials to class I also brought supplementary bibliography (often in the form of a bag of books to pass around). From the dreams of ancient American cultures, we turned freshly to the Puritans (not without mention of the gap: literature in Spanish following Mexican and southwestern explorations; the figure of Esteban, a black explorer entering the heartland in 1537, a century before the Puritans; the Viking Sagas; the journals of Columbus—these were all laid out briefly as potential subjects for individual projects). We spoke of the Puritans' myth of the expulsion from Eden, Exodus, Canaan, using short extracts from Bradford, Winthrop, Mather, Rowlandson, Bradstreet, Taylor. When we spoke of the Declaration of Independence, we read Wheatley and Hammon. And so on, through the nineteenth and early twentieth centuries, we alternated reference to events, short passages from works, with full discussion of one of our key texts.

By firmly subordinating familiar historical and literary material to our seven key books, we drew out of all the themes, stories and images central to an understanding of the American Dream. These seven books summed up and made memorable the struggles of immigrant people on this continent.

Booklist

Willa Cather, *O Pioneers!*
Rebecca Harding Davis, *Life in the Iron Mills*
Maxine Hong Kingston, *Chinamen*
Mark Holloway, ed., *Heavens on Earth*
W. E. B. DuBois, *The Souls of Black Folk*
Tillie Olsen, *Yonnondio*
Roderick Nash, *Wilderness and the American Mind*

Syllabus

Week 1   Indian origin myths, prehistoric immigration
    2   Puritans, Colonial New England: Cather, *O Pioneers!*
    3–4   Declaration of Independence, Federalist Papers
    5   Emerson, Whitman, Thoreau
    6   The railroads, frontier, manifest destiny
    7   Slavery, the Civil War
    8   European immigration, industrialism, the Gilded Age
    9   Utopias. *Heavens on Earth*
    10–11 Black experience. DuBois, *The Souls of Black Folk*
    12   Women. Olsen, *Yonnondio*
    13   Women in the Twentieth Century
    14   The life of the environment: Nash, *Wilderness and the
          American Mind*
    15   Summary

Assignments

The interview assignments

I aked each student to do two interviews, tape-recorded, of at least a half-hour each, one with a recent immigrant (last ten years) and one with a pre-World War II immigrant. After students identified their subjects, I assigned ten prepared questions centering on the American dream and its fullfillment or frustration, gave some abbreviated oral history interview technique instruction emphasizing the right to depart from prepared questions, and required each tape to be accompanied by a signed release form. Students were not required to transcribe tapes. I audited each tape, supplying written commentary, and played appropriate sections of tape in class. My twenty-four students interviewed people from Siberia, Tarnopol, Panama, Barbados, Poland, Italy, Cuba, Trinidad, Ireland, Prussia, Shanghai, and the U.S.S.R. The interviewees included parents, neighbors, and fellow-students.

The individualized project

This project had its origin in letters of introduction in which students wrote to me about their own backgrounds and fields of interest. Each person developed a different project: one student transcribed the diary of a nineteenth-century Long Island school girl from its manuscript at the Queensborough Public Library, supplying an essay in introduction; one student chose a day in November at random, bought two copies of the *New York Times*, mounted each sheet back and front on heavy paper and circled each article that impinged on the American Dream. Then she selected an essay about the development of the issue and its relation to the rest of the news that November day. A third student wondered if the rich dream, and examined biographies for the answer. Another wrote a biographical account of her mother, using her taped interviews as a starting point; another wrote an essay about the contributions of her large family to American life, following parents, sisters, and brothers from Panama to Barbados to New York, using family letters. I tried to encourage writing projects that permitted the use of primary source material.

Observations
This assignment insures that everyone comes to class with something valuable to contribute. The observations I assign are full sentences stating what the reader notices in a work, excluding inference and judgment. For the best and only published account of this method of teaching about literature and writing, see Marie Ponsot and Rosemary Deen, *Beat Not the Poor Desk: Writing: What to Teach, How to Teach it and Why*, (Boynton/ Cook Publishers, 1982).

64
DECODING AMERICA
Vera Norwood
Spring, 1983
University of New Mexico
Albuquerque, NM 87131

Course Objectives

This course focuses on learning to read the codes—personal, cultural, linguistic, historical—of different American voices. From the linguistic level of code switching in bilingual writings to the rhetorical level of using different types of discourse to appeal to different audiences, literature uses doubleness to communicate and withhold, to expose and protect, to affirm and alter. Decoding such doubleness is a cultural process, a way of learning the voice of another's experience, of perceiving its differences and likenesses. Decoding is, at the same time, a critical process, a way of focusing on voice and strategies of presentation, on concern for audience, and rehetorical impact.

A Note on the Origins of the Course

The original syllabus was developed from an outline prepared by a group at the Reconstructing American Literature Institute. The outline contained primarily literary readings, with few secondary sources. I found in attempting to turn it into a course that more background information on sociolinguistics and American cultural history was required for students to understand the goals of the course. These materials I added. Primary drafters on the syllabus were Jean Ferguson Carr, James Payne, and myself.

Booklist

E.L. Doctorow, *The Book of Daniel*
Frederick Douglass, *Narrative of the Life of Frederick Douglass*
Benjamin Franklin, *Autobiography*
Zora Neale Hurston, *Their Eyes Were Watching God*
Tomas Rivera, *Y no se lo trago la tierra*
Leslie Marmon Silko, *Ceremony*
Other readings are available as handouts or reserve.

Syllabus

I. Code Switching and Contexts
Class 1   Class overview and handout, "Aunt Cat."
      2   William Labov, "The Logic of Nonstandard English,"
               Poverty and Language, ed. Frederick Williams; Ezekial
               Mphahlele, in *Harvard Educational Review* (1964); Paul
               Laurence Dunbar, "We Wear the Mask," "Sympathy,"
               "A Letter," "Little Brown Baby"
      3   Guadalupe Valdes Fallis, "Code-Switching in Bi-Lingual
               Chicano Poetry," *Hispania* (December, 1976); Jose
               Montoya, "El Louie," *Aztlan*, ed. Stan Steiner
      4   View videotape of "By This Song I Walk" Alan Dundes,
               "Texture, Text and Context," *Southern Folklore Quarter-
               ly* (December, 1974)
II. Levels of Discourse
      5   Jonathan Edwards, "Sinners in the Hands of an Angry God,"
               selections from "Personal Narrative"; Einar Haugen,
               "The Ecology of Language," *The Ecology of Language*
III. Oral and Written Discourse
      6   Ralph Waldo Emerson, "The American Scholar," "The
               Poet"

7   Herman Melville, "Benito Cereno"
8   Dennis Tedlock, "Yellow-Woman Tales"; "Pueblo Liter-
        ature: Style and Verisimilitude," *New Perspectives on the
        Pueblos*, ed. Al Ortiz
9   Written assignment: "Texture, Text and Context in Leslie
        Silko's 'Yellow Woman.'" Be prepared to discuss your
        analysis
IV.   One Voice/Mass Voice
10   Walt Whitman, "O Captain, My Captain," and selected Civil
        War Poems
11   Walt Whitman, "Song of Myself" (selections)
V.   Private/Public
12   Selections from Emily Dickinson's poems and letters
13   Michelle Rosaldo, "Women, Culture and Society: A Theo-
        retical Overview"; Karen Sachs, "Engels Revisited:
        Women, The Organization of Production and Private
        Property," *Women, Culture and Society*, eds. Rosaldo
        and Lamphere
VI.   Cultural Codes—Dominant and Sub
14-15   Franklin, *Autobiography*
15-16   Douglass, *Narrative of the Life of Frederick Douglass*
16   Paulo Friere, selections from *The Pedagogy of the Oppressed*
17   Sherwood Anderson, "I Want to Know Why"; Nathaniel
        Hawthorne, "The Birthmark"; Charlotte Perkins Gilman,
        "The Yellow Wallpaper"
18   Judith Fetterley, *The Resisting Reader: A Feminist Approach
        to American Fiction*, pp. xi-xxvi, 12-33; Annette
        Kolodny, "A Map for Re-Reading: Or, Gender and the
        Interpretation of Literary Texts," *New Literary History*
        (1979-80)
19   Dell Hymes, "Models of the Interaction of Language and
        Social Life," *Directions in Sociolinguistics*, eds. Hymes
        and Gumperz
20   Using Franklin or Douglass or Gilman as the text, apply
        Hymes's "Speaking" ethnography to the text as a form
        of analysis
VII.   Conscious Doubleness
21-22   Hurston, *Their Eyes Were Watching God*; Claudia Mitchell-
        Kernan, "Signifying and Marking: Two Afro-American
        Speech Acts," *Directions In Sociolinguistics*, eds. Hymes
        and Gumperz.
22-24   Rivera, *Y no se lo trago la tierra*; Fernando Penalosa, *Chicano
        Sociolinguistics*, Chaps. 7-8
25-26   Silko, *Ceremony*; taped interview with Silko.
27-28   Doctorow, *The Book of Daniel*; Roland Barthes, "Dominici,
        or the Triumph of Literature," *Mythologies*
29-30   Papers due; presentations on papers.

65
LAW AND LITERATURE
IN ANTEBELLUM AMERICA
Brook Thomas
1981
University of Hawaii
Honolulu, Hawaii 96822

Course Objectives

The purpose of this course is to understand the interrelation between law and literature at a specific moment in American history, especially how both react to the historical transformations occurring as American society changes from agrarian to an industrial economy. This period has been called the "formative era of American law" because it laid the foundation for our present legal system. By the end of the course we should have a better understanding of the forces shaping the development of that legal system. We should also have a better understanding of how the same forces helped to shape the course of American literature. Furthermore, it is probably fair to say that more people get their understanding of the function of the law from how it is portrayed in literature or popular arts drawing from literature (such as Grade B Westerns' portrayal of the conflict between the law and the individual, which draws on James Fenimore Cooper) than from a study of American legal history. Part of our task will be to see how accurately the literature of the period portrays the function of the law in American society, whether it challenges the dominant legal ideology, supports it, or both. Finally, we will bring the methods of literary ideology, to bear on a study of important legal decisions to try to understand the rehetoric of the law and the unstated assumptions contained in its rhetoric and metaphors.

For purposes of organization the course will concentrate on comparing three major legal figures with three literary figures, all having biographical connections. Cooper will be paired with James Kent, the Chancellor of New York and the author of the famous *Commentaries on American Law*. Nathaniel Hawthorne will be paired with Joseph Story, a Supreme Court justice, a professor of law at Harvard, and the foremost legal scholar of his day. Herman Melville will be paired with his father-in-law, Lemuel Shaw, the Chief Justice in Massachusetts for thirty years and the most influential state judge of the period. Other writers and works will also be read, most notably Harriet Beecher Stowe's *Uncle Tom's Cabin*.

Booklist

James Fenimore Cooper, *The Pioneers*
Edwin S. Corwin, *The "Higher Law" Background of American Constitutional Law*
Nathaniel Hawthorne, *The House of the Seven Gables*
Morton Horwitz, *The Transformation of American Law 1780–1860*
Herman Melville, *Complete Short Works*
Harriet Beecher Stowe, *Uncle Tom's Cabin*

Books and Essays on Reserve

Maurice Baxter, *Daniel Webster and the Supreme Court*
Joseph Dorfman, "Chancellor Kent and the Developing American Economy"
Gerald Dunne, *Justice Joseph Story and the Rise of the Supreme Court*
Ralph Waldo Emerson, *Works*
Dixon Ryan Fox, *The Decline of Aristocracy in the Politics of New York*
H. Hayford, ed., *The Somers Mutiny*
Theodore Horton, *James Kent: A Study in Conservatism*
Leonard Levy, ed., *Jim Crow in Boston*
———, *The Law of the Commonwealth and Chief Justice Shaw*
Walker Lewis, *Speak for Yourself, Daniel*
C. Peter Magrath, *Yazoo*
Marvin Meyers, *The Jacksonian Persuasion*
Joseph Story, *The Miscellaneous Writings of Joseph Story*
Robert Sullivan, *The Disappearance of Dr. Parkman*
Henry David Thoreau, *Works*
Mark Tushnett, *The American Law of Slavery*

Syllabus

Week 1   Corwin, *The "Higher Law" Background of American Constitutional Law.* This short work outlines the tradition of political philosophy underlying the Constitution. It will provide us with needed background.

2–3   Cooper, *The Pioneers;* Fox, *"Property or People" (The Decline of Aristicracy);* Dorfman, "Chancellor Kent and the Developing American Ecomony." We will read *The Pioneers* along with the account of the New York Constitutional Convention of 1821 in Fox. *The Pioneers,* a book about the role of law in American society, portrays the death of one way of life and the ascendancy of another. It was written one year after the Convention, in which Kent, with Cooper's sympathies, unsuccessfully defended the old, Federalist system. To compare Cooper's work with Kent's legal philosophy will let us see both as different, yet similar, reactions to the conditions leading to the 1821 Convention. *The Pioneers* also offers one of the most powerful portrayals of an impartial judge in our literature. The depiction of Judge Temple will allow us to start an examination of how the judicial character was portrayed in the literature of the time.

4-5   Morton Horwitz, "The Emergence of an Instrumental Conception of Law," "Transformation in the Conception of Property," "Subsidation of Economic Growth through the Legal System," "Competition and Economic Development," "The Relations Between the Bar and Commercial Interest"; Emerson, "Nature," "Self-Reliance" (*Works*). Horwitz's book will be our guide to the legal history of the period. We will eventually read the entire book. The firt two chapters are extremely important because they show how American law transformed itself as America developed from a basically agrarian to an increasingly commercial economy. There is obvious relevance of this discussion for *The Pioneers*, in which the same transformation is fictionally presented through a conflict over the right to own a piece of property. Horwitz's discussion also makes way for a look at two of Emerson's most famous essays, which we will read for next time, "Nature" and "Self-Reliance." We will read these essays along with three of Horwitz's chapters which show in detail how the instrumental concept of the law helped to bring about a "release" of economic energy, and consider Emerson's doctrine of higher laws in part as a reaction to the legal system's change from a higher law to an instrumental concept, his theories of Nature and self-reliance in part as reaction to a rapidly expanding market economy which made the value of all commodities extremely unstable.

6-7   Hawthorne, *The House of the Seven Gables*; Walker Lewis, "The White Murder" (*Speak for Yourself, Daniel*); Horwitz, "The Development of Commercial Law," (*Transformation*); Joseph Story, "Characteristics of the Age," "History and Influence of the Puritans" (*Miscellaneous Writings*). Our first task will be to compare Hawthorne's Judge Pyncheon with Cooper's Judge Temple and his resolution of a conflict over the land with Cooper's. For the first session we will also read accounts of the famous 1830 Salem Murder Trial that Hawthorne used as a source for his romance, paying careful attention to the role of Justice Joseph Story and Daniel Webster. Having introduced a possible connection between Hawthorne and Story and Webster, we will read about their considerable role in the development of commercial law, concentrating especially on the landmark Dartmouth College and Charles River Bridge cases described in Horwitz. The Story essays will let us compare the responses of Salem's most famous judge and its most famous writer to the role the law played in American and Salem history.

8-10   Thoreau, "Slavery in Massachusetts" (*Works*); Emerson, "The Fugitive Slave Law" (*Works*); Stowe, *Uncle Tom's Cabin*; Herman Melville, "Benito Cereno" (*Complete Short Works*); Levy, "The Law of Freedom," "The Fugitive Slave Law," "Segregation" (*Law of the Commonwealth*); Mark Tushnett, "Slave Law and Its Uses," *The American Law of Slavery*. These three weeks will deal with the test slavery posed to the American legal system and the literary response to it. It was Shaw's rulings upholding the Fugitive Slave Law that in part prompted Thoreau's, Emerson's, and Stowe's works. We will also try to understand how accurately slave law was portrayed in the literary works by looking at actual laws in the South.

11-12   Melville, "Bartleby, the Scrivener," "The Paradise of Bachelors and the Tartarus of Maids" (*Complete Short Works*); Thoreau, "Civil Disobedience" (*Works*); "The Triumph of Contract" (*Transformation*). From a literary response to slave laws we will turn to a literary response to laws creating a system that some called "wage slavery" in the North. The wage system was based on the notion of free individuals whose selling of their labor was guaranteed to be fair by the sanctity of contract. We will examine the assumptions of contractarian ideology and how they are portrayed by Melville and Thoreau. Be cause the reading for these two weeks is light, I will also ask for an abstract and outline of papers.

13-14   Melville, "Billy Budd" (*Complete Short Works*); Horowitz, "The Rise of Legal Formalism" (*Transformation*); Robert Sullivan, selections from *The Diisappearance o Dr. Parkman*. We will read "Billy Budd" and examine the legal reasoning represented by Captain Vere in light of Horwitz' discussion of "The Rise of Legal Formal ism" and in light of Shaw's controversial decision in the Webster murder case, one of the most sensational trials in the nineteenth century.

Assignments

1. A glossary of key legal terms, figures, and cases of the time. I will provide the list; you provide the identifications. For example, you will need to explain an instrumental concept of the law, a natural rights concept, legal formalism, vested rights, etc.
2. Brief outlines of the transformation of American property law, commercial law, and contract law.
3. A ten-page paper. Possible topics:
    a. How the legal rights of women affected their portrayal in a work of literature at the time.
    b. Analyze the portrayal of the law in a work of literature in the period that we did not read in class.
    c. Compare a historical source with the literary work in terms of the law, as we did with the White murder and *The House of the Seven Gables*. Examples would be the Somers mutiny and "Billy Budd" or the *Amistad* case and "Benito Cereno".
    d. Do a "literary" analysis of the rhetoric of a famous decision such as *Marbury vs. Madison, Roberts vs. Boston*. Pay careful attention to the metaphors used to describe the function of the law.
    e. A topic of your choice. But see me first.

66
SURVIVALS—A THEMATIC COURSE:
Reading list created at the Yale Institute on Reconstructing American Literature
Martha Chew, Beverly Vlark, Brian Gallagher, Joan Hedrick, and Eleanor Tignor
June, 1982
Yale University

Introduction

We argue against a monolithic notion of "survival" for two reasons:
1) Because it does nothing to open up the canon of American literature—within the canonical works there are innumerable emblems of survival (e.g., Natty Bumppo, Ishmael, Nick Carraway) which could (and would) be used to delineate "survival" as essentially a white male rite of passage.

2) Because a singular notion of survival could easily tempt the student to read solipsistically, seeing American literature only in relation to the particular conditons of his/her survival.

Rather, we argue for "survivals" as a theme befitting the complex and varied literature of a pluralistic society. Often such survivals are achieved in the face of racial, gender, and class oppressions, thereby giving our literature *as a whole* a dialectical character. For example, the Indian myths and tales should be seen in conjunction with a work of the Euro-American colonization like *Of Plymouth Plantation*, or Douglass's *Narrative* with Emerson's "Self-Reliance." Similarly, many works reflect a clash of cultures (e.g., *Tell Me a Riddle, In Love and Trouble, Huckleberry Finn*). In this respect, it is crucial to study works written outside the dominant literary tradition (and often in subversion of it) within their contexts, lest their form be misunderstood—i.e., it is just as much the form as the content which represents an instance of a literary survival. Conversely, works representing different kinds of survivals can be grouped together in terms of their affinities (e.g., "Song of Myself" and Dickinson's poems). (An aside: as a means of studying the affinities and discontinuities, the "conjunctions and disjunctions" within the American literary tradition, it would be useful to have a new kind of journal, something like a *Comparative American Literature.*)

Within the body of literature we have chosen on "survivals" there are a number of sub-themes—e.g., the quest for education, the resistance of materialism, religious adaptations as survival strategies, the ambiguities of "passing" (and its allied issue, "masking," a particularly useful sub-theme for linking minority and women's literatures), the economic basis of racism and sexism (which so shapes the worlds within the texts of writers who are not white, male and middle/upper-class), the creative use of anger (particularly for the creation of a "voice" which demands its right to be heard and the importance of being heard), and the importance of self-definition (which crucially involves the right to create one's own *necessary* literary forms). Naturally, the theme of survivals implies its obverse, and we have therefore included several works which represent "destructions" (e.g., *Miss Lonelyhearts*).

Two further observations:

1) Affinities are not equations—e.g., to note affinities between, say, black and white women writers is not to suggest the interchangeability of the two groups but only to demark an area of overlap.

2) Conventional literary approaches can be retooled for more effective use—e.g., the much maligned concept of "regionalism" could be given a cross-cultural function if one studies the myths and stories of the Indians of the Northeast in relation to the literature of the Puritan colonizers and, as another unit (which attempts to break down the segregation of Indian literature), the Indian literature of the Southwest in relation to the literature of Spanish settlement and Chicano literature.

Reading List

Seventeenth and eighteenth centuries
Selections from *Singing for Power: The Song Magic of the Papago Indians*
Selections from *Traditional American Indian Literatures*
William Bradford, from *Of Plymouth Plantation*
Anne Bradstreet, selected poems
Jonathan Edwards, "Sinners in the Hands of an Angry God"
Benjamin Franklin, *Autobiography*
Excerpts from the First Trial of Anne Hutchinson (1636)
Cotton Mather, "The Trial of Martha Carrier"
Mary Rowlandson, *Narrative of the Captivity and Restoration*
Susanna Rowson, *Charlotte Temple*
Phillis Wheatley, selected poems
Michael Wigglesworth, *Diary* (1650)

Nineteenth century
"The Battle Hymn of the Republic"
Linda Brent, *Incidents in the Life of a Slave Girl*
William Wells Brown, *Clotel*
Calamity Jane, *Letters to Her Daughter*
Charles Chesnutt, "The Wife of His Youth"
Rose Terry Cooke, selected stories
Stephen Crane, "The Open Boat"
Emily Dickinson, selected poems
Frederick Douglass, *Narrative* (1845)
Paul Laurence Dunbar, "We Wear the Mask"
Ralph Waldo Emerson, "Self-Reliance," "The American Scholar,"
     "Experience"
Charlotte Forten, *Journal*
Mary Wilkins Freeman, "The Revolt of 'Mother'"
Sarah and Angelina Grimké, *Appeal to the Christian Women of the
     Southern States*
Frances Ellen Watkins Harper, selected poems
Nathaniel Hawthorne, "My Kinsman, Major Molineux"
Henry James, *Daisy Miller*
Sarah Orne Jewett, *The Country of the Pointed Firs*
Henry David Thoreau, "Civil Disobedience"
Mark Twain, *Huckleberry Finn*
Thorstein Veblen, selections from *The Theory of the Leisure Class*
David Walker, *Appeal*
Walt Whitman, "Song of Myself," selected poems

Twentieth century
John Berryman, "In Homage to Anne Bradstreet"

Blues lyrics, including selections from *The Blues Line* and *The Book of Negro Folklore*

Gwendolyn Brooks, "Kitchenette Building," "Sadie and Maud"

Sterling Brown, "Strong Men," "Old Lem," and other selections from *Southern Road*

Willa Cather, "A Wagner Matinee"

Frank Chin, ed., selections from *Aiiee*

Lucille Clifton, "Turning" and other selected poems

Hart Crane, selections from *The Bridge*

W.E.B. DuBois, *The Souls of Black Folk*

Charles Fuller, *A Soldier's Play*

Jean C. George, *Julie of the Wolves*

Susan Glaspell, "A Jury of Her Peers"

Susan Griffin, "I Like to Think of Harriet Tubman"

Langston Hughes, "Still Here," "Mother to Son," other selected poems, *Best of Simple*, *The Ways of White Folks*

Zora Neale Hurston, *Their Eyes Were Watching God*

James Weldon Johnson, *God's Trombones*

Nella Larsen, *Passing*

Lesbian Poetry; an Anthology, ed., Elly Bulkin and Joan Larkin, selections

The Maimie Papers, ed. R. Rosen and S. Davidson

Toni Morrison, *Sula*

Vladimir Nabokov, *Pnin*

Tillie Olsen, *Tell Me a Riddle*

Grace Paley, "The Loudest Voice"

John Rechy, *The Sexual Outlaw*

Adrienne Rich, "I Am an American Woman" and other selected poems

Anne Sexton, *All My Pretty Ones*

Leslie Silko, "Lullaby," "Indian Song: Survival"

John Steinbeck, *The Grapes of Wrath* (including the film)

Wallace Stevens, "Sunday Morning," "The Comedian as the Letter C," "Peter Quince at the Clavier"

Luis Valdez, *El corrido de Jesus Pelado Rascuachi* (film)

Alice Walker, "A Letter of the Times" and other selected stories

Margaret Walker, "For My People"

Nathanael West, *Miss Lonelyhearts*

Edith Wharton, "The Bunner Sisters"

William Carlos Williams, "Meditations on History"

Edmund Wilson, selections from *American Jitters*

Richard Wright, selections from *Eight Men*

Mitsuye Yamada, "Invisibility Is an Unnatural Disaster: Reflections of An Asian American Woman"; Audre Lorde, "The Master's Tools Will Never Dismantle the Master's House," and other selections from *This Bridge Called My Back*

67
CRITICISMS OF AMERICAN CULTURE
Jean Fagan Yellin
Fall, 1982
Pace University
New York, NY 10038

Introduction to Course

"We hold these truths to be self-evident, that all men are created equal; that they are endowed by their creator with certain unalienable rights, that among them are life, liberty, and the pursuit of happiness."
—Thomas Jefferson

"The history of reform is always identical, it is the comparison of idea with fact."
—Ralph Waldo Emerson

Historically, American radical critics have embraced the stated national ideals of "life, liberty, and the pursuit of happiness"; addressing the realities of inequality in America, they have developed critiques asserting the necessity of basic social change if we are to realize our national goals. In this course, students examine texts expressing radical critiques of inequalities grounded in class, race, and sex from three periods: the pre-industrial 1830s–1850s, the industrialized turn of the century, and the Great Depression of the 1930s. Each period is introduced by a case-study: first of a radical periodical—*The Liberator*; next of a radical's life—Eugene V. Debs; last of a radical cause—the Scottsboro Case. Readings stress primary criticisms of inequalities of race, class, and sex written during each historic period. Writing assignments require students to explore correlatives in American life today. Study of each period is completed by examining a work of literature by an artist not usually relegated to the context of "radical social criticism"—Melville, Dreiser, and Wright. This large design is meant to invite students to explore tensions between the three periods sketched, between past and present, within each period between mainstream culture and radical critiques, among various radical critiques, between historical and literary texts, between "propaganda" and "art."

Criticisms of American Culture is a three-credit one-semester lecture-discussion course designed as the final requirement in an honors level interdisciplinary academic minor in the humanities. Ideally, students electing this course have completed an urban internship and a sophomore-level team-taught interdisciplinary (His/Eng) course studying mainstream American culture, a course addressing an apsect of American civilization that is taught within a traditional humanistic discipline.

The syllabus that follows represents the third version of this course that has been offered. Before it was presented, a *Reader* was assembled to make available texts otherwise accessible only on library reserve. Next time around, three changes will be made in this syllabus. First, the weakest reading assignment, Fine's *Sit-Down: The General Motors Strike of 1936–37* will be replaced, perhaps by Henry Kraus, *The Many and the Few: A Chronicle of the Dynamic Auto Workers* (c/o Books on Demand, University Microfilms). Second, the optional interview with a self-styled radical critic of American life today—which proved confusing—will be dropped; all students will be asked to complete the interview with someone currently identified with a radical cause. Third, because few students enter the classroom with ideal prerequisites, brief historical lectures will precede the case studies that inaugurate the examination of each period.

Originally, this course was developed with the assistance of the National Endowment for the Humanities (EN-20798-74-372); it was implemented with the aid of the Endowment (EN--0010), the American Express Foundation, and Pace University. Its contents, however, do not necessarily represent the views of the Endowment, the Foundation, or the University.

Booklist

Books in which entire text is assigned
Frederick Douglass, *Narrative of the Life of Frederick Douglass*
Theodore Dreiser, *Sister Carrie*
W.E.B. DuBois, *The Souls of Black Folk*
Upton Sinclair, *The Jungle*
Richard Wright, *Native Son*; *American Hunger*
Jean Fagan Yellin, ed., *NYC 280 Reader*

Books in which a portion of the text is assigned
Edward Bellamy, *Looking Backward*
[Linda Brent, pseud.], *Incidents in the Life of a Slave Girl*, ed. L. Maria Child
Dan Carter, *Scottsboro: A Tragedy of the American South*
Sidney Fine, *Sit-Down: The General Motors Strike of 1936–37*
Ray Ginger, *The Bending Cross: A Biography of Eugene Victor Debs*
Joanne Grant, ed., *Black Protest*
Herbert Gutman, *Work, Culture, and Society in Industrializing America*
Hutchins Hapgood, *The Spirit of the Ghetto*
Truman Nelson, ed., *Documents of Upheaval: Selections from William Lloyd Garrison's The Liberator, 1831–1865*
Harriet Robinson, *Loom and Spindle: Or, Life Among the Early Mill Girls*
Alice Rossi, ed., *The Feminist Papers*

Short stories (can be located in various anthologies or on library reserve)
Herman Melville, "Benito Cereno," "The Paradise of Bachelors and the
 Tartarus of Maids"

Syllabus

I. 1830s–1850s
Class 1   Backgrounds.
      2   Case study: Focus on a radical publication—*The Liberators*.

> "Tell a man whose house is on fire to give a moderate alarm; tell him to
> moderately rescue his wife from the hands of the ravisher; tell the
> mother to gradually extricate her babe from the fire into which it has
> fallen; but urge me not to use moderation in a cause like the present."
>   —William Lloyd Garrison

Nelson, *Documents of Upheaval:* "Introduction" (ix–xii),
 "What Shall Be Done?" (10–11), "A Colored Phila-
 delphian" (27), "Insurrection in Virginia" (28–31),
 "Woman and the Cause" (54), "The Prudence Crandall
 Case" (64–69), "Reign of Terror" (79–95), "Garrison
 Blasts Beecher" (introduction only, 96), "Children's
 Crusade" (114–18), "Short Catechism" (128–30),
 "Lovejoy Climax" (introduction only 131), "Fire and
 Hammer of God's Word" (140–44), "Schism" (163–68),
 "World's Anti-Slavery Convention" (169–72),
 "Fraternal Community" (177–81), "Constitutional
 Argument" (200–01), "Revolutionary Separatism and
 Protest" (202–07), "Resistance to Tyranny" (215–17),
 "Uncle Tom and an Anti-Tom Convention" (239–40),
 "Garrison Calls for Success to Insurrectionists" (263–75),
 "Phillips on Lincoln's Election" (274), "Valedictory"
 (275–82)
      3–4   A black perspective:

> "What, to the American slave, is your Fourth of July?"
>   —Frederick Douglass

Douglass, *Narrative*; Brent, *Incidents In the Life of a Slave
 Girl*: Introduction, Preface, chapters 1-2, 4–7, 10–12,
 14–21, 24, 27–30, 32, 39, 41, appendix
      5–6   A feminist perspective:

> "All I ask of our brethren is, that they will take their feet from off our necks, and permit us to stand upright to that ground which God designed us to occupy."
>
> —Sarah Grimké

Margaret Fuller, "The Great Lawsuit"; Angelina Grimké, *Appeal to the Christian Women of the South, Letters to Catharine Beecher*; Sarah Grimké, "Letters on the Equality of the Sexes and the Condition of Women," numbers 3, 8, 15; Seneca Falls "Declaration of Sentiments and Resolutions"; Sojourner Truth, "Ain't I a Woman?" (*Feminist Papers*), "What Time of Night It Is"; Lucy Stone, "Marriage Under Protest," "Disappointment is the Lot of Woman"; Elizabeth Cady Stanton, "Address to the New York State Legislature"; M.W. Chapman, *Right and Wrong*, "Lines: Inscribed to the Intolerant, Throughout New England and the Coast Thereof," "The Times That Try Men's Souls"; Hutchinson Family, "Woman Suffrage Song," "A Hundred Years Hence," "Let Us All Speak Our Minds"; J. A. Collins, "The Anti-Slavery Call"; Frances E. W. Harper, "The Two Offers"; L. Maria Child, "Preface," *Appeal in Favor of that Class of Americans Called Africans*, "Woman's Rights" (*NYC 280 Reader*)

7   A class perspective:

> "It is only a proper amount of work that is a blessing; too much of it...makes a man a spinning-jenny, or a ploughing-machine...He ceases to be a man, and becomes a thing."
>
> —Theodore Parker

Gutman, "Work, Culture and Society in Industrializing America, 1815–1919 "(*Work, Culture and Society*). Critiques of class in antebellum America—read two: W. E. Channing, "On the Elevation of the Laboring Classes"; Theodore Parker, "Thoughts on Labor"; Wendell Philips, "Labor and the Eight-Hour Movement", "The Case for Labor" (*NYC 280 Reader*). Workers' reminiscences—read one: Louisa May Alcott, "How I Went Out to Service" (*NYC 280 Reader*); Robinson, *Loom and Spindle*, chaps. 2–5. Communitarianism as a solution to the problem of class in America—read one: Alcott, "Transcendental Wild Oats"; *The Harbinger* (*NYC 280 Reader*).

8   A review of 1830s–1850s: Writing—Special Log assignment: discuss an aspect of either of Melville's tales in light of one or more of the assigned readings. Round-table discussion based on Log entries. Melville, "Benito

Cereno," "The Paradise of Bachelors and the Tartarus
of Maids"
II.   Turn of the Century
9   Transition. Film: "The Inheritance"
10   Case study: Focus on a radical's life—choose either option A
         or B. Reading for Option A and B: Jack London, "What
         Life Means to Me" (*NYC 280 Reader*). Option A:
         Eugene Victor Debs

"... while there is a lower class, I am in it, while there is a criminal
element, I am of it, and while there is a soul in prison, I am not free."
—Eugene Victor Debs

Ginger, *The Bending Cross*, pp. 18–19; chapter 7, pp. 181–83;
chapters 10, 13, 14, 17, 18, 20; pp. 457–59. Option B:
Find someone who identifies himself/herself as a radical
critic of American life today. *Interview* that person about
his/her life, and *write up* your interview—relating it to
to some of the work in this course—in about 1,500 words
(five double-spaced pages) of graceful standard English.
Hand in an original and one copy; the original will be
returned to you. *Participate* in a special round-table
discussion based on your paper.
11   A class perspective:

"This class struggle will continue just so long as one man eats his bread
in the sweat of another man's face."
—William Haywood

Hamlin Garland, "Under the Lion's Paw"; Jack London,
"The Apostate"; Lincoln Steffens, "Tweed Days in St.
Louis"; Edwin Markham, "The Man With the Hoe"
(*NYC 280 Reader*); Bellamy, *Looking Backward*, chaps.
2, 3, 5, 28; Hapgood, *The Spirit of the Ghetto*, pp. 18–43,
181–94
12–13   Sinclair, *The Jungle*. Logs due for check
14–15   A black perspective:

"We will not be satisfied to take one jot or tittle less than our full
manhood rights."
—W.E.B. DuBois

DuBois, *The Souls of Black Folk*; "The Niagra Movement
Declaration of Principles" (*Black Protest*); Frances E.W.
Harper, "Aunt Chloe," "The Deliverance," "Aunt
Chloe's Politics," "Learning to Read," "Church Build
ing," "The Reunion"; Paul Laurence Dunbar, "We
Wear the Mask"; Ida B. Wells Barnett, *A Red Record*;

Frederick Douglass, "Lynch Law in the South"; F.B. Williams, "The Accusations Are False"; "K.K.K. Terror" (*NYC 280 Reader*)

16   A feminist perspective:

"The strongest reason why we ask for a woman voice in government under which she lives; in the religion she is asked to believe; equality in social life, where she is the chief factor; a place in the trades and professions, where she may earn her bread, is because of her birth-right or self-sovereignty; because, as an individual, she must rely on herself."
                                        —Elizabeth Cady Stanton

Emma Goldman, "The Tragedy of Woman's Emancipation"; Margaret Sanger, "My Fight for Birth Control" (*Feminist Papers*); Hapgood, *The Spirit of the Ghetto*, chap. 3; Charlotte Perkins Gilman, from *Women and Economics* (*Feminist Papers*), "The Socialist and the Suffragist"; H. Marot, "A Woman's Strike—An Appreciation of the Shirtwaist Makers of New York"; Rose Schneiderman, "Triangle Memorial Speech"; Elizabeth Cady Stanton, "The Solitude of Self"; Kate Chopin, "The Story of an Hour," "A Respectable Woman"; Willa Cather, "A Wagner Matinee,"; Mary Wilkins Freeman, "The Revolt of 'Mother'"; Mary White Ovington, "The White Brute" (*NYC 280 Reader*)

17–18 A review of the turn of the century:
Writing—Special Log assignment: discuss as aspect of *Sister Carrie* in light of one or more assigned readings. Roundtable discussion based on Log entries. Dreiser, *Sister Carrie*

III. The 1930s
19   Transition. Film: "Union Maids"
20   Case study: Focus on a radical cause—Choose either option C or D. Option C: The Scottsboro Case

"Free Tom Mooney and the Scottsboro Boys!"
                                        —Radical slogan

Carter, *Scottsboro*: Preface, chapters 1, 2, 5, 7, 8, epilogue; Countee Cullen, "Scottsboro, Too, Is Worth Its Song" (*NYC 280 Reader*). Option D: Identify a cause that has moved people to take radical action and find someone identified with this cause. *Interview* that person about the cause, and *write up* your interview—relating it to some of the work in this course—in about 1,500 words (five double-spaced pages) of graceful standard English. Hand in original and one copy; the original will be returned to you. *Participate* in a special round-table discussion based on your paper.

21   A black perspective:

> "Let America be America again.
> (It never was America to me.)
> And yet I swear this oath—
> America will be!"
>
> —Langston Hughes

"Why We March"; Angelo Herndon, "You Cannot Kill the Working Class"; L.B. Granger, "The Negro—Friend or Foe of Organized labor?" (*Black Protest*); Ted Poston, "The Making of Moma Harris"; W.E.B. DuBois, "Segregation"; James Weldon Johnson, "Negro Americans, What Now?"; Sterling Brown, "Strong Men"; Margaret Walker, "For My People"; Robert Hayden, "Gabriel," "Speech"; Langston Hughes, "Let America Be America Again," "Ballad of Lenin," "Sharecropper," "Park Bench"; Richard Wright, "Between the World and Me" (*NYC 280 Reader*)

22   A feminist perspective:

"Finally it boils down to this: Women must be activized in the interests of the people, and the people must be activized in the interests of women."

> —M. Inman

M. Inman, "In Woman's Defense"; Edna St. Vincent Millay, "Rendezvous"; Phyllis McGinley, "Why, Some of my Best Friends Are Women," "The 5:32"; Muriel Rukeyser, "More of a Corpse Than a Woman," "Night Feeding," "Poem Out of Childhood"; S. Nowicki, "Rank and File Organizing"; Meridel LeSueur, "I Was Marching," "Salvation Home," "Sequel to Love," "They Follow Us Girls," "Women on the Breadlines"; Tillie Lerner (Olsen), "The Strike"; Genevieve Taggard, "Interior"; Dorothy Parker, "The Standard of Living" (*NYC 280 Reader*)

23-24   A class perspective:

> "They say in Harlan County
> There are no neutrals there;
> You'll either be a union man
> Or a thug for J.H. Blair.
> Which side are you on?"
>
> —Ella Mae Wiggins

Fine, *Sit-Down*, chaps. 1-6, 11

25-26   Review of the 1930s:
        Writings—Special Log assignment: discuss an aspect of
           Wright's novels in light of one or more assigned read-

ings. Round-table discussion based on Log entries.
Wright, *Native Son*; *American Hunger*
27–28   Transitions and conclusions. Film: "Salt of the Earth." Logs
due

Logs

Throughout this semester, you are to keep a weekly Log in which you record your reactions and responses to the week's work in this course. Weekly entries should run approximately 300–600 words. They must be written in standard English. You need not type these unless you wish; you may write in ink but do make them legible; use a special loose-leaf notebook. Three Log assignments are more specific than the others: see classes 8, 17, 25.

Papers

You will write one paper. You must choose Option B—a case study of a radical's life; or Option D—a case study of a radical cause.

MODEL CHRONOLOGY

The following chronology was prepared by Jean Fagan Yellin of Pace University in connection with her course, "Criticisms of American Culture" (see syllabus #67, above.) We present it both for its inherent use and as a model for chronologies that should be developed for all of United States history and culture.

1829   David Walker, *Appeal . . . to the Coloured Citizens of the World, but in Particular and very expressly to those of the United States of America*

1831   Workingmen's Parties organized in Philadelphia, Boston, and New York (dwindle by 1834)
First Convention of People of Color in Philadelphia
Nat Turner insurrection in Virginia
Virginia legislature debates emancipation
William Lloyd Garrison establishes *The Liberator*
Edgar Allan Poe, Poems; *The Narrative of Arthur Gordon Pym*, 1838; *Tales of the Grotesque and Arabesque*, 1840; *The Raven and Other Poems*, 1845.

1833   American Anti-Slavery Society organized
Slavery abolished throughout British Empire
Lydia Maria Child, *Appeal in Favor of that Class of Americans Called Africans*

1834   New York City Locofocos (anti-monopoly Jacksonians) elect trade unionist to Congress
National Trade Union organized (1834–37)
New England Association of Farmers, Mechanics, and other Workingmen organized (1834–37)

1835   Seminole War (1835–42)
Anti-Black, anti-abolitionist violence: riots against anti-slavery females in Boston; Garrison escapes lynching; Murrell Affair in Mississippi; Post office sacked for anti-slavery mail in Charleston; Amos Dresser whipped in Nashville

1836 Philadelphia building trades workers win ten-hour day
Congress passes gag rule against anti-slavery petitions
Ralph Waldo Emerson, *Nature; The American Scholar*, 1837;
"Divinity School Address," 1838; *Essays*, 1841, 1844, *Representative Men*, 1850
Richard Hildreth, *Archy Moore*; first American abolitionist novel

1837 Elijah Lovejoy murdered and his anti-slavery press destroyed at
Alton, Illinois
Economic depression; 600 banks close; "flour riots" in New York
City
First Anti-Slavery Convention of American Women held in New
York City; Second Convention mobbed following year in
Philadelphia and Pennsylvania Hall burnt to ground; final
Convention held in Philadelphia, 1839
Mt. Holyoke Seminary opens as first women's college in United
States

1838 Cherokees begin 1,200 mile forced march under U.S. Army
evacuation drive
Mass meeting of Afro-Americans in Philadelphia protests
Pennsylvania disfranchisement
Mirror of Liberty, first Afro-American magazine; (earliest
Afro-American Newspaper: *Freedom's Journal*, 1827)
Sarah Grimké, *Letters on the Equality of the sexes and the Condition
of Women*

1839 Theodore D. Weld, ed., *American Slavery As It Is: Testimony of a
Thousand Witnesses*

1840 Ten-hour day established for government workers; in New
England, workers unsuccessfully demand ten-hour day
throughout decade
American and Foreign Anti-Slavery Society splits from American
Anti-Slavery Society
Liberty Party, first anti-slavery political party, nominates
Presidential ticket
Charles Remond and William Lloyd Garrison to London for
World Anti-Slavery Convention; refuse their seats when
Lucretia Mott and other female delegates are not seated
because of their sex; Mott and Elizabeth Cady Stanton discuss need for women to call their own convention.
The Dial, organ of Transcendentalist Club, begins publication

1841 Utopian community founded at Brook Farm; Nathaniel
Hawthorne in residence April to November; reorganized in
1845 under Fourierist principles, one of approximately forty
associations established in decade (earliest: Sylvana Phalanx,
1842; longest-lasting: North American Phalanx, 1843–54)
Frederick Douglass meets William Lloyd Garrison at Nantucket
anti-slavery meeting

Supreme Court frees African slave rebels of Spanish slaveship
Amistad
Slaves revolt on board the *U.S.S. Creole*; sail to Bahamas for
asylum and freedom

1842   Supreme Court permits slaveowner to recover fugitive under
1793 act
Nathaniel Hawthorne, *Twice Told Tales; Mosses from an Old
Manse*, 1846; *The Scarlet Letter*, 1850; *The House of the Seven
Gables*, 1851; *The Blithedale Romance*, 1852; *The Snow Image*,
1852; *The Marble Faun*, 1860

1843   Henry Highland Garnet, "Address to the Slaves" calls for active
resistance
Baptist church splits over slavery issue; Methodist Episcopalians
follow in 1844, Presbyterians in 1847
Margaret Fuller, "The Great Lawsuit," revised as *Woman in the
Nineteenth Century*, 1845; writes for New York *Tribune*,
1844; reports on and participates in Italian revolution in 1848

1844   Joseph Smith, leader of Mormon Church, killed by mob at
Nauvoo, Illinois; Brigham Young leads exodus to West in
1846
William Lloyd Garrison advances slogan, "No Union With
Slaveholders"
New Agrarians demand free land
Boston Afro-Americans protest segregated schools; file suit in
1849; Massachusetts Supreme Court establishes "separate
but equal" precedent; Boston Jim Crow schooling ends in
1855
New England Afro-Americans form "Freedom Association" to
aid fugitive slaves

1845   Henry David Thoreau to Walden Pond
Lowell Female Labor Reform Association formed
Frederick Douglass, *Narrative*; expanded to *My Bondage and My
Freedom*, 1855; *Life and Times*, 1881, 1892

1846   Mexican War (1846–48); victory gives United States territories of
California, Arizona, New Mexico, and Texas
Convention of New England Workingmen at Lynn,
Massachusetts, adopts resolution against black slavery
Herman Melville, *Typee; Omoo*, 1847; *Mardi, Redburn*, 1849;
White-Jacket, 1850; *Moby-Dick*, 1851; *Pierre*, 1852; *The
Piazza Tales*, 1856; *The Confidence Man*, 1857
John Greenleaf Whittier, *Voices of Freedom*
Oliver Wendell Holmes, Poems

1847   Liberia established as independent republic
Irish immigration peaks following great potato famine
Frederick Douglass begins publication of *The North Star*

Karl Marx and Frederick Engels, *The Communist Manifesto*; first
American publication in English is in *Woodhull & Claflin's
Weekly*, 1871

1848 Perfectionist community established at Oneida; Icarian
communities established
Worker's uprisings in France and Germany put down; German
immigrants to U.S. include William Weitling and Joseph
Weydemeyer, friends of Marx and Engels; in 1867 form first
U.S. Marxist organization, the General German Working-
man's Association (later Section One of New York, First
International)
Feminists meet on women's rights at Seneca Falls, New York;
adopt Declaration of Sentiments which includes first formal
demand for women's suffrage in U.S.; split in 1869 over issue
of supporting Fourteenth Amendment which inserts word
"male" into Constitution
Free Soil Party organized
Wisconsin disfranchises black residents
Thoreau, "Civil Disobedience"; *A Week on the Concord And
Merrimack Rivers*, 1849; *Walden*, 1854

1848 James Russell Lowell, *A Fable for Critics*
William Collins Foster, *Songs of the Sable Harmonists*

1849 California gold rush
Elizabeth Blackwell becomes first woman physician in U.S.
Harriet Tubman escapes from slavery in Maryland; makes first
Underground Railroad trip, 1850
Francis Parkman, *The Oregon Trail*

1850 Women's rights leaders meet during Boston Negro Rights
Convention, plan First National Women's Rights Conven-
tion; hold yearly conventions until 1860
Susan B. Anthony joins feminist ranks; arrested and tried for
voting, 1873
Fugitive Slave Law and Compromise of 1850
Walt Whitman prints first free verse poem "Blood Money" on
slavery

1851 Fugitive slave cases: Shadrack, Simms; Christiana Affair; Jerry
rescue
Sojourner Truth addresses Akron, Ohio Women's Rights
Convention
William Nell, *Service of Colored Americans in the Wars of 1776 and
1812; The Colored Patriots in the American Revolution*, 1855

1852 Death of Fanny Wright, pioneering abolitionist, feminist,
founder of utopian colony Nashoba
The Pro-Slavery Argument, an explicit defense of institution of
chattel slavery

Harriet Beecher Stowe, *Uncle Tom's Cabin*

Martin R. Delany, *The Condition, Elevation, Emancipation and Destiny of the Colored People of the United States, Politically Considered*

1853   William Wells Brown, *Clotel*; first Afro-American novel published

Blacks petition Massachusetts Constitutional Convention to join state militia

1854   Fugitive slave case: Anthony Burns; mobs attack Boston courthouse in effort to free him; 2,000 United States troops return him to his master; Burns freed by purchase 1855

Kansas-Nebraska Act

William Lloyd Garrison burns Constitution

Lincoln University, first black college, founded as Ashmun Institute

Republican party formed

1855   Abolition of slavery in Peru leaves Western Hemisphere free except Cuba, Brazil, and the United States

Walt Whitman, *Leaves of Grass*; *Democratic Vistas*, 1870

1856   John Mercer Langdon becomes Township clerk, Lorain County, Ohio, first Afro-American to win elective office

Lawrence, Kansas sacked

Charles Sumner caned on floor of U.S. Senate

Wilberforce University founded by Methodist Episcopal church

1857   In Dred Scott decision, United States Supreme Court upholds Fugitive Slave Law and denies United States citizenship to Afro-Americans; Fourteenth Amendment makes Afro-Americans citizens, 1868

Business panic, mobs in New York and Philadelphia

1858   Campaign for U.S. Senate seat in Illinois waged by Lincoln and Douglas

Treaties concluded for trade with China and Japan

Transatlantic cable laid

John Brown at Convention in Chatham, Canada West

Oberlin-Wellington rescue case: Black fugitive John Price freed by students and professor

Frances Ellen Watkins Harper, "The Two Offers"; *Iola Leroy*, 1892

1859   John Brown leads raid at Harper's Ferry; Thoreau and Emerson speak in his defense; Brown is executed with four black co-conspirators

Georgia Legislature acts to allow sale of free blacks picked up as vagrants

Clothilde, last African slave ship, docks in Alabama

Anglo-African Magazine begins publication, serializes Martin R.
  Delany's *Blake*
Harriet E. Wilson, *Our Nig: Or Sketches from the Life of a Free
  Black*, first novel published by an Afro-American woman
Charles Darwin, *Origin of the Species*

1860   Lincoln elected President; South Carolina secedes
       New York Afro-Americans appeal for equal suffrage rights

1861   Russian Czar emancipates serfs
       National Convention of Workingmen meets in Philadelphia
       Confederacy fires on Ft. Sumter; Civil War begins (to 1865)
       Linda Brent, *Incidents in the Life of a Slave Girl*
       Rebecca Harding Davis, "Life in The Iron Mills"; *Margaret
         Howth*, 1862

1862   Abolition of slavery in District of Columbia
       Union army accepts black troops
       Afro-American Robert Smalls (seaman on gunboat) turns
         Confederate ship over to Union

1863   Unions revive; trades' assembly organized at Rochester, New
         York; National Labor Union organized in 1864
       Draft riots in New York City
       Lincoln signs Emancipation Proclamation; Thirteenth
         Amendment, abolishing slavery, 1865; Civil Rights Bill 1866;
         First Reconstruction Act in 1867

1876   American Centennial
       Federal troops withdrawn from former Confederacy
       Native Americans defeat General Custer at Battle of Little Big
         Horn
       End of First International (organized London 1863)
       Marxist Working Men's Party of the U.S. founded; renamed
         Socialist Labor Party in 1877

1877   "Molly McGuires" (Irish Unionists) hanged in Pennsylvania
       Nationwide railroad strike: "The Railroad War"

1878   Greenback Party polls 1,000,000 votes
       Woman Suffrage Amendment introduced into United States
         Senate; becomes effective as Nineteenth Amendment in 1920
       Knights of Labor, founded 1869, established on national scale

1879   Black exodus from South to Kansas
       Henry George, *Progress and Poverty*
       George Washington Cable, *Old Creole Days; The Negro Question*,
         1888

1880   National Farmers Alliance organized; forerunner of Populist
         Party
       Joel Chandler Harris, *Uncle Remus*

1881   Booker T. Washington opens Tuskeegee

Revolutionary Socialist Labor Party formed by direct actionists in
split from Socialist Labor Party, renamed International
Working People's Association, expounds Bakuninist anar-
chism

Founding of Federation of Organized Trades, predecessor of
American Federation of Labor

Jim Crow railroad law in Tennessee inaugurates modern
segregation movement; Florida, Mississippi, Texas,
Louisiana, Alabama, Kentucky, Arkansas, Georgia, South
Carolina, North Carolina, and Virginia follow by 1900;
Maryland and Oklahoma by 1907

Henry James, *Portrait of a Lady; The Bostonians; The Princess
Cassamassima*, 1886; *The Wings of the Dove*, 1902; *The
Ambassadors*, 1903; *The Golden Bowl*, 1904

1882   First Labor Day Parade held in New York City

1883   Brooklyn Bridge opened

Supreme Court declares Native Americans "aliens" and "de-
pendents"

Mark Twain, *Life on the Mississippi; Huckleberry Finn*, 1884; *A
Connecticut Yankee in King Arthur's Court*, 1889; *The
Tragedy of Pudd'nhead Wilson*, 1894; *The Man that Corrupted
Hadleyburg*, 1900

1884   Equal Rights Party nominates Belva Lockwood, first woman
Presidential candidate

William Dean Howells, *The Rise of Silas Lapham; A Hazard of
New Fortunes*, 1890; *An Imperative Duty*, 1893; *A Traveller
from Alturia*, 1894; *Through the Eye of a Needle*, 1907

1886   Strike at McCormick Harvester Company in Chicago

Demonstrations for eight-hour day (later commemorated as May
Day); Chicago meetings lead to bombing at the Haymarket;
four leaders hanged; remaining pardoned by Governor
Altgeld in 1893

New York streetcar strike

Statue of Liberty dedicated

Twenty Afro-Americans killed at Carrollton, Mississippi

Founding of New York City United Labor Party; nomination of
Henry George for mayor

German Socialists Wilhelm Liebknecht, Edward Aveling and
Eleanor Marx Aveling tour U.S.; Avelings publish *The
Working Class Movement in the U.S.*

1887   First vote on woman suffrage taken in U.S. Senate; defeated
two-to-one

Thomas N. Page, *In Ole Virginia*

Mary Wilkins Freeman, *A Humble Romance; A New England Nun*,
1891

1888 Society of Christian Socialists organized; dwindles by 1896
Edward Bellamy, *Looking Backward*; book sparks organization of
(socialist) Nationalist Clubs; movement spreads to twenty-
one states; defunct 1894

1890 McKinley Tariff
Sherman Anti-Trust Act
Sherman Silver Purchase Act; repealed 1893
Ellis Island opened as immigration depot
Socialist Party led by Daniel DeLeon (organized 1877)
United Mine Workers of America founded
Feminists merge organizations and focus on suffrage; form
National American Suffrage Association; plan state-by-state
campaigns
Wyoming enters Union as first state with full woman suffrage
Afro-American National League founded to combat discrimina-
tion; program foreshadows NAACP
U.S. Troops kill 200 Native Americans at Wounded Knee
Mississippi begins systematic exclusion of Afro-Americans from
politics; voting tests circumventing Fifteenth Amendment
adopted in South Carolina, Louisiana, North Carolina,
Alabama, Virginia, Georgia and Oklahoma by 1910
William James, *The Principles of Psychology; Varieties of Religious
Experience*, 1902
Jacob Riis, *How the Other Half Lives*
Emily Dickinson, *Poems*
Ignatius Donnelly, *Caesar's Column*

1892 Homestead steel strike; anarchist Alexander Berkman shoots cap-
italist Henry Clay Frick
Strike at Coeur d'Alene, Idaho led by Western Federation of
Miners' Bill Haywood
Ida B. Wells-Barnett launches anti-lynching campaign with pub-
lication of *Southern Horrors; A Red Record*, 1895; *Mob Rule in
New Orleans*, 1900
Populists (People's Party) hold first national convention

1893 Financial panic
World's Columbian Exposition opens at Chicago
Passage of Illinois Factory Act outlawing employment of children
under fourteen at night or for longer than eight hours during
day; State Supreme Court rules eight-hour provision un-
constitutional in 1895; Illinois passes child labor bill in 1903
Male voters grant woman suffrage for first time (in Colorado)
F.J. Turner, "The Significance of the Frontier in American
History"
Stephen Crane, *Maggie: A Girl of the Streets; The Red Badge of
Courage, 1895*

1894 "Coxey's Army" of unemployed to Washington
Strike at Cripple Creek, Colorado led by Western Federation of
    Miners; union defeated in violent strike, 1904
Pullman Car Company Strike: "The Debs Rebellion"
Henry Demarest Lloyd, *Wealth Against Commonwealth*

1895 Carrie Chapman Catt revitalizes woman suffrage struggle
First National Conference of Colored Women leads to founding
    of National Association of Colored Women
Booker T. Washington, "Atlanta Exposition Address"
The Appeal to Reason (1895–1929)

1896 Bryan-McKinley campaign; coinage of silver at 16:1
Christian Commonwealth Colony founded in Georgia (until
    1900)
Strike at Leadville, Colorado
In *Plessy v. Ferguson*, U.S. Supreme Court denies that southern
    segregation conflicts with Thirteenth and Fourteenth
    Amendments; articulates "separate but equal" doctrine
Atlanta Conferences for the Study of the Negro Problem (to 1907)
Utah and Idaho franchise women; no states follow until 1910
Sarah Orne Jewett, *Country of the Pointed Firs*
Paul Laurence Dunbar, *Lyrics of Lowly Life*; *The Love of Landry*;
    The Strength of Gideon, 1900; *The Fanatics*, 1901; *The Sport
    of The Gods*, 1902

1897 American Negro Academy founded
Alaska gold rush begins
Strikes in soft coal industry
Thorstein Veblen, *The Theory of the Leisure Class*

1898 Spanish-American War (opposed by Anti-Imperialist League);
    United States gains Hawaiian Islands, Puerto Rico, and
    Philippines; Philippine rebellion against United States 1899
    is defeated 1902; Philippines become independent republic
    1946
Louisiana introduces "Grandfather Clause," automatically regis-
    tering as voters males whose fathers or grandfathers qualified
    to vote in 1867; others (Afro-Americans) must comply with
    educational or property requirements
Race riot in Wilmington, North Carolina

1899 Boxer Rebellion in China; intervention by Great Powers; agita-
    tion for "open door" policy
Frank Norris, *McTeague*; *The Octopus*, 1901; *The Pit*, 1903
Edwin Markham, "The Man With the Hoe"
Charles Waddell Chesnutt, *The Conjure Woman*; *The Wife of His
    Youth*; *The House Behind The Cedars*, 1900; *The Marrow of
    Tradition*, 1901; *The Colonel's Dream*, 1905

Sutton Griggs, *Imperium in Imperio*; *Overshadowed, 1901; Unfettered, 1902; The Hindered Hand*, 1905; *Pointing the Way*, 1908

Kate Chopin, *The Awakening*

1900   Gold Standard Act

Race riot at New Orleans

National Negro Business League founded

Sigmund Freud, *The Interpretation of Dreams*

Booker T. Washington, *Up From Slavery*

Theodore Dreiser, *Sister Carrie* (suppressed until 1912); *Jennie Gerhardt*, 1911; *The Financier*, 1912; *An American Tragedy*, 1925

1901   McKinley shot; Roosevelt succeeds to Presidency

United States Steel formed by Judge Gary, Carnegie, Schwab, and Morgan; first billion-dollar corporation

Socialist Party formed

Western Federation of Miners conduct strike at Telluride, Colorado; militia sent in 1904

Roosevelt recommends regulation of trusts and corporations

Isaac Kahn Freedman, *By Bread Alone*

John Spargo edits *The Comrade*

1902   Pennsylvania anthracite coal strike

American occupation of Cuba ended; Republic of Cuba proclaimed

McClure's publishes Ida M. Tarbell, "History of the Standard Oil Company," launching muck-raking journalism

Chinese Exclusion Act broadened (repealed 1943); 1907 immigration act checks entrance of Japanese

Thomas Dixon, *The Leopard's Spots*; *The Klansman*, 1905; filmed by D.W. Griffith as *Birth of a Nation* (1914) sparks NAACP protests

1903   Ford Motor Company formed; establishes assembly line production, 1911

First motor airflight by Wright brothers; Lindbergh flies solo from New York to Paris, 1927

W.E.B. DuBois, *The Souls of Black Folk*

Jack London, *The People of the Abyss*, 1903; *The War of the Classes*, 1905; *The Iron Heel*, 1907

1904   New York subway opened

Panama Canal brought under American auspices; completed 1914

Lincoln Steffens, *The Shame of the Cities*; *Autobigraphy*, 1931

1905   Organization of revolutionary industrial union International Workers of the World (One Big Union) by Daniel DeLeon, Eugene Debs, Bill Haywood, Lucy Parsons, Mother Jones, and others

Critics of Booker T. Washington organize Niagara Movement,
   forerunner of NAACP
Socialist-oriented Rand School of Social Science established New
   York City; Ferrar School founded 1911
Russia defeated by Japan in Pacific war, puts down revolutionists
Einstein's theory of relativity revolutionizes concepts of space and
   time
Willa Cather, *The Troll Garden*; *O Pioneers!*, 1913; *Song of the
   Lark*, 1915; *My Antonia*, 1918
Edith Wharton, *The House of Mirth*; *The Age of Innocence*, 1920
Daniel DeLeon, *Socialist Reconstruction of Society*

1906 San Francisco earthquake and fire
Railway Rate Act
IWW strikes at General Electric, Schenectady, New York; at
   Goldfield, Idaho; at Portland, Oregon
Moyer, Haywood, Pettibone arrested for dynamite murder; trials
   1907
Equal Rights Convention held in Georgia
Race riots in Atlanta, Georgia; W.E.B. DuBois, "Litany of
   Atlanta"
Roosevelt orders discharge of three companies of black troops
   following violence in Brownsville, Texas
Intercollegiate Socialist Society organized
Henry Adams, *The Education*
Upton Sinclair, *The Jungle*; publication sparks Pure Food and
   Drug Act (amended 1912)
John Spargo, *The Bitter Cry of the Children* strengthens campaign
   against child labor; first federal law passed 1916, declared
   unconstitutional 1918

1907 Immigration peaks at 1,285,349 arrivals from southern and
   eastern Europe
American fleet sent around the world (to 1909)

1908 Harriet Stanton Blatch founds Women's Political Union in New
   York
Demonstration of working women on New York's east side
   inaugurates International Women's Day
Race riots in Springfield, Illinois
First professional organization of Afro-American women founded:
   National Association of Colored Graduate Nurses

1909 IWW free speech fight at Spokane, Washington; repeated at San
   Diego, Fresno, Everett
NAACP organized; campaigns against lynching; Association for
   the Study of Afro-American Life and History organized
   1915; National Urban League organized 1919
New York waistmakers strike: "The uprising of 20,000"
United States' flag planted at North Pole

Gertrude Stein, *Three Lives: The Autobiography of Alice B. Toklas*, 1933
William Carlos Williams, *Poems*
Washington enfranchises women; California, Oregon, Kansas, and Arizona follow by 1912

1910 First woman suffrage parade in New York City
Milwaukee socialist Victor Berger elected to Congress
Jane Addams, *Twenty Years at Hull House*

1911 Triangle Shirtwaist Fire in New York, resulting from unsafe working conditions, kills 146 workers, sparks unionization of garment industry
McNamara case
Supreme Court orders disolution of Standard Oil trust and American Tobacco Company as monopolies
The Masses (suppressed 1917, resumes publication as *The Liberator*)

1912 Eugene Victor Debs polls million votes for Socialists
IWW leads victorious textile strikers at Lawrence, Massachusetts; "the children's crusade"; Ettor-Giovanetti trial
IWW strike at Paterson, New Jersey
Federal employees win eight-hour day
Alice Paul organizes Congressional Union; focuses suffragist efforts in Washington, D.C.; National Womens Party formed 1916
Illinois becomes first state east of Mississippi to enfranchise women; in 1917 New York assures suffragist victory; Nineteenth Amendment effective in 1920

1913 James Weldon Johnson, *The Autobiography of an Ex-Colored Man*
Washington, D.C., suffrage parade is mobbed
Ratification of Sixteenth (income tax) and Seventeenth (popular election of United States Senators) Amendments to U.S. Constitution

1914 Massacre at Ludlow, Colorado
First World War (to 1918); United States declares neutrality; enters war in 1917; Socialists oppose United States involvement; Debs sentenced to ten-year term, enters prison in 1919

1929 United States stock market crash, part of world-wide financial crisis, begins Great Depression
Soviet Russia, established following 1917 revolution, begins First Five Year Plan (completed 1932)
Cotton mill workers strike at Gastonia, North Carolina
Oscar DePriest enters Congress; first Afro-American Representative since 1901
William Faulkner, *Sartoris*, first of the Yoknapatawpha County novels

Thomas Wolfe, *Look Homeward, Angel*; *Of Time and The River*, 1935; *The Web and The Rock*, 1939; *You Can't Go Home Again*, 1940

1930 Drought in far western states
Hoover plan for unemployment relief
Trade Union Unity League organized
Wali Farad founds Black Muslim movement; Elijah Muhammad assumes leadership in 1934
Workers demonstrate for unemployment insurance; National Unemployed Councils convene in Chicago
NAACP-organized campaign blocks nomination of Judge Parker to Supreme Court
Hart Crane, *The Bridge*
John Dos Passos, *U.S.A.* (vol. 2, 1932; vol. 3, 1936)
Mike Gold, *Jews Without Money*
Langston Hughes, *Not Without Laughter*; *The Dream Keeper*, 1932; *The Ways of White Folks*, 1934

1931 Arrest of "Scottsboro Boys" on rape charges sparks most celebrated case since Sacco-Vanzetti (1920-27); last of nine defendants freed in 1950
Spanish revolution ends monarchy; Civil War in Spain (1936-39); Abraham Lincoln Brigade organized in United States, joins International Brigades fighting fascism; Franco dictatorship victorious in 1939
Japan invades Manchuria; attacks Shanghai in 1932; resigns from League of Nations in 1933
Edmund Wilson, *Axel's Castle*; *The American Letters*, 1932; *Travels in Two Democracies*, 1936; *The Triple Thinkers*, 1938; *To The Finland Station*, 1940; *The Wound And The Bow*, 1941
Robert Cantwell, *Laugh and Lie Down*; *Land of Plenty*, 1934

1932 Franklin Delano Roosevelt elected to first of four terms
"Bonus Army" of World War veterans marches on Washington; attacked by United States troops
Unemployed demonstrate in major United States cities
Tenants battle police in Bronx, New York; prevent evictions
Erskine Caldwell, *Tobacco Road*; *God's Little Acre*, 1933; *You Have Seen Their Faces* (with Margaret Bourke-White), 1937
James T. Farrell, *Young Lonigan*; *Studs Lonigan*, 1934; *Judgment Day*, 1935

1933 Adolph Hitler becomes Chancellor of Germany; Reichstag fire
American banks and stock exchange close; federal government insures bank deposits
The "Hundred Days" of the New Deal: AAA, NRA, PWA, CCC
Section 7A (NIRA) grants workers the right to organize and to bargain collectively; union ranks swell

1,200,000 Americans take part in strikes; from mid-1933 to end of
1934, troops called out against strikers in sixteen states
Twentieth ("lame duck") Amendment
United States recognizes U.S.S.R.
Tennessee Valley Authority created for flood control and sale of
cheap electricity
NAACP inaugurates court attack on Jim Crow in education; this
culminates in *Brown v. Board of Education*, 1954
Angelo Herndon sentenced to twenty years
Josephine Herbst, *Pity Is Not Enough*, 1933; *The Executioner
Awaits*, 1934; *Rope of Gold*, 1939

1934 Polish-German nonagression pact signed
Outbreak of Italian-Ethiopian War (to 1935)
Strike at Auto-Lite in Toledo ends in union victory; paves way for
auto workers organizing drive at General Motors
Teamsters strike, organize in Minneapolis
Longshoremen strike West Coast, Texas, and New Orleans;
"Bloody Thursday" in San Francisco results in general strike
(first since Seattle general strike in 1919)
Nationwide textile strike
Southern Tenant Farmers Union organized
Lillian Hellman, *The Children's Hour; Days to Come*, 1936; *The
Little Foxes*, 1939; *Watch On The Rhine*, 1941
Zora Neale Hurston, *Jonah's Gourd Vine; Men and Mules*, 1935;
Their Eyes Were Watching God, 1937
Moscow trials begin in U.S.S.R. (to 1938)

1935 Beginnings of Congress of Industrial Organizatons
Federal Social Security Act passed
National Labor Relations Board created under Wagner Act;
replaces earlier institutions lacking power to enforce right to
organize
National Recovery Act declared unconstitutional by Supreme
Court; AAA found unconstitutional in 1936
WPA established, inaugurates Federal Arts Projects
Nationwide soft coal strike
Milk farmers strike in Illinois, Wisconsin, Indiana, Iowa
Harlem race riots
American Artists Congress meets in New York City; American
Writers Congresses in 1935, 1937, 1939, 1941
John Steinbeck, *Tortilla Flat; In Dubious Battle*, 1936; *Of Mice
And Men*, 1937; *The Grapes of Wrath*, 1939
Ellen Glasgow, *Vein of Iron*

1936 Japan and Germany sign anti-Comintern pact; proclaim "Rome-
Berlin Axis"
Afro-American Olympic champion Jesse Owens wins four gold
medals in Berlin

Rubber workers strike Goodyear at Akron, Ohio; first success in
  CIO organizing drive
American Labor Party formed in New York

1937   Proposed reform of Supreme Court precipitates controversy;
         Wagner Act found Constitutional
       Almost two million unionists involved in 4,470 work stoppages;
         double number of previous year
       Philip Murray, Steel Workers Organizing Committee chairman,
         addresses National Negro Congress inviting black support of
         new unions
       United States Steel accords bargaining rights to SWOC-CIO;
         union strikes little Steel; ten killed in Memorial Day
         massacre at Republic works in South Chicago
       United Auto Workers strike General Motors; sit down at Flint,
         Michigan; "Battle of Bulls Run"
       "Labor Holiday" in Lansing, Michigan
       William H. Hastie appointed first Afro-American federal judge
         Maritime workers strike on West Coast
       Pullman Company recognizes Brotherhood of Sleeping Car Por-
         ters and Maids (organized by A. Philip Randolph in 1925,
         following organizing efforts by Friends of Negro Freedom,
         National Association for the Promotion of Labor Unionism
         Among Negroes, and American Negro Labor Congress)
       Ernest Hemingway, *To Have and Have Not; For Whom the Bell
         Tolls*, 1940

1938   Mexican government takes over properties of American and Brit-
         ish oil companies
       Hitler invades Austria, demands Sudeten area of Czechoslovakia;
         Munich Conference
       House of Representatives forms Committee to investigate Un-
         Americanism
       Cotton pickers strike in California
       Fair Labor Standards Act becomes law; 25¢ minimum wage and
         time-and-a-half pay for work over forty hours
       Richard Wright, *Uncle Tom's Children*; *Native Son*, 1940; *Black
         Boy*, 1945

1939   Hitler invades Czechoslovakia; Italy annexes Albania; border war
         between Japan and Russia in Manchuria; German-Russian
         non-aggression pact; Fino-Russian war (Russia annexes part
         of Finland in 1940); Germany invades Poland; start of World
         War II (to 1945)
       United States declares national emergency
       Tom Mooney pardoned after twenty-three years in jail
       Marian Anderson, denied use of Constitution Hall by D.A.R.,
         sings to 75,000 at Lincoln Memorial
       WPA workers strike

Auto workers strike Chrysler

James Agee and Walker Evans, *Let Us Now Praise Famous Men*

1940 End of "phoney war"; Germany invades Denmark, Norway, Low Countries, and France

Battle of Britain

Selective Service Act Passed by one vote in House of Representatives

Trotsky, exiled from U.S.S.R. since 1928, killed by assassin in Mexico

Death of Marcus Garvey, leader of black nationalist Universal Improvement Association in 1920s

1941 Auto workers strike, unionize Ford

Roosevelt announces "Four Freedoms"

Roosevelt and Churchill proclaim Atlantic Charter

Germany invades U.S.S.R., overruns Balkans

Fair Employment Practices Commission established; prohibits discrimination in defense industries

Japanese bomb Pearl Harbor; United States declares war

READING LIST

The following reading list was prepared for the Institute held at Yale University, June, 1982, by the project on Reconstructing American Literature. While the reading list was directed to particular Institute sessions, we felt that it also constituted a useful anthology about the issues involved in reconstructing our teaching of American literature.

Babín, María Teresa. "Contemporary Puerto Rican Literature in Translation." In *Minority Language and Literature: Retrospective and Perspective*, ed. Dexter Fisher. New York: Modern Language Association, 1977.

Baker, Houston, A., Jr. "Generational Shifts and the Recent Criticism of Afro-American Literature." *Black American Literature Forum* (Spring, 1981).

Baym, Nina. "Melodramas of Beset Manhood: How Theories of American Fiction Exclude Women Authors." *American Quarterly* (1981).

Bethel, Lorraine. "'This Infinity of Conscious Pain': Zora Neale Hurston and the Black Female Literary Tradition." In *But Some of Us Are Brave*, eds. Gloria Hull, Patricia Bell Scott, and Barbara Smith. Old Westbury, N.Y.: 1981, The Feminist Press.

Bronstein, Miriam. "The Voice of the Chicana in Poetry." *Denver Quarterly* (Fall, 1981).

Bruce-Novoa, Juan. "Hispanic Literature in the United States." *Chicano Poetry: A Response to Chaos*. Austin: University of Texas Press, 1982.

———. "Introduction" to *Chicano Authors: Inquiry by Interview*. Austin: University of Texas Press, 1980.

———. "Introduction" to *Chicano Poetry: A Response to Chaos*.

———. "Righting the Oral Tradition." *Denver Quarterly* (Fall, 1981).

———. "The Space of Chicano Literature." *The Chicano Literary World 1974*. N.M.: New Mexico Highlands Univ., 1975.

Cawelti, John. "Literary Formulas and Their Cultural Significance." In *The Study of American Culture: Contemporary Approaches*, (ed. Luther S. Luedtke. DeLand, Fla.: Everett-Edwards, 1976.

Cervantes, Lorna Dee. "Beneath the Shadow of the Freeway." *Emplumada*. Pittsburgh: University of Pittsburgh Press, 1981.

247

"A Conversation With Leslie Marmon Silko." *Sun Tracks* 3, no. 1 (Fall, 1976).

"A Conversation With N. Scott Momaday." *Sun Tracks* 2, no. 2 (Spring, 1976).

Dorris, Michael. "Native American Literature in an Ethnohistorical Context." *College English* (October, 1979).

Ellis, Grace W. "The Southern Writer and the New York *Times*." Typescript, 1981.

Gates, Henry Louis, Jr. "Preface to Blackness: Text and Pretext." In *Afro-American Literature: The Reconstruction of Instruction*, eds. Dexter Fisher and Robert B. Stepto New York: Modern Language Association, 1979.

Gelfant, Blanche. "Mingling and Sharing in American Literature: Teaching Ethnic Fiction" *College English* (1981).

Heilbrun, Carolyn. "Women, Men, Theories and Literature." *Profession* (1981).

Hemenway, Robert, "Are You a Flying Lark or a Setting Dove?" In *Afro-American Literature: The Reconstruction of Instruction*.

Kelley, Mary. "The Sentimentalists: Promise and Betrayal in the Home." *Signs* (1979).

Kolodny, Annette. "A Map for Rereading, or, Gender and the Interpretation of Literary Texts." *New Literary History* (1980).

――――― . "Dancing Through the Minefield." *Feminist Studies* (1980).

――――― . "Turning the Lens on 'The Panther Captivity': A Feminist Exercise in Practical Criticism." *Critical Inquiry* (1981).

Lauter, Paul. "Sex and Race in the Shaping of the American Literary Canon: A Case History from the Twenties." *Feminist Studies* (1983).

――――― . "Working-Class Women's Literature—An Introduction to Study." In *Women In Print*, Vol. I, eds. Joan Hartman and Ellen Messer-Davidow. New York: Modern Language Association, 1982.

Lurie, Nancy Oestreich. "Historical Background." In *The American Indian Today*, eds. Stuart Levine and Nancy Oestreich Lurie. New York: Penguin, 1970.

Martin, Jay. "National Development and Ethnic Poetics." In *The Study of American Culture: Contemporary Approaches*.

Montoya, Jose. "El Louie." In *Aztlan: An Anthology of the Mexican-American Literature*, eds. Louis Valdez and Stan Steiner. New York: Vintage, 1972.

Ong, Walter J., S.J. "Oral Culture and the Literate Mind." In *Minority Language and Literature*.

Ortiz, Simon J. "Towards a National Indian Literature." *MELUS* (1981).

Paredes, Raymund. "The Evolution of Chicano Literature." *MELUS* (1978).

Ramsey, Jarold. "The Teacher of Modern American Indian Writing as Ethnographer and Critic." *College English* (October, 1979).

Reilly, John M. "Literature and Ideology." *MELUS* (1981).

Roemer, Kenneth. "Native American Oral Narratives: Context and Continuity." In *Smoothing the Ground: Essays on Native American Oral Literature*, ed. Brian Swann. Berkeley: University of California Press, 1983.

Ruoff, A. Lavonne Brown. "American Indian Oral Literatures." *American Quarterly* (1981).

Smith-Rosenberg, Carroll. "The Female World of Love and Ritual." *Signs* (1975).

Sollars, Werner. "Theory of American Ethnicity." *American Quarterly* (1981).

Sommers, Joseph. "Critical Approaches to Chicano Literature." In *Modern Chicano Writers: A Collection of Critical Essays*, eds. Joseph Sommers and Tomás Yberra-Frausto. Englewood Cliffs, N.J.: Prentice-Hall, 1979.

Stepto, Robert B. "Teaching Afro-American Literature: Survey or Tradition." In *Afro-American Literature: The Reconstruction of Instruction*.

Thackeray, William W., " 'Crying for Pity' in *Winter in the Blood*." *MELUS* (1980).

Tompkins, Jane P. "Sentimental Power." *Glyph* (1981).

Walker, Alice. "In Search of Our Mothers' Gardens." *Ms* (1974).

Washington, Mary Helen. "Teaching *Black-Eyed Susans*." In *But Some of Us Are Brave*.

Williams, Sherley. "The Blues Roots of Contemporary Afro-American Poetry." In *Afro-American Literature: The Reconstruction of Instruction*.

Ybarra-Frausto, Tomás. "The Chicano Movement and the Emergence of a Chicano Poetic Consciousness." *New Scholar* (1972).

"Yellow-Woman and Whirlwind Man" and "Yellow-Woman and the Giantess," ed.
Franz Boas, in *Keresan Texts*, 2 vols. American Ethnological Society, Publications #8 (1928);
Leslie Marmon Silko, "Yellow Man," "Lullaby," "Coyote Holds a Full House in His Hands";
A. Lavonne Brown Ruoff. "Ritual and Renewal: Keres Traditions and the Short Fiction of Leslie Silko." *MELUS* (1978).

Zamora, Bernice. "Penitents." In *Restless Serpents. Diseños Literarios* (1976).

FEMINIST CLASSICS FROM THE FEMINIST PRESS

Antoinette Brown Blackwell: A Biography, by Elizabeth Cazden. $16.95 cloth, $9.95 paper.

Between Mothers and Daughters: Stories Across a Generation. Edited by Susan Koppelman. $8.95 paper.

Brown Girl, Brownstones, novel by Paule Marshall. Afterword by Mary Helen Washington. $7.95 paper.

Call Home the Heart, a novel of the thirties, by Fielding Burke. Introduction by Alice Kessler-Harris and Paul Lauter and afterwords by Sylvia J. Cook and Anna W. Shannon. $7.95 paper.

Cassandra, by Florence Nightingale. Introduction by Myra Stark. Epilogue by Cynthia Macdonald. $3.50 paper.

The Convert, a novel by Elizabeth Robins. Introduction by Jane Marcus. $5.95 paper.

Daughter of Earth, a novel by Agnes Smedley. Afterword by Paul Lauter. $5.95 paper.

The Female Spectator. Edited by Mary R. Mahl and Helen Koon. $5.95 paper.

First Feminists: British Women Writers from 1578-1799. Edited with an introduction by Moira Ferguson. $12.95 paper.

Guardian Angel and Other Stories, by Margery Latimer. Afterwords by Louis Kampf, Meridel Le Sueur, and Nancy Loughridge. $7.95 paper.

I Love Myself When I Am Laughing ... And Then Again When I Am Looking Mean and Impressive, by Zora Neale Hurston. Edited by Alice Walker with an introduction by Mary Helen Washington. $9.95 paper.

Käthe Kollwitz: Woman and Artist, by Martha Kearns. $7.95 paper.

Life in the Iron Mills, by Rebecca Harding Davis. Biographical interpretation by Tillie Olsen. $4.95 paper.

The Living Is Easy, a novel by Dorothy West. Afterword by Adelaide M. Cromwell. $6.95 paper.

The Maimie Papers. Edited by Ruth Rosen and Sue Davidson. Introduction by Ruth Rosen. $15.95 cloth, $7.95 paper.

The Other Woman: Stories of Two Women and a Man. Edited by Susan Koppelman. $8.95 paper.

Portraits of Chinese Women in Revolution, by Agnes Smedley. Edited with an introduction by Jan MacKinnon and Steve MacKinnon and an afterword by Florence Howe. $4.95 paper.

Reena and Other Stories, by Paule Marshall. $8.95 paper.

Ripening: Selected Work, 1927-1980, by Meridel Le Sueur. Edited with an introduction by Elaine Hedges. $14.95 cloth, $7.95 paper.

The Silent Partner, a novel by Elizabeth Stuart Phelps. Afterword by Mari Jo Buhle and Florence Howe. $6.95 paper.

These Modern Women: Autobiographical Essays from the Twenties. Edited with an introduction by Elaine Showalter. $4.95 paper.

The Unpossessed, a novel of the thirties, by Tess Slesinger. Introduction by Alice Kessler-Harris and Paul Lauter and afterword by Janet Sharistanian. $7.95 paper.

Weeds, a novel by Edith Summers Kelley. Afterword by Charlotte Goodman. $6.95 paper.

The Woman and the Myth: Margaret Fuller's Life and Writings, by Bell Gale Chevigny. $8.95 paper.

The Yellow Wallpaper, by Charlotte Perkins Gilman. Afterword by Elaine Hedges. $2.95 paper.

OTHER TITLES FROM THE FEMINIST PRESS

Black Foremothers: Three Lives, by Dorothy Sterling. $6.95 paper.

But Some of Us Are Brave: Black Women's Studies. Edited by Gloria T. Hull, Patricia Bell Scott, and Barbara Smith. $16.95 cloth, $9.95 paper.

Complaints and Disorders: The Sexual Politics of Sickness, by Barbara Ehrenreich and Deirdre English. $3.95 paper.

The Cross-Cultural Study of Women. Edited by Mary I. Edwards and Margot Duley Morrow. $8.95 paper.

Dialogue on Difference. Edited by Florence Howe. $8.95 paper.

Everywoman's Guide to Colleges and Universities. Edited by Florence Howe, Suzanne Howard, and Mary Jo Boehm Strauss. $12.95 paper.

Household and Kin: Families in Flux, by Amy Swerdlow et al. $14.95 cloth, $6.95 paper.

How to Get Money for Research, by Mary Rubin and the Business and Professional Women's Foundation. Foreword by Mariam Chamberlain. $5.95 paper.

In Her Own Image: Women Working in the Arts. Edited with an introduction by Elaine Hedges and Ingrid Wendt. $17.95 cloth, $8.95 paper.

Las Mujeres: Conversations from a Hispanic Community, by Nan Elsasser, Kyle MacKenzie, and Yvonne Tixier y Vigil. $14.95 cloth, $6.95 paper.

Lesbian Studies: Present and Future. Edited by Margaret Cruikshank. $14.95 cloth, $8.95 paper.

Moving the Mountain: Women Working for Social Change, by Ellen Cantarow with Susan Gushee O'Malley and Sharon Hartman Strom. $6.95 paper.

Out of the Bleachers: Writings on Women and Sport. Edited with an introduction by Stephanie L. Twin. $7.95 paper.

Reconstructing American Literature: Courses, Syllabi, Issues. Edited by Paul Lauter. $10.95 paper.

Rights and Wrongs: Women's Struggle for Legal Equality, by Susan Cary Nicholas, Alice M. Price, and Rachel Rubin. $5.95 paper.

Salt of the Earth, screenplay by Michael Wilson with historical commentary by Deborah Silverton Rosenfelt. $5.95 paper.

The Sex-Role Cycle: Socialization from Infancy to Old Age, by Nancy Romer. $6.95 paper.

Witches, Midwives, and Nurses: A History of Women Healers, by Barbara Ehrenreich and Deirdre English. $3.95 paper.

With These Hands: Women Working on the Land. Edited with an introduction by Joan M. Jensen. $17.95 cloth, $8.95 paper.

Woman's "True" Profession: Voices from the History of Teaching. Edited with an introduction by Nancy Hoffman. $17.95 cloth, $8.95 paper.

Women Have Always Worked: A Historical Overview, by Alice Kessler-arris. $14.95 cloth, $6.95 paper.

Women Working: An Anthology of Stories and Poems. Edited and with an introduction by Nancy Hoffman and Florence Howe. $7.95 paper.

Women's Studies in Italy, by Laura Balbo and Yasmine Ergas. A Women's Studies International Monograph. $5.95 paper.

When ordering, please include $1.50 for postage and handling for one book and 35¢ for each additional book. Order from: The Feminist Press, Box 334, Old Westbury, NY 11568. Telephone (516) 997-7660.